Facts and Explanatic Studies...and beyond

The politicizing of facts and factual claims has led some to abandon all talk of a meaningful distinction between a fact and a strongly held political commitment. This book argues that what we need, instead, are better accounts of facts and their relationship to explanation—accounts that take seriously the dependence of facts on communities of practice and on consensus procedures of measurement, but do not abandon the epistemic distinctiveness of facts.

Bringing clarity and order to the discussion by disclosing both key commonalities and significant differences between the ways we talk about facts and explanations, Patrick Thaddeus Jackson argues that although intrinsically more contestable than facts, social-scientific explanations can nonetheless be related to facts in ways that allow researchers to evaluate explanations based on whether and to what extent they accord with the relevant facts in each situation. Ardently defending a pragmatist account of knowledge that has no patience with either "alternative facts" or "anything goes" relativism, the author develops a set of concepts that enables tricky philosophical problems to be dissolved. After examining facts, causal explanations, and interpretive explanations, the book culminates in an account of the priority of interpretation in the evaluation of any explanation—and any seemingly factual claim.

Defining the terms of the debate and grounding better conversations about the issues, this book will appeal to all scholars interested in the philosophy and methodology of the social sciences, international studies, international relations, security studies, and anyone teaching or studying research methods.

Patrick Thaddeus Jackson is Professor of International Studies and Chair of the Department of Global Inquiry in the School of International Service at American University in Washington, D.C. He is the author of one of the foundational (and award-winning) books on philosophy of science in international studies (*The Conduct of Inquiry in International Relations*), and has been working on problems related to knowledge and explanation for much of his career, including developing and teaching multiple courses for both undergraduate and graduate students. For approximately 15 years he also has taught philosophy of science and research design in short-term intensive graduate courses around the world for the European Consortium on Political Research, the International Political Science Association, and MethodsNET.

"Jackson's *Facts and Explanations* is a must-read for scholars and students, regardless of epistemology or political persuasion. It makes a convincing case that how we claim to know matters as much as, if not more than, what we claim to know. In making this case, Jackson marshals an impressively broad body of literature on knowledge, fact, and science, providing a singular perspective that combines the complexities of hundreds of years of thought and the many conflicting messages of the 21st century in an elegant and parsimonious way. We will all be stronger analysts more capable of navigating international studies…and beyond for having read this book."

Laura Sjoberg, *Royal Holloway, University of London, UK*

Facts and Explanations in International Studies ...and beyond

Patrick Thaddeus Jackson

LONDON AND NEW YORK

Designed cover image: gettyimages.com

First published 2025
by Routledge
4 Park Square, Milton Park, Abingdon, Oxon OX14 4RN

and by Routledge
605 Third Avenue, New York, NY 10158

Routledge is an imprint of the Taylor & Francis Group, an informa business

British Library Cataloguing-in-Publication Data
A catalogue record for this book is available from the British Library

ISBN: 9781032595320 (hbk)
ISBN: 9781032597041 (pbk)
ISBN: 9781003455912 (ebk)

DOI: 10.4324/9781003455912

Typeset in Times New Roman
by Newgen Publishing UK

For Nick Onuf,
a fellow accidental tourist.

Contents

There's no denying
With the rage we keep supplying
The division is multiplying

We're turning tables
Cutting cables to assemble our own teams
With endless feedback
Every little quack can build into a scream

When talk is cheap—we can't refuse
When every tweet—is breaking news
The price is steep for what we're bound to lose
We've got the bottom feeder blues

—Randy McStine

Preface and Acknowledgments

For a long time now I have been bothered by two opposing positions on issues of fact, truth, and knowledge. One position, which I might call the strong sociology of knowledge position, maintains that there is nothing more to validity than the power to compel acceptance, whether that power is understood to be centralized in a government or other organization, or diffused throughout some structured subset of society. "Fact" means just what is taken to be fact, and "truth" means just what is taken to be true; knowledge is consensus, or imposition, or some subtle combination of both. Taken out of context, Nietzsche's quip that the truth is a coin that has been passed around so many times that the face has worn off of it captures much of this view, and directs our attention away from the question of whether any particular claim *is* valid to the question of whether that claim is upheld or maintained or promulgated or believed, and what effects that has.

I find much attractive in this position, especially in light of the myriad claims that are handed to us as facts and truths which, upon closer examination, turn out to be deceitful and cynically self-serving. And certainly for the analysis of the effects of political rhetoric on action, the validity of any claims proffered by politicians is pretty much beside the point. But I worry that *completely* assimilating considerations of validity to issues of power or consent leaves us in the untenable situation of having to regard *all* claims—even basic descriptive claims—as arbitrary impositions, so that (e.g.) whether an object is round or square depends on someone's power to enforce their will over someone else. And once we get beyond descriptive claims to explanatory claims, matters get even more confusing, as we have no way of distinguishing between a strongly held belief or commitment on the one hand, and a valid knowledge-claim on the other. This includes, of course, knowledge-claims about how validity is nothing but an arbitrary imposition of power.

At the same time, I find the opposite position—that the validity of facts, truth, and knowledge depend on their being correctly connected to a mind-independently real external world—to be equally problematic. From this perspective, facts are just features of the world, and knowledge consists of the proper arrangement of those facts, aided by whatever conceptual structures and theories we produce en route to better and better approximations of reality. Here there is no question of arbitrary imposition, and power is sidelined in favor of an autonomous notion of validity: what makes a claim valid is not whether it is accepted, but whether it corresponds to the facts.

But the problem with this position is that it founders on the notion of "correspondence," and comes apart when faced with the evident actuality of different communities understanding things in different ways—or the same community understanding things in different ways over time. If we persist in treating valid knowledge as requiring correspondence, we make such epistemic diversity difficult if not impossible to comprehend, and we give license to those who claim valid knowledge to dismiss, or even aggressively destroy, rival claims. After all, if I have knowledge that corresponds to the facts and you do not, why should I bother to listen to you? And if you persist in your obviously false beliefs after I have presented to you my clearly true knowledge, then there must be something wrong with you.

My dissatisfaction with both sides of this debate is thus equally about the philosophical inconsistencies of each position, and about the ethical and political consequences that each position warrants. Both positions, it seems to me, countenance a pronounced *intolerance*, insofar as each makes it possible for adherents of particular claims to simply ignore the claims made by others. Neither position is especially interested in dialogue and discussion, since each has its rhetorical backstop—correspondence on the one hand, arbitrary imposition on the other— to serve as an unquestionable parameter constraining conversation. And neither, I think, are adequate to what is arguably the most pressing challenge of our time: the simultaneous erosion of non-partisan factuality as a common ground for social and political action *and* the triumphant proclamations by partisans of all sorts that they and they alone have facts, truth, and valid knowledge.

Contrary to reports, we do not live in a "post-truth world," a world where the question of truth (and the related questions of factual validity) has become irrelevant. We live in a confusing cacophony of inconsistent partisan perspectives all of which claim to be true. Everyone wants facts; they just insist that the facts be, and are, on their side. This is actually more dangerous than a world where no one cared about validity, since if no one cared about validity we would have to look for other grounds for our actions. Instead we go into battle with all sides claiming validity— so is it any surprise when political compromises become harder and harder to find?

When I set out on the path that led to this book I had two main and more immediate concerns that brought my dissatisfaction with both positions into sharp relief. Both make appearances in the chapters to follow. One involved the electoral victories of campaigns based on outright falsehoods, especially in places like the United States and the United Kingdom where in previous decades politicians who simply made things up that were convenient for their partisan positions generally did not attain their country's highest political offices. The notion that "the facts" had become *political*—that Weber's vocations for politics and for scholarship had been collapsed—struck me as needing a response. But that response couldn't be a blunt assertion that valid knowledge corresponded to the facts, in part because of my other concern: the utter *weakness* of the facts in the face of determined political opposition. Knowledge that was to be effective needed to be something other than a simple statement of the facts; it had to go *beyond the facts* in providing some kind of instructions for future action. So what was needed was a double clarification: about the nature of facts, and about the relationship of explanations of various sorts to factually true claims.

For while I did not think that my thinking through these matters was going to lead to a book. I wrote and published two papers on these themes, and in significantly remixed form they appear in the text below:

Chapter 3 is a remixed version of "Causal claims and causal explanations in international studies," *Journal of International Relations and Development* 20:4 (2017), pp. 689–716.
Chapter 5 is a remixed version of "The Dangers of Interpretation: C.A.W. Manning and the 'going concern' of international society," *Journal of International Political Theory* 16:2 (2020), pp. 133–152.

I also published a piece in *Renewal* 29:2 (2021) entitled "'Alternative Facts', Scientific Claims and Political Action," which covers ground similar to what I discuss in Chapter 1. But I thought that those pieces were sufficient until I gave a talk at the London School of Economics in November 2022 (preceded by a similar talk earlier that week at Aberystwyth University, and one in Oslo the previous month) and realized, halfway through that talk, that I was actually delivering the core of Chapter 2. So I returned to the project, had a supportive conversation with Rob Sorsby (my editor at Routledge) at the ISA meeting in March 2023, and here we are.

To be clear, I have written this book largely to clarify my own thinking about these issues, and to see if a combination of Wittgensteinian philosophy of (ordinary) language, Deweyian pragmatism, and a broadly Weberian sensibility would be sufficient to chart a third position on facts and explanations that would avoid the problems of the two with which I was dissatisfied—and whether that third position would be adequate to the problem of pluralized inconsistent truths and weaponized/counterfeit "facts." I am largely satisfied with where I have ended up; I hope that you will be too, or that at any rate you will find my exploration provocative. In the end what matters to me is not whether or not you agree with me, but whether we can have a reasonable conversation about the issues involved. By all means, disagree! But do so without caricature, and without dismissal.

My wife Holly has been living with this project as long as I have, and she was often my first interlocutor. A subordinate theme of my explorations here has been attempting to figure out just what she is doing when she climbs into the pulpit almost every Sunday and delivers a typically trenchant sermon. Thinking through the relationship between facts, scripture, and the genre of the sermon was a vital component of the final argument on display here. As always she has my first and most heartfelt thanks and appreciation—and my love.

The examples involving dogs scattered throughout the text refer both to our older dog Olaf and our younger puppy Zorri. I will leave it as an exercise for the reader to determine which is referenced when.

The book's epigraph is from the song "Bottom Feeder Blues" by Randy McStine, and used with his kind permission; explore more of his music at www.randymcstine.com. The book's index was meticulously prepared by Stephan Przybylowicz at Twin Oaks Indexing.

Many of the concepts and notions here were initially developed in a number of instructional settings over the past several years: my courses on pragmatism and relational social theory at the ECPR Winter Schools, several Zoom-mediated workshops during the COVID-19 pandemic, and my AU Honors course "Theories of Inquiry." I thank all of the students in those classes for helping to co-constitute a space where thinking could take place, and for providing an early audience for the formulations that appear in the text. Along these lines let me also give a special thanks to my colleagues at Aberystwyth University; my annual visits and the extended conversations they anchor provided a significant impetus to my thinking.

More concretely, several colleagues read and commented on significant parts of the manuscript in draft: Sujin Heo, Ian Reynolds, Ilan Baron, Cathy Elliott, Gregorio Bettiza, and Tony Lang. They all pressed me in important ways and deserve thanks for the level of clarity achieved. Whether they agree with me or not in the end is, as you might expect, far less important to me than the fact that we have had and continue to have conversations about these issues. Sujin Heo and Ian Reynolds also provided important research support, and always managed to make good on the most unusual extra-disciplinary requests ("what is the state of the art in the science of crowd counting?").

Because of my personal academic trajectory, I start my thinking about matters like the ones here from within international studies—which is how I name the broader global inter-discipline that encompasses, but is not reducible to, that subfield of U.S. Political Science called "International Relations." But the issues I am pondering here are in no way specific to international studies. Hence the book's title. I urge you not to spend any time trying to figure out whether this is an "IR" book in any sense of that term. Instead, simply follow the argument, and see if you find it compelling, regardless of academic field or discipline. I did not construct this book as an intervention into any field- or discipline-specific debate, but as a philosophical reflection on issues that are, I would posit, of concern to all of us. I ask you to read it in that spirit, and see where your thinking takes you—where it takes *us*.

1 Facts

The inauguration of Donald Trump as President of the United States in January 2017 was perhaps inevitably going to be an occasion for controversy. Trump's victory in the 2016 presidential election had been an incredibly narrow one, coming down in some accounts to about 80,000 votes in three states: Michigan, Pennsylvania, and Wisconsin (Bump 2016). Indeed, Trump had lost the *popular* vote to his opponent Hillary Clinton by 2.87 million votes; Clinton received 48 percent of votes cast nationally, while Trump received 45.9 percent (Sabato, Kondik, and Skelley 2017, 5). Presidential elections in the United States are not, however, decided by the popular vote totals, but by the Electoral College, and there Trump's margin of victory was decisive: 304 votes for Trump, 227 for Clinton, and 7 "faithless" votes for other candidates—the largest number of electors switching their votes to a candidate other than the one who won the election in their state, excepting only the 1872 election in which one of the candidates had died after the election but before the electoral college met (FairVote.org 2016).[1] Trump was only the fifth person in U.S. history to become president while losing the popular vote, setting the stage for all manner of discussions about the nature of his public support.

Indeed, a month before the inauguration, Trump and his transition team had claimed that Trump's electoral college margin was one of the biggest in history, but this was simply untrue. Trump's margin in the electoral college was actually one of the *smallest* margins in history, falling in the bottom 20 percent of all U.S. presidential elections (Goldstein 2016). This was not the first time that the Trump administration had asserted untrue claims as though they were true, but all of those occasions were quickly overshadowed by the celebrated controversy over the number of people who attended Trump's inauguration. The day after the inauguration, press secretary Sean Spicer used his first official session with members of the press to castigate them for repeating falsehoods about the inauguration crowds, and provided some numbers of his own—numbers that were easily, and more or less immediately, shown to be incorrect (Cillizza 2017). Kellyanne Conway, who had

---

[1] Ten electors attempted to cast votes for someone other than the candidate who won the election in their state, but only seven of those votes were recorded because of state laws requiring electors to vote for the candidate to whom they are "pledged" (FairVote.org 2019).

DOI: 10.4324/9781003455912-1

been Trump's campaign manager and was subsequently appointed Counselor to the President, sought to defend Spicer on the television program *Meet the Press* the next day, replying to a charge that Spicer had himself uttered falsehoods: "You're saying it's a falsehood, and they're giving—our press secretary, Sean Spicer, gave alternative facts to that" (Blake 2017).

Thus was born the phrase "alternative facts." Immediately a source of great controversy—Chuck Todd, the host of *Meet the Press*, quickly replied "Alternative facts are not facts; they're falsehoods"—the phrase quickly achieved some pop-cultural notoriety in the U.S., with the late-night television comedy program *The Tonight Show* creating a recurring segment called "Two Truths and an Alternative Fact," and a slew of memes making their appearance more or less overnight (Guido 2017). Conway herself subsequently defined the phrase as meaning "additional facts and alternative information," giving as examples "Two plus two is four. Three plus one is four. Partly cloudy, partly sunny. Glass half full, glass half empty. Those are alternative facts" (Nuzzi 2017). That did not put an end to the contro-versy, however, and "alternative facts" quickly joined "fake news" in the lexicon of terms used by political commentators across the spectrum to describe the Trump administration's often strained relationship with the news media.

In the gap between Conway's initial statement and her subsequent elaboration lies a plethora of subtle conceptual and philosophical distinctions. If "alternative facts" are simply "additional facts," then the situation is unproblematic: here are some facts, there are some other facts, and the only discussion would be about which set of facts is most appropriate for resolving the question at hand. Conway's examples point in this direction, since *both* elements of the pairs she mentions are, arguably, facts, and can be true at the same time: half-full and half-empty are both factually correct ways to describe a glass containing half as much liquid as it could possibly contain, and 2 + 2 and 3 + 1 both equal 4. "Party sunny" and partly cloudy" are a little more complicated, because although both terms refer to situations in which between 3/8ths and 5/8ths of the sky is covered by opaque clouds (if you want to get really technical), the sky can't be "partly sunny" at night because the sun isn't visible, but it can be "partly cloudy" (Soniak 2017). The key point is that with *additional* facts, there is no visceral reaction the way there is with *alternative* facts.

Why?

"Alternative facts" considered as something other than additional facts disrupts one of the central intuitions that we have about factual claims: that they are in some sense *incontrovertibly* and *incontestably* true. If something is a fact, there is no need to append "...for me" or "...for us" to the statement, because the statement is just *true*. If I make a claim that I regard as a fact, and someone disagrees with the statement, then they have either misunderstood what I was saying, or they are claiming that what I asserted wasn't true—and implicitly, that some other, contra-dictory statement is true. Lurking behind or alongside that disagreement is a tacit assertion that the rival statement can be demonstrated to be true in an *imperson-ally* compelling way: that I can be brought to acknowledge the truth of the rival statement, and abandon my earlier assertion, through some process of reasoning and observation that terminates in my agreeing that the rival statement is true while my original statement is not. I say "the ratio of the diameter of a circle to its circumference is 2.14159"; you say "no, it's the irrational number pi, which approximates to 3.14159265…" Only one of us can be correct, because only one of these statements is factually true, and once we understand terms like "circle" and "ratio" and "circumference" the same way, there *can be* no sensible controversy about which statement is true and which is not.

Take Conway's pairing of "half-full"/"half-empty." Against the background of our ordinary ways of talking, which are embedded in our ordinary ways of existing in the world, it's clear that these are equivalent factual claims: they are different ways of describing the same situation, and both statements would be proven false if we were referring to, say, a glass that contained no liquid, or a glass that was filled to the brim. The background of "ordinary ways" is critical here, because it's not as though the statement "the glass is half-empty" *could* be true outside of those ordinary ways. Ordinarily, by "half-empty" we mean something like "there is an amount of liquid in the glass which is one-half of the amount that could potentially be in the glass," and we ordinarily evaluate claims like this by looking at the glass, rather than by, for example, pulling out some measuring cups and checking to see just how much the glass can hold. In a different context—say, in a laboratory context—"half-empty" might call for just such a measurement procedure, and if you had grown up using the word "half" to mean something different from what *I* mean by it (perhaps you say "half" wherever I would say "one-quarter"), and we'd have to proceed differently than we would in a situation in which we share that practical background. If we share definitions and procedures, agreement on facts follows relatively seamlessly—so seamlessly that we might not even notice that any sort of procedure has been followed or any sort of definition was involved.

But it has. If I assert that "2 + 2 = 4" or "1 + 3 = 4," I am relying on definitions of these symbols, and on a procedure—specifically, the procedure of addition—which, if you don't share, will make it difficult if not impossible for you to evaluate my claims and *either* agree that they state facts *or* conclude that they do not. This is a subtle, but important, point. It's not that a statement like "2 + 2 = 4" is somehow true or not true depending on whether we share definitions and procedures; rather, the prerequisite for saying whether the statement is true or not is a sharing of definitions and procedures. As long as we have what Ludwig Wittgenstein once referred to as "agreement in judgments" (Wittgenstein 1958, para. 242), we are in a position to evaluate whether "2 + 2 = 4" is true or not, and we are *also* in a position to perform the same kind of evaluation of "2 + 2 = 7" and "1 + 3 = 6" and "1 + 3 = 4." Once we share definitions and procedures, the truth or falsity of these statements is *not a matter of opinion*, and it is *not something we can sensibly disagree about*. The claims are either true, or they are not.

This is what it means for a factual claim to be *impersonally* true. Factual statements are those we cannot help agreeing with, unless we decide to drop out of the background consensus about definitions and procedures that makes factual claims possible in the first place. Whether the sky is partly cloudy right now is not something we can disagree about, as long as we share a definition of "partly cloudy" and a procedure for determining how much of the sky is obscured by opaque clouds. Whether the sky is partly sunny…well, if it's nighttime now, and we're adhering to the strict technical definition, then it can't possibly be the case that the sky is partly sunny; but if it's not nighttime, because "partly sunny" and "partly cloudy" have the same operative definitions, the sky could well be both "partly cloudy" and "partly sunny" at the same time—just the way that the glass can, unproblematically, be both half-full and half-empty at the same time. All of these statements are factual claims, resulting from the consistent application of definitions and procedures in an impersonal way. And there is no contradiction between applying a set of definitions and procedures that concludes that the glass is half-full, and another set that concludes that the glass is half-empty; these are merely additional facts, resulting from the use of different definitions and procedures, and once we have (background) consensus on which set to use, reaching agreement is relatively straightforward.

The problem is that this relative harmony only obtains for *additional* facts, where the definitions and procedures underpinning each statement of fact are distinct and different. That is the case with Conway's examples, but it is not the case with Spicer's original assertions. At one point in his remarks, Spicer asserted that 420,000 people had ridden public transit trains the day of Trump's inauguration, and only 317,000 had used public transit for Barack Obama's second inauguration; both claims were immediately refuted by the official records of the Washington Metropolitan Transit Authority, which recorded 570,557 metro trips on the day of Trump's inauguration, and 782,000 for Obama's second inauguration (Morris 2017). Spicer also gave some crowd size numbers that were asserted without any basis of support:

> We know that from the platform where the President was sworn in, to 4th Street, it holds about 250,000 people. From 4th Street to the media tent is about another 220,000. And from the media tent to the Washington Monument, another 250,000 people. All of this space was full when the President took the Oath of Office.
>
> (Cillizza 2017)

These numbers are quite different from the "carrying capacity" numbers provided by sociologists Clark McPhail and John McCarthy, who estimate that the *entire* National Mall area between the U.S. Capitol and the Washington Monument would only hold 524,103 people if all areas of the Mall were packed to a density of 5 square feet per person, "allowing slow passage through the crowd with repeated apologies" (McPhail and McCarthy 2004, 16–17).[2] In addition, photographs of the National Mall quite clearly indicate that not all of the space was full of people,

2 McPhail and McCarthy estimate that the National Mall could hold 1.3 million people if the entire area were filled to "about the density of a packed elevator or subway car, leaving hardly any space to wriggle through," and that "it might be possible to shoehorn 1 million people into the National Mall (at 2.5 square feet per person), but only if they stood more or less perfectly still"—an unrealistic expectation for people attending a public event for a long period of time (McPhail and McCarthy 2004, 17), particularly for U.S. citizens whose notion of personal space is somewhat more expansive

and side-by-side photographic comparisons show a considerably larger crowd at Obama's first inauguration than were at Trump's (Morris 2017).[3] This led crowd scientists Marcel Altenburg and Keith Still to estimate the size of the crowd on the Mall itself at Trump's inauguration at about 160,000, a third of the number of people who attended the Women's March on Washington the day after the inauguration; they also estimated the total attendance at Trump's inauguration as between 300,000 and 600,000 people, or about one-third as many people as attended Obama's first inauguration (Frostenson 2017; Wallace and Parlapiano 2017).

In this light, Spicer's numbers look less like additional facts and more like inaccuracies or falsehoods. Unless he was using words like "people," "holds," and "full" in ways that are quite at variance with ordinary usage, the claims that he was making were simply not factually accurate ones. Granted, he *might* have been using these words in different ways, and he *might* have been presuming a different procedural background for the notion of "counting." Counting is, after all, "an epistemic achievement that involves categorical judgments" about "*what* to count and, correlatively, of what *counts as* something to be counted" (Martin and Lynch 2009, 246). Put another way, counting is a procedure that only seems simple until you have to do it, and at the moment of application, there are inevitably judgments to be made. In particular, the carrying capacity assessments made by crowd scientists provide a check on whatever numbers one might obtain by, say, scrutinizing aerial or satellite photographs looking to enumerate individual people: if such scrutiny and enumeration produce results that are incompatible with the carrying capacity estimates, crowd scientists throw out the enumeration, presuming some kind of error in the photograph. Indeed, the most charitable reading of Spicer's numbers is that they were formed by an error of extrapolation: the crowd closest to the front of the inauguration was extremely tightly packed, and assuming that the rest if the crowd was packed that tightly would yield numbers much higher than the experts came up with. But that procedure would be quite different from the procedure used by crowd scientists, and would also be quite different from how most listeners would likely presume that Spicer got his numbers.

The point is that Sean Spicer's numbers were *presented* as facts, but if treated as factual and evaluated with the procedures used by crowd scientists, his claims are quickly shown to be false. Had he been presenting additional facts—the results of the impersonal application of a set of definitions and procedures different from those presumed by crowd scientists and perhaps from those presumed by ordinary listeners—then it would be possible to have a discussion about the relative merits of different ways of counting crowds, and the different factual results that those operational processes produced when enacted, in order to gain insight into how

than that in other parts of the world. Spicer's numbers would suggest that the Mall held 720,000 people the day of Trump's inauguration; McPhail and McCarthy's carrying capacity estimates suggest that in order to hold that many people, the crowd density would have had to be quite extreme all throughout the area.

3 Those photographs also show, quite clearly, that the areas that Spicer claimed were full were not full, for any commonly accepted definition of "full."

many people attended Trump's inauguration. But there is no evidence that this was the case. Conway's declaration that these were "alternative facts" only applies to Spicer's remarks if they are treated not like the "half-empty"/"half-full" pair, or like "partly cloudy"/"partly sunny," but instead as something far more troubling: a kind of "fact" that would be true not for all speakers of a particular language or users of a particular procedure, but only for some of those people listening to the claims. The *impersonally true* quality of a fact would evaporate, in favor of a kind of anarchy of knowledge-claims: X is a fact merely because I say that it is a fact and you agree with me, and the claim needs no basis other than that agreement in order to be accepted as true. True for us, at least.

"There are four lights"

For many contemporary philosophers, the problem here is *epistemic relativism*, in which two or more contradictory claims could both be factually true at the same time, for members of different communities. Some point to a nightmare scenario in which, for example, the melting point of tin would not be the same in "Kansas City, Cologne, and Kandahar" (Hickman, Neubert, and Reich 2009, 156), because the existence of different ways of calculating that number. Contemporary scientific metallurgy, which calculates the melting point of tin to be about 232 °C/450 °F, would thus be reduced to a mere opinion, as epistemic relativism would destroy the impersonally true quality of any and all facts. Some even go a step further, suggesting that the strong linkage (on which I have relied in the preceding discussion) between background definitions and procedures on the one hand, and factual statements on the other, is *already* an invitation to epistemic relativism. Relating factual statements to the practical procedures that we use to evaluate them would mean that "ways of talking…can't be said to be truer than one another, or more faithful to the way things are in and of themselves than one another" (Boghossian 2007, 44). For such thinkers, the only kind of factuality that will do is a factuality that is *so* impersonal that *any person whatsoever* would have to acknowledge it.

But this response goes too far, in response to an imagined problem of epistemic relativism that never rears its head in the way that such philosophers fear that it will. The problem with Spicer's numbers is not that they don't correspond to "the way things are in and of themselves" while the numbers provided by crowd scientists do. The problem—the problem with "alternative facts"—is that while Spicer's numbers might appear at first glance to be the results of an established procedure of counting, they are not, and the use of any of our existing established crowd-counting procedures shows the claims to be false…but Spicer asserted them anyway, and he and the rest of the Trump administration stood by them in subsequent days. "Alternative facts" are a social and political problem, not an epistemic one.

This is perhaps best and most clearly illustrated with an example drawn from fiction. The two-part episode "Chain of Command" aired during the sixth season of the television show *Star Trek: The Next Generation*. In this episode, Captain Jean-Luc Picard is captured by the hostile Cardassians and subjected to a variety of methods of torture in an attempt to break his will and force him to reveal classified information. The most psychologically dramatic of these methods involves the interrogator showing Picard four lights while insisting that there are five lights, and inflicting intense pain on Picard if he disagrees.[4] Picard, whom we have gotten to know in previous seasons as a man who cares deeply about truth and justice, predictably refuses, leading to powerfully acted scenes of intense torment (Lapidos 2009). At the end of the episode Picard, still refusing to submit, is rescued, and as he is being removed from the room for medical treatment, shouts out, "There are four lights!"—although he subsequently confesses to a fellow officer that he was on the verge of giving in at the time of his rescue.

What we see depicted in the episode is a graphic illustration of the kind of clash that follows from the abandonment of the impersonally true character of factual claims. Picard sees, and says, that there are four lights; his interrogator says that there are five lights; and between the two statements there is only the exercise of coercive power and the imperative of authority. What is lacking here is any impersonal way to determine how many lights there are, and each statement—four versus five—becomes an exercise of power and resistance rather than a factual claim.[5] In that torture chamber, there are only Picard's claims and his interrogator's claims, and each is only acceptable to one of the two parties. This is the situation of "alternative facts."

But what is depicted on the screen is *not* epistemic relativism of the "anything I say is true" sort. For one thing, there are not simply two perspectives on the number of lights that there are. Instead, there are *three*: Picard's, the interrogator's, and the viewer's. The scenario is compelling in no small part because of the similarity of background assumptions—definitions and procedures—between the viewer and Captain Picard. That similarity means that, from *our* perspective as viewers, there *is* an impersonally true factual claim to be made about how many lights there are: there are, *in fact*, four lights. Imagine if the on-screen depiction had shown a number of lights that we would normally call five: if the scene had been shot from the perspective that the interrogator wanted Picard to assume. Picard's refusal to say that there were five lights wouldn't appear as heroic and steadfast if we the viewers did not have an impersonal truth to fall back on. So the problem is not that there *really are*, in some universal sense, only four lights. The problem is that *given our existing, conventional background*, the correct answer about how many lights there are is four, not five, and Picard's interrogator is trying to use force and violence to coerce Picard into assenting to a statement that is a falsehood *given that background*.

---

4 This is, of course, a homage to the scene in George Orwell's novel *Nineteen Eighty-Four* in which Winston Smith is tortured until he admits that his torturer is holding up five fingers even though his torturer, we are told, is only holding up four fingers.

5 It was for precisely this reason that Thomas Hobbes (1651, 93, 198–200) suggested that the sovereign needed to control the interpretation of contracts and the understanding of Scripture, lest social order break down into the state of nature in which everyone would be their own arbiter of truth and meaning. Thanks to Tony Lang for emphasizing this point.

Shift the situation slightly, and imagine that Picard was being taught to speak Cardassian, and was shown a number of lights and asked how many there were. "Four," he says. The teacher, utilizing a Cardassian teaching method of corporal punishment, raps Picard on the knuckles with a stick from an ithian tree, and says, "No, there are five." If Picard continues to insist that there are four lights in *this* situation, then he would be just speaking incorrectly, and failing to use the proper Cardassian word. Or imagine that Picard was unaware that a common Cardassian game, when someone asks how many of some object there are, involves giving a number that is different from the number of objects that you actually think there are, and then when the other speakers agrees, giving yet another number, and so on: "How many lights are there?" "Six." "Okay, six." "No, three." "Okay, three." "No, five." Okay, five." If Picard insists that there are four lights, he wouldn't be playing the game correctly, because he would be utilizing a different procedure than his interlocutor expected and presumed.

Of course neither of those two scenarios are what is going on in the episode "Chain of Command." We the viewers are given a multitude of signs and indicators that what we are watching is neither an instructional setting nor a lack of understanding of the local norms and conventions. We are instead watching someone—Picard—who knows (just as we know) that *in fact* there are four lights, being forced, ultimately unsuccessfully, to say that there are five. Picard's knowing that there are four lights, like our knowing that there are four lights, is inextricably intermixed with the background assumptions that we bring to bear on the situation: assumptions about what counting is and what the word "four" means in such a procedure. That doesn't make Picard's, or our, claim that there are four lights a matter of opinion, or something that we simply assert and impose on others; instead, the conclusion that there are four lights rather than five or any other number of lights is a *logically necessary* conclusion, as long as we are playing the counting game the way we normally play it.

This is an important distinction. Epistemic relativism would be a scenario in which "human agreement decides what is true and what is false," and accordingly, judgments about whether a factual claim was correct would be arbitrary matters of power and influence. The Picard situation is different from epistemic relativism, not because there is some fact about how many lights there are that is ultimately divorced from human convention, but because "it is what human beings *say* that is true and false; and they agree in the *language* they use" (Wittgenstein 1958, para. 241). In this situation, as long as we have agreement in practice about our definitions and procedures, there is no room for ambiguity in determining how many lights there are, and therefore no room for an arbitrary decision. The interjection of such an arbitrary decision—by the interrogator—into the situation therefore, properly, appears to us as a violation of the very notion of factuality, and an unwarranted exercise of power. The claims "there are four lights" and "there are five lights" do not have equal epistemic status, because we the viewers can *clearly see* that there are four lights and not five lights. The claim that there are five lights in such a situation is thus something other than a factual claim, and even if Picard had been coerced to say that there were five lights, that would not make the claim factually true.

Sensible Controversies

Both the situation with Captain Picard and the situation with Trump's inauguration raise the issue of the appropriate response to a claim that is presented as factual, particularly a claim of which we are skeptical. Picard can see that there are four, not five, lights, and a variety of observers could see that there weren't three-quarters of a million people gathered for the inauguration ceremony. But both of those "seeings" are a bit more complex than they might at first seem to be, because the act of "seeing" is far from an unproblematic operation of letting the facts speak for themselves. Consider what is involved in "seeing" how many lights there are on a wall: at a minimum, the observer brings a *definition* of "light" and a *procedure*— "counting"—to bear on the visual input that comes from their eyes.[6] If someone makes a claim that is intended to be factual—and not, say, intended as a joke—and we don't agree with it, it follows that we have at least two lines of investigation we can sensibly follow:

1) Perhaps the speaker is operating with a different definition, in this case of "light," than we were expecting.
2) Perhaps the speaker is operating with a different procedure, in this case for "counting," than we were expecting.

To these lines of investigation we can add a third:

3) Perhaps the speaker *made a mistake* in the application and enacting of the definition and procedure.

A mistake, in this case, could mean that the speaker was confused by something in the environment, perhaps because they were trying not to look at their questioner and so only took a quick glance at the wall. We would react to such a mistake by asking the speaker to take another look, which is the rough equivalent of checking one's work before proceeding: measuring the board a second time before cutting it, checking the temperature again before putting the cookies in the oven, and so on. If the speaker then corrected themselves, we'd chalk the original claim up to

---

6 I am setting aside for the moment the question of precisely *when* these definitions and procedures are brought to bear. Contemporary neuroscience would largely say that the aggregation of raw sensory input into perceived objects happens long before we become conscious of it (e.g. Libet et al. 1983); many if not most contemporary philosophers would agree (e.g., McDowell 1998a, 462–65). Unless it were the case that certain definitions and procedures were somehow hard-wired into the neurological hardware of human beings, the answer to this question would not affect my argument—and if some definitions and procedures *did* turn out to be hard-wired, that would only mean that they were not optional for *any of us*, and could then serve as a court of final appeal for factual claims.

a mistake and simply discard it. But notice that even the determination that the original claim was a "mistake" depends on a presumptively shared background of definition and procedure, so that the speaker can replace their initial misstatement by applying and enacting the definition and procedure "correctly" and dismissing their initial claim as resulting from not properly following the rules, as it were. So this third line of investigation—"Did you make a mistake?"—supervenes on the question of whether the speaker is using the same definition ("I do not think that word means what you think it means") and procedure ("that's not how you do it") as we expect.

Presuming, then, that the speaker has not made a mistake, we are left with only two sensible lines of investigation: an investigation of definitions and an investigation of procedures. Imagine for a moment that we are trying to determine how many people can be in a room at the same time, perhaps because we are looking to schedule a meeting there; you say that 40 people can fit in the room, and I say that only 20 can. If we are both making claims that are intended to be factual, and if neither of us has made a mistake, then it follows that we must not be using the same definition or the same procedure, because both of us can't be right at the same time unless we differ on one of those two aspects. If we agree on what a "person" is and on what "fit" means, and if we agree on how to determine how many people can fit in a room, then we *can't* disagree about the answer. But if we disagree about what a person is[7] or what fit means—say, if one of us is thinking in terms of social distancing during a pandemic, such that people need to maintain a six-foot or two-meter gap between one another, and the other one of us is not thinking in those terms—we might well come to different answers. A similar situation would follow if we were operating with different notions of "fit," each stemming from a distinct cultural context. And if your procedure for determining how many people fit in a room means measuring the area of the floor and dividing that by the size of a chair, while mine means looking at the posted room capacity as authorized by the fire marshal, we might again come to different answers. Those different answers would be a consequence of our differences of definition and/or procedure, and each of us would be correct given our background assumptions.

Because we are assuming that both of us are making statements that are intended to be factual claims, the appropriate response to our disagreement is to inquire more closely into our respective definitions and procedures. A factual claim is supposed to be *impersonally* true, but that doesn't mean that it is supposed to be somehow true for any speaker operating with any definition and procedure; all it means is that the claim is true for speakers operating with the definitions and procedures

---

7 This might seem a little less likely nowadays, when the notion of the individual person has been pretty firmly established globally, but one might see traces of this kind of a disagreement in definition if we shift the situation slightly: suppose that the meeting is a meeting of ambassadors, and the question is "How many ambassadors can fit in this room?" One party to the discussion might well look to answer this question by just focusing on the persons of the ambassadors themselves, and another might look instead at the various staff members each ambassador would bring with them to an important diplomatic meeting.

that are involved in making it in the first place. The impersonal truth of the claim also presumes that those definitions and procedures are being used competently, which is to say in a way that others recognize as correct—and not just correct *for you* or *for me*, but correct *impersonally*, for *anyone* using those definitions and procedures. The shared character of the relevant definitions and procedures is what makes possible the "fact-checking" of a claim that is intended to be factual: someone else can check our work, so to speak, by applying the procedures and definitions and seeing if they get the same result. This is part of what is meant by the oft-repeated contention (e.g., Popper 1979; see also King, Keohane, and Verba 1994; Gerring 2012) that claims intended to be factual are *fallible*, that is, falsifiable by the appropriate kind of evidence.[8] A true factual claim can thus be regarded as a claim that has survived precisely this kind of scrutiny about the definitions and procedures involved in making it, and how they were applied.

After all, how many people can fit in a room, or how many people can fit on the National Mall in Washington, D.C., is not some given aspect of nature, but is inextricably entwined with our definitions and procedures. The answer is different for different definitions of "fit" and different procedures of determining capacity. Those different answers can *all* be facts, despite their disagreement, as long as all parties to the dispute are applying their definitions and procedures in ways that are neither idiosyncratic nor arbitrary—in other words, in ways that are not dependent on the individual observer. Evaluating a statement intended to be a factual claim means evaluating that claim in terms of its definitions and procedures, and not simply in terms of whether we agree with it or whether we "believe" the speaker. Hannah Pitkin points out that making a claim that is intended to be factual means "announcing what attitude we are prepared to take toward those who disagree with us, what kind of support we would be able to muster for our assertion if challenged, how we regard that assertion and intend to use it, how it is to be used and considered by others" (1973, 239); that attitude in turn permits disagreement on definitions and procedures, and on whether they have been correctly applied, but does not permit the simple expression of a personal preference. What matters is the *logic* of the claim, which in turn has to be compelling for anyone who uses the same definitions and procedures in the same way. There is thus no special problem with the conclusion that there can be different factual answers to the question of how many people can fit in a room—as long as those different answers depend on differences of definition and procedure, and not on differences of opinion or sentiment.

In other words, saying that facts are contingent on, and a product of, particular definitions and procedures is not the same as saying that facts are arbitrary or subjective. "40 people can fit in this room if we are following established social distancing guidelines and determining 'fit' by arranging chairs in the room" is nothing but a fuller elaboration of the statement "40 people can fit in this room," provided of course that the speaker is using that definition and that procedure. Likewise, "20

---

8 There is another aspect to falsification, involving the replacement of one set of procedures and definitions by another, the resulting changes in which claims are factually true, and whether this constitutes progress in knowledge. I will take up that aspect in the next chapter.

people can fit in this room if we look at what the fire marshal said" makes explicit what was implicit in the initial statement "20 people can fit in this room." Making those implicit definitions and procedures explicit *eliminates the apparent contradiction* between the statements: they can *both* be true at the same time, now that we understand them better and more fully. And while it would be incorrect, or at least deeply misleading, to say that one statement was true for one person while the other statement was true for the other person, it would be entirely correct to say that the truth of each statement depends on the definitions and procedures from which the claim that it makes arises. The difference between those two formulations is that while the former (different statements can be true for different people) makes the truth of a statement a function of the *speaker*, the latter (claims resting on different definitions and procedures can be simultaneously true even if they appear to be different) makes the truth of a statement a function of the *logic* of the claim, understood in context. That latter formulation also opens the possibility of recognizing the truth of a statement even while disagreeing with, or rejecting, the parameters of the claim it makes: "sure, if we ignored social distancing guidelines, it is true that 40 people would fit in here, but we should adhere to social distancing guidelines."

All of this is in turn afforded by the presumption that both of the statements in question were intended to be factual claims.[9] Because the claim is not simply that I "think" that 40 people will fit in the room, but that 40 people *can* fit in the room, it certainly looks as though the intention here is to make a factual claim that would be impersonally true. But "surface grammar can at best be a guide to pragmatic structure" (Kukla and Lance 2009, 32), and words can be deceiving—which is why context is so important in making sense of a claim. If the claim is being made in the context of two people working to schedule a meeting, it is a safe bet that the statement is intended to be a factual claim, because in that context it would make little sense for someone to make a statement about a room's capacity with any other intention. Matters are more ambiguous if the statement is made in the course of a conversation between two bored undergraduate students in a residence hall lounge at 2am, or in some other context divorced from any immediate practical use of the information that the claim provides. Making sense of the statement means making sense of the context in which it is made, and a different understanding of the context may well result in a different understanding of what the stated claim is intended to do. Outside of a context in which a factual intention can be safely presumed, the possibility of treating the claim as a candidate for being impersonally true quickly evaporates and, indeed, insisting on treating the claim as one intended to be factual might be more disruptive than productive, or at least might be seriously out of sync with the actual situation.

Sean Spicer's claims about the number of people attending Trump's inauguration were delivered from the podium of the briefing room in the White House, in front of an audience of journalists. The ordinary presumption in such a setting

---

9 Bernardo Teles Fazendeiro (2023, 10–11) makes a similar point, although I am not entirely satisfied with the notion of "meaningful truth" that he juxtaposes to "factual truth." The reasons why will emerge in the following chapters.

is that the press secretary is operating as a reliable source of information about the administration's activities, giving the assembled reporters a sense of what the president and the rest of the federal government are doing. While the position of press secretary is a political position, and the press secretary is expected to adhere to and uphold the administration's position on controversial issues, much of the outcry about Spicer's performance of the role involved his apparent disregard for the truth of even the most innocuous of statements (Terris 2017). "Message discipline" took the place of any kind of commitment to factuality, and even when it came to statements about numbers—statements that could be easily fact-checked by third-party observers—Spicer consistently adhered to the position that the Trump administration was bigger, better, and in every way superior to any other administration or any other politician in history. Although appearing to offer factual claims, Spicer's statements all too often did not; they appeared to be offered as impersonally true, but did not stand up to any scrutiny. Whatever their worth as *political* statements intended to rally the president's supporters, as factual claims, they were all too often entirely valueless. But by *appearing to be* factual claims, and by being offered in a setting where factual claims would ordinarily be expected, they are perhaps best understood not as factual claims at all, but as "counterfeit" facts (Shotter 1993a, 138): statements that appropriate the form of impersonally true claims but which actually deliver the very kind of idiosyncratic and arbitrary assertions that Picard's Cardassian interrogator sought to coerce him into agreeing with.

Descriptive Claims

At this point in the discussion it may be useful to be more explicit about the concepts I have been developing through the preceding examples. I have distinguished between *statements* and *claims*: statements are an arrangement of words, but a claim is what a statement expresses. We might call a claim the *meaning* of a statement, with the important qualification that any given statement might have different meanings depending on how we read it. "That's an affectionate cat" might be ironic if the cat is presently hissing and clawing at my arm, or it might be a metaphor or a bit of slang if applied to something that we wouldn't ordinarily call a cat in the first place. Which claim we think the statement is making—what its meaning is—depends on the context and how we position the statement in that context: what we regard as the *intention* of the claim. Intention here means not any kind of subjective motivation on the part of the speaker, but what we take the future state of affairs envisioned by the statement to be (Anscombe 1963, 35–36); with a communicative action like making a statement, that future state affairs involves how people will respond to the statement. The words of that statement could be a joke, or they could be commentary, or they could be a number of other things, and each of those comes with a different envisioned future response. But those words, that statement, might also, in certain contexts, be understood as making a claim intended to be factual: that the animal in question, a cat, is affectionate. In that context, the envisioned future state involves treating the matter as settled and acting towards the animal accordingly.

The important role of intention here suggests the need for a term to characterize a claim that is a) intended to be factual but b) might or might not be factually true. The problem is that the word "factual," used to characterize a claim, *already* presumes that the claim is true, and thus bypasses the question of intention in order to focus on validity. I might, however, intend a claim to be factual, but be in error: the cat I called "affectionate" starts aggressively biting my finger, and I realize that I mistook a moment of affection for a broader affectionate disposition, or perhaps I confused the definitions of the words "affectionate" and "aggressive." Claims intended to be factual are fallible claims, but they cannot be contested on just any grounds. If a claim is intended to be factual, we have recourse to the kind of structured controversies I have been discussing: controversies about definitions, controversies about procedures, controversies about mistaken observations or other incorrect applications of definitions and procedures. All of those presume that the claim was intended to be factual, *even if it is not actually factual, but false.* It would make little sense to evaluate a satirical or ironic claim by closely examining definitions and procedures, and arguably such claims can't be factually true or false because they were never intended as such. So I will reach back into archaic English usage for a term to characterize claims as intending to be factual: *factic*, which might be contrasted with (say) "ironic" or "aesthetic." The first question to be asked when evaluating a potentially factual claim, then, concerns its intention: is the claim factic, or not? If so, *then* we can proceed to a discussion of definitions and procedures, whether they are shared by the speaker and her audience, and whether those procedures have been enacted and those definitions have been used in the accepted manner.

But not just any procedures, and not just any definitions. While it may not have escaped notice that (almost) all of the examples I have discussed thus far are descriptions,[10] I want to draw this point out by looking more closely at the act of description itself. The features I have claimed for facts—in particular, the notion of an impersonal truth that can be arrived at through a careful comparison of definitions and procedures in order to ensure that speaker and audience are using the same notions in the same way—depend on the way that description works. The act of description involves using shared definitions and procedures in order to bring an object before us. A "fact" is then a true factic description, and since true factic descriptions depend on shared definitions and procedures, it follows that a fact is *a description with which no competent speaker of the relevant language can disagree.* If I put forth a true factic description, then I have used the accepted definitions and procedures in their ordinary, established ways, and no one else who

---

10 The mathematical equations I mentioned earlier as additional but not alternative facts are, perhaps, not descriptions. The epistemic status of mathematical expressions is a very complex issue; for an overview, see Hacking (2014). For most of the remainder of this book I will simply set this question aside by focusing on claims made in languages other than pure mathematics.

proceeds in a similar fashion can arrive at a different conclusion than I have—unless one of us has made a mistake.

I will start with a homely example: On my desk in front of me is a wax candle, a pillar candle that has an elephant on it. The elephant's head, ears, trunk, and front legs are formed from wax that extends out from the surface of the candle, so that the elephant appears to be walking out of the candle towards me—and the lower half of the outside of the candle is molded so as to suggest a grassy plain on which the elephant appears to be walking. The candle material is generally a whitish-brown; the elephant's tusks are white, its eyes black.[11] I have just described the candle to you; perhaps you can picture it in your mind.

Describing something—and, in particular, describing something *to someone*—means focusing attention on the object being described, which makes the person doing the describing recede into the background. In describing an object to you I am in the first instance putting myself in a situation of receptiveness and attentiveness to the object, to certain particular attributes of the object as they show themselves to me; I am, so to speak, *attuned* to the object, and when I offer a description of the object to you, I am working to make you similarly attuned. Description rests on a way of comporting oneself towards an object that emphasizes observation (Gifford 1991). So I use words that are intended to call your attention to those attributes of the object that I want you to notice, and if it works, you notice not the description or the describer, but the object itself.

When I describe the candle on my desk to you, what I intend to do is to bring the candle before us in a way that makes it available for things we might want to do with it. A good description gives us a shared basis for future action, although the description itself doesn't typically tell you precisely what that future action will be: did I describe the candle to you because I want to give you information about what's on my desk so that you have a mental image of me writing this book, or because I want to you to go into my house to get something from my desk and I was concerned that you might grab the wrong thing, or because I want to use that candle and my act of describing it as an example in this chapter and intermittently throughout the rest of the book?[12] Although in this case the last option is closest to the truth, the point is that you usually can't simply read the *purpose for which I am describing something to you* off of the statements themselves. You can produce a wider understanding of my statements, of course, based on your understanding of the situation in which we find ourselves—for example, if we are talking about our mutual love of elephants, my description of the candle on my desk might be meant as evidence that I really do love elephants: see, I even have an elephant candle on

---

11 There are other things on my desk, including books, papers, framed photographs, a Marillion Weekend 2019 mug, and a bobblehead of Chirrut Îmwe, but describing those to you would take us rather far afield.

12 Or because René Descartes (1993) uses a description of a lump of wax at a key point in his argument about the unreliability of the senses when it comes to providing knowledge, and for those who have read or one day will read Descartes on this point I wanted to gesture at some tension between his account and mine?

my desk! But any of the potential purposes to which a description might contribute are in a way secondary to what we might call the *primary intention* of an act of description: to bring the object before us and, in this instance, to lift the candle out of the general background of "stuff here in the room" and make it available to us in a distinct and distinctive way.

This characterization of description holds whether I am confining myself to the visual register or whether I am utilizing other senses as well. I did not talk about how the candle responds to my touch or how it tastes, but I could have done so without modifying anything crucial about the act of description. Likewise I could have used a balance to determine how much the candle weighed, or a ruler to determine just how tall it is and how far the elephant head extends from the surface, or I could have used the full resources of a laboratory to detail the exact chemical composition of the candle. All of those tool-aided "prosthetic" ways of engaging the world and the objects in it would not make the resulting account any less of a description.[13] Indeed, I neglected to mention that I was looking at the candle through the lenses in my glasses, since prosthetic tools like glasses have become so commonly accepted nowadays that they literally "go without saying." In any case, the point is that whether one uses "unaided" or prosthetically "enhanced" tool-assisted senses make no difference to the character of the act of description.

Notice also that the description I offered used words that are part of a common stock of meaningful notions, including "elephant," "whitish-brown," "wax," and "candle." Of course it did; how else would I make myself understood except by using words that were already a part of our common language? If you had no idea what a "candle" was, my describing the object on my desk to you as a candle would do no good, since it would not help bring the object before us in any useful way. So description depends on a shared descriptive vocabulary; we have to in some sense "speak the same language" before I can use words in that language to describe something to you. Although words like "elephant" and "candle" do not have completely determinate boundaries of application—it's difficult and perhaps impossible to come up with precise definitions of "candle" and "elephant" that would cover *all* correct uses of those words in *all* circumstances—there is certainly sufficient agreement in practice to make my description meaningful to you.[14] Describing the object as a candle means, for example, that it isn't a pair of scissors, and describing the animal represented on the candle as an elephant means that it is not a six-legged creature with horns and wings. To say that we share a descriptive vocabulary means only that we have this kind of sufficient agreement, enough so that "a whitish-brown wax pillar candle with an elephant on it" *means something* in a way that "snorlax wiffleball crabtree" does not.

13 On such "prosthetics," see (Shotter 1993b, 21–23; and Haraway 1990).
14 The evidence that sufficient agreement in practice exists is, of course, whether the description of the candle I offered a few paragraphs earlier accomplished its intended goal. Although agreement in practice is *presumed* in every act of describing, it is always an open question in each individual situation whether or not that agreement actually obtains.

The point is that the vocabulary out of which a description is constructed is always and already part of a community of language-users that extends beyond the individual offering the description. And this is where the potential for a descriptive claim to be *impersonally* true comes from: it can be true for everyone who uses that vocabulary in a similar enough way to be judged a competent speaker of that language. Descriptions are always descriptions *from* a location within a community, and are in a certain sense *tied to* that community. This holds even if I am describing something when no one else is around to hear and receive my description. Suppose I am taking a walk and come upon a rabbit nibbling on the grass.[15] In describing the situation in that way, even just to myself ("A rabbit!"), I am drawing on a common descriptive vocabulary involving walks and rabbits. I am already indebted to a particular descriptive vocabulary even before I tell anyone, even myself, about the encounter. Indeed, my perception of the rabbit *as a rabbit* (and my walk *as a walk*, and the grass *as grass*, etc.) is not some neutral emanation from the world, but depends on the same complex inheritance of concepts and practices that enable me subsequently to describe it to you (McDowell 1998b, 491). I can't even see and understand the rabbit *as a rabbit* without first having learned what a rabbit is, which is to say, having learned how to correctly use the word "rabbit" to describe some objects but not others.

One has to be a competent language-user in order to make a valid descriptive claim. The encounter and my descriptions of the object I encountered depend, crucially, on a shared descriptive vocabulary. That vocabulary comes with notions of correct use that prevent me—if I am acting correctly as a competent speaker of the language—from saying that I encountered a rabbit on my walk if there was no rabbit. The descriptive vocabulary we share does enable me to construct the statement "I saw a rabbit on my walk!" even if I did not actually see a rabbit—maybe I saw a fox, maybe I saw a squirrel, maybe I saw no animals at all—but the rules of properly using the words in our shared vocabulary mean that such a factic claim made under those circumstances would simply be *wrong*. Describing an object does not mean that one can say anything that one wants to, but that what one says has to somehow respond or relate to the object itself. Otherwise, if the object is no longer in play, we are not really describing correctly; we might instead be making things up, or perhaps we are just using misusing words. And this makes it difficult, perhaps impossible, for the act of description to fulfill its primary intention and bring an object before us in a useful way; any secondary intentions that the act of description also has would likewise run into problems. If I claim that the candle is on my desk when the correct way to describe its location using our shared vocabulary is "on the shelf," I haven't given you a particularly helpful sense of where to look for it. Only a true factic description—a fact—properly constructed from our shared descriptive vocabulary provides a solid basis for future action.

---

15 For this example, and the general point about the conceptual embeddedness of observatives, I am indebted to Kukla and Lance (2009, 76–78).

To this point I have been proceeding as though there were only one descriptive vocabulary which we all shared, but the actual situation is considerably more complicated than that. Because descriptive vocabularies are tied to communities of competent speakers, rather than springing full-grown from objects themselves, it is always possible to approach *any* object with a different vocabulary and generate a different description of the object. Whether I am focusing on the candle's physical appearance or its chemical composition (and whether I am bringing to bear the physical and conceptual instruments appropriate to the measurement of appearance or composition) is related to the secondary purpose for which I am describing the candle; that secondary purpose suggests the vocabulary in which my description should be couched. From the point of view of someone looking to produce more light in the room, the important question is likely whether or not the candle will burn if lit, and not whether the elephant on the candle is an aesthetically pleasing representation that fits with the rest of the room's décor, or precisely what kind of material the candle is made of. Each of these descriptions involve a concretely situated describer with a particular purposive "take" on the situation, and a descriptive vocabulary, including a community of competent speakers sustaining that vocabulary, to match: interior designers focusing on the candle's aesthetic qualities, chemists interested in its chemical make-up, and people sitting in the dark looking for a way to illuminate the room. None of these descriptions of the candle are any more basic or fundamental than any other, and each description is constructed from a different descriptive vocabulary for a different purpose (as in Pitkin 1973, 257). But all of them depend on speakers using definitions and procedures in a way that is acceptable to a particular community.

So it is possible to correctly—factually—describe the object on my desk in a number of different ways, depending on the descriptive vocabulary that is used to construct the description. All descriptions are constructed out of a shared vocabulary that picks out some but not all aspects of the object described. That in turn means that there is no such thing as an ultimate or final description that would *completely* bring the object before us in all of its inexhaustible richness; there are only different purposive "cuts" highlighting different features of the world and the objects in it.[16] Certainly the chemist, the interior decorator, and the person looking for illumination are not describing the object on my desk in the same way, but that doesn't mean that correct descriptions constructed out of their separate descriptive vocabularies are *contradictory*. Instead it means that they are *complementary*, setting the object before us in different ways for different purposes. The interior decorator and the chemist are constructing different descriptions of the object, but those descriptions are in no way inconsistent with one another; the candle can, without any special consideration, be both made from dyed paraffin wax *and* nicely coordinated with the other elephant-themed decorations in the room. Each descriptive vocabulary comes with its own material for constructing correct descriptions, but this does not mean that there is no such thing as a correct description. Instead

---

16   I have borrowed the notion of a purposive "cut" from Barad (2007).

there are many correct descriptions, many different—additional, not alternative!—facts, arising from the various descriptive vocabularies we might bring to bear, and the different purposes for which we are engaged in description in the first place.[17]

Competent Speakers

The account of description I have been sketching depends quite crucially on the notion of a "competent speaker." This is worth pulling apart a bit, because otherwise it can easily lead to the mistaken conclusion that anyone who disagrees with my description of an object is simply "incompetent." But such a conclusion is unwarranted. The key thing about the notion of a "competent speaker" is whether when faced with a disagreement we find, upon further investigation, a sufficient gap between our own definitions and procedures and those of the speaker that we do not judge the speaker to be a competent speaker of our language—although they might be a perfectly competent speaker of some *other* language. Between two competent speakers of the same language, facts are necessarily shared, so there can be no sensible disagreement: the candle either has or does not have an elephant on it, and any other use of those words is incorrect, a mistake. Between competent speakers of different languages, there can be additional facts, which is to say true factic claims that are made using different vocabularies and highlighting different aspects of the objects that they describe: the candle is made of wax *and* coordinates nicely with the décor of the room. As long as we are working with factic claims, there are *only* those two options, along with the possibility that a particular claim is simply incorrect—and determining that a factic claim is not true also depends on our using words in the same way, because only then can we figure out if the words of this statement properly claim a fact.

So when would we ever characterize a speaker as "not a competent speaker of our language"? It's not enough to notice that they are using words in ways that differ from our own ways of using those words, because that could arise from a number of different situations: maybe they are tired, or impaired, engaged in some piece of wordplay other than the one we expected—looking for rhymes, say, or conforming their sentences to particular rhythmic patterns. Instead, we have to make a judgment that they are trying but failing to use words in the correct way: that they are, in some sense, still *learning* our language, and that their mistakes arise from their incapacity to "say what they mean." The clearest examples of this can probably be seen when a student studies a foreign language and gives incorrect answers to descriptive questions ("Where is the candle?") because they have, for instance, confused

---

17 Note that the phrase "the object on my desk" isn't some kind of objective/neutral substrate on which other descriptions can somehow supervene. "The object on my desk" is just another descriptive vocabulary, useful for some purposes and not for others. The conceptual slippage that leads to the categorical privileging of some particular descriptive vocabulary as closer to "reality" than others—a slippage at the heart of John Searle's (1995) distinction between "brute" and "institutional" facts—is something I will take up in subsequent chapters. Needless to say I do not think that this distinction does very much for us.

the words "desk" and "floor," and say "the candle is on the floor" when it is on the desk. In such a situation, the proper response is to correct the error, pointing out that the correct descriptive use of the words is different than the speaker thought that it was: that the word for the place where the candle is at the moment is "desk" and not "floor." Of course, the speaker could be mistaken in another way, and they could erroneously think that the candle was on the floor, but in that situation we wouldn't doubt their linguistic competence, but their eyesight or their memory. Instead, linguistic competence is *presumed* when we seek to correct the speaker, because if the speaker wasn't trying to use the words "floor" and "desk" in the same way that we do, it would do little good to insist that the candle was on the desk, and imploring the speaker to simply look at where the candle was wouldn't lead to their reformulation of the statement to make a true factic claim unless the speaker already knew how to use those words correctly.

Once again, the context and the situation are crucial for figuring out the correct response to a statement that seems to offer a factic description that is nonetheless false. If I am still learning the language, then my mistaken use of words calls for a pedagogical correction about the correct use of words. In such a context, a statement that looks to be making a factic descriptive claim but is false can be treated as a teachable moment. Otherwise, all you can do is ask me to look again— and if, having done so, I keep insisting that the candle is on the floor, you might wonder whether I am engaged in an act of factic description as opposed to having some quite different intention for my words. Or you might start to doubt whether I am actually a competent speaker of the language at all. Or perhaps you are the one making the mistake?

The point is that a judgment about whether someone is a competent speaker of a language is a judgment that is made in course of our interaction, and cannot be ascertained in advance. When we speak, we *presume* that our listeners are competent speakers of the language that we are using, just as we *presume* that we ourselves are. As our conversation unfolds I may come to doubt whether we are using words in the same ways, and if I attribute that difference to one of us still being a learner of the language while someone else already knows the correct way to use the words in question, then the situation shifts from one of disagreement about the facts to one of *training* (Wittgenstein 1958, paras. 85–86). Otherwise, if we all continue to presume that we are all competent speakers, our disagreement is subject to common adjudication, because we all share a common language that we all know how to use correctly. Factic claims are fallible in specific ways, and factic claims that stand up to fact-checking are facts.

Of course, this possibility of coming to a consensus about the facts depends on our treatment of statements as making factic descriptive claims, because such claims have a primary intention of bring an object before us, and that in turn means that they can be evaluated *observationally*. The attunement to the object that is an indispensable part of good observation ensures that when we all consider the candle, our evaluation of claims about the candle are something other than just our fanciful speculations, but are in important ways addressed to the candle itself—and if I say that the candle is square, you can evaluate that claim by referencing the candle. The possibility of consensus also depends on a shared descriptive vocabulary, which the parties to the conversation can of course work out in the course of the discussion; if we start off with terms like "white" and "brown" which don't unequivocally describe the candle, we can certainly evolve a new shared vocabulary, in which terms like "whitish-brown" have a place. In doing so we have, in effect, produced a new way of using words, a "language"[18] of which we can now be competent speakers and a vocabulary we can use to generate true factual claims. Alternatively, we could continue to tussle over which of us was using the words in question correctly, using the notion of linguistic competence as a marker: "You're just using that word wrong, the candle is brown."

When we are dealing with languages that are more restricted and specialized than ordinary or natural language, such as the technical language used by practitioners in some specific field, the recourse to a judgment about competence can happen even faster. Consider the claim that democracies do not fight one another; many scholars of international affairs would agree that the "absence of war between democracies comes as close as anything we have to an empirical law in international relations" (Levy 1989, 88). When faced with potential counterexamples—the war between Spain and the United States in 1898, for example, or the "football war" between Honduras and El Salvador in 1969—the usual response from researchers (e.g., Russett 1993; Oneal and Russett 2000) is to question whether these countries are properly described as "democracies" in the time-period in question (did they have all of the attributes of a mature democracy?) or whether the conflict in question is properly described as a "war" at all (were there a sufficient number of battlefield deaths, with 1000 usually serving as the cut-off point for classifying a conflict as a war?). An ongoing line of inquiry in the area of democratic peace research is whether the absence of war between democracies is best described in "monadic" or "dyadic" terms: whether democracies simply fight fewer wars than non-democracies, or whether democracies simply don't fight wars against one another (Rousseau et al. 1996). All of these can be most easily understood as issues of language use, as the various parties to these debates operate with different definitions and procedures, and also respond to disagreement as though the speaker simply doesn't speak the language properly. Indeed, numerous scholarly disputes can be understood this way, as struggles over the correct way to describe something *as* something, and as efforts to educate others in what one considers the correct way to do so.

As such, we should understand "being a competent speaker" as an *ongoing achievement* rather than a quality that someone either does or does not possess in a permanent way (Medina 2004, 355–56). Whether we are talking about ordinary natural language or specialized technical language, I show that I am a competent speaker of a language by using words in a way that others judge as correct. Sometimes that means shifting to a pedagogical ground, so to speak, and correcting someone else's incorrect word usage, or being corrected ourselves. The judgment

---

18 Wittgenstein would likely call this a "language-game" rather than a "language."

of competence thus serves to delimit the boundary of the community of speakers—which is also the boundary of the community among which the kind of true factic description I have been discussing in this chapter can be shared.

All of which means that when faced with a statement that we seek to treat as making a factic claim—as intending to be evaluated according to its factuality—we need to be careful to consider the community of competent speakers among whom that claim makes sense. A factic claim can only be true or false within that community, because it is quite literally meaningless outside of that language.[19] A true factual description is one that competent speakers of the relevant language cannot disagree with, because to do so would be to use words in a different way; if someone *does* disagree with such a claim, we either question their linguistic competence or wonder if they are speaking a different language, we investigate their definitions and procedures, or we wonder if they have made a mistake. Those are the only sensible options for dealing with a factic description. So when Sean Spicer insists that there were more people at Trump's inauguration than at Obama's inauguration, he is either mistaken, or he is using words in a different way than we are, or he is not a competent speaker of our language and needs to be corrected. There is simply no warrant for *accepting* his claim, given the usual meanings of words like "more" and "people," unless we drop the initial presupposition that his statement was intended as a factual description. And treating the statement as a factic description in the first place is not a decision we can make based on the words of the statement itself, but instead involves a much broader set of considerations about the kind of situation that the speaker and the audience alike find themselves in.

---

19   And if a true factual claim is translated into another language, then statements in that other language that make the same factual claim are true as well. If "the candle is on the desk" is true, then "die Kerze steht auf dem Schreibtisch" is also true. In later chapters I will take up more interesting cases, in which translation is not so simple.

2   Descriptions

On March 11, 2020, the World Health Organization's Director-General, Dr. Tedros Adhanom Ghebreyesus, declared that the WHO had "made the assessment that COVID-19 can be characterized as a pandemic" (Ghebreyesus 2020). At that point, only about 4000 people had died, and globally there were only about 118,000 cases reported in 114 countries—a small fraction of the millions of cases and deaths that would soon occur. Indeed, the declaration was explicitly based on a forecast of how bad things could get if countries did not take some drastic steps to "detect, test, treat, isolate, trace, and mobilize their people in the response." At the same time, the Director-General's statement held out hope that global outbreak of the coronavirus *could* be controlled; he explicitly linked his declaration to a whole litany of strategies that the WHO had been recommending for weeks, arguing that with sufficient political leadership and preparedness, "all countries can still change the course of this pandemic."

Dr. Ghebreyesus's use of the term "pandemic" in this context is notable. The WHO stopped using "pandemic" as an official designation after the organization was criticized for seeming too alarmist during a 2009 swine flu outbreak (Nebehay 2020). At that time, to be classified as a pandemic, a disease had to show "community-level outbreaks" in two different world regions, as this would indicate a sufficiently global spread of the underlying virus that disease rates would be almost certain to rise dramatically all around the world (World Health Organization 2009). "Pandemic is not a word to use lightly or carelessly," Dr. Ghebreyesus admitted, tacitly recognizing the historical context. "It is a word that, if misused, can cause unreasonable fear, or unjustified acceptance that the fight is over, leading to unnecessary suffering and death" (Ghebreyesus 2020). But neither he nor the WHO offered a replacement definition, so the declaration instead seemed like a way to call attention to the seriousness of the outbreak rather than to provide any precise characterization of how severe COVID-19 was or could become.

Yet the statement appears to be intended as factual. Dr. Ghebreyesus did not say that the WHO *believed* or *felt* that COVID-19 was a pandemic, but that COVID-19 *was* a pandemic, and should be correctly described as such, at least according to the WHO's assessment. The WHO was in effect asking the audience and the media, and the world as a whole, to trust its conclusion: to accept that the WHO's scientists

DOI: 10.4324/9781003455912-2

had correctly applied a definition and a procedure, even though the details were not spelled out. The request was not simply "trust the WHO," but "trust that the WHO has made an appropriate determination," along with an implicit invitation to check the WHO's work. The newsworthiness of the event relied on the notion that the WHO's assessment was something to be taken seriously, and was more than just an arbitrary declaration that might constitute a misuse of the term. There is a close linkage between the presumptive factuality of the WHO's assessment and the authority that it is supposed to carry; this was not just some random collection of people deciding that a pandemic was upon us, but a responsible agency making a determination that was supposed to be understood as impersonally true.

The centrality of decision and authority to this process might suggest that we are no longer operating in the realm of facts at all, because a competent speaker of the language might well disagree with the WHO's assessment. "Pandemic" is one of those words that does not have a precise operational definition but which nonetheless carries immense emotional weight.[1] And successfully character- izing something as a pandemic brings along social and political consequences, including justifying any number of emergency measures. We might think that this is precisely a place where a formal and exact specification might be helpful, as that would enable the kind of decentralized process described in the previous chapter: agreement on definitions and procedures would move us closer to a situ- ation in which any competent speaker—and not just the officials of the WHO— could assess the situation for themselves, much as any competent speaker of our language could determine for themselves whether the book were on the shelf or on the floor. But medical professionals, public health scholars, and government agencies operate with different definitions, and these different definitions have important implications—including whether the speaker's assessment of the risk of widespread disease outbreak concludes that an outbreak is likely or not (Singer, Thompson, and Bonsall 2021). Do we therefore have a situation in which there is no fact of the matter, and no way to determine the truth or falsity of a claim about whether something is a pandemic? Was Dr. Ghebreyesus expressing an *opinion*, despite the seemingly factic form of the sentence he used?

Play Ball

A closer examination of the act of description is thus called for. The concep- tual issues involved here may be easier to see in a situation where the stakes are not quite as high, such as in a sporting competition in which officials of various types are called on to make determinations about events that take place during the course of the game. In the game of baseball, for example, these officials are called "umpires," and one of their most important jobs is determining "balls and strikes": whether the pitcher has thrown the baseball inside the strike zone where a

---

1 It turns out that there are a lot of words like this—which should not be surprising if we remember from the previous chapter that rules for competent language use are socially negotiated.

batter has a fair chance of hitting it (a strike), or whether the baseball was outside of that zone and the batter should therefore not be penalized for not swinging at it (a ball). The definition of the strike zone is clearly given in the official rules of Major League Baseball:

> The STRIKE ZONE is that area over home plate the upper limit of which is a horizontal line at the midpoint between the top of the shoulders and the top of the uniform pants, and the lower level is a line at the hollow beneath the kneecap. The Strike Zone shall be determined from the batter's stance as the batter is prepared to swing at a pitched ball.
> (Official Playing Rules Committee 2021, 152)

The official rules also specify that if the batter does not swing their bat, only the umpire may determine whether a thrown baseball has passed through the strike zone or not, and that this decision is final (ibid., 95).[2] The umpire's decision is extremely consequential, because a batter who amasses three strikes is out, while a batter who amasses four balls gets to advance to first base.

What we have here is a situation in which the definition is clear—clear enough that the strike zone can be drawn on a picture of any batter standing at home plate prepared to swing at a pitch—but despite this clarity, different people might not agree on whether a given pitch is a ball or a strike. Pitched baseballs move extremely quickly, covering the 60 feet 6 inches between the pitcher and home plate in less than half a second, and sometimes in the time it literally takes to blink your eyes (Quinton 2017). At that speed, different observers might reasonably disagree about the precise location of the baseball when it crossed home plate. Understandably, the pitcher would prefer that every pitch they throw be a strike, while the batter would prefer that anything they didn't swing at be a ball, and this obvious and strategic interest raises doubts about any involved player's reporting of the facts; they might actually be *seeing* the pitch *as* a strike or a ball, seeing what in some sense they wanted to see (Balcetis and Dunning 2006). The clarity of the definition of the strike zone alone is insufficient to resolve the ambiguity. Competent speakers of the baseball language might not agree, and this would bring the game to a halt.

Instead, the umpire's determination of whether a pitch was a ball or a strike resolves the impasse, and allows play to proceed. Part of playing baseball competently means accepting both the definition of the strike zone and the procedure for determining the correct description of a particular pitch—and accepting that that procedure is not decentralized or distributed. It is not enough for a pitched ball to pass through the strike zone in order for it to be a strike; the pitch also needs to be "called"—described by the umpire as—a strike. Because the umpire's decision cannot be appealed, after a determination has been made we *do* have a situation in which a competent speaker of the relevant language cannot disagree with the

---

2 Any legal pitch that "[i]s struck at by the batter and is missed" is a strike, regardless of whether the baseball was inside the strike zone or not (Official Playing Rules Committee 2021, 152).

claim. Indeed, umpires are explicitly empowered by the rules to eject anyone from the game who argues balls and strikes with them, so a public disagreement about whether a pitch was a ball or a strike comes with a penalty—a penalty that we might well regard as a pedagogical instrument for training players and managers in the correct use of the word "strike."

But as anyone who has ever watched or been to a baseball game knows, things are not quite so simple.[3] Because everyone else can see home plate and the baseball (perhaps not as well as or from the precise vantage-point of the umpire, but still), everyone else can in principle *accept* the definition of the strike zone but *reject* the procedure for determining whether a pitch was a strike or not. The unsurprising result is consternation on the part of the spectators, and the players and managers, when the umpire calls a pitch a strike that does not look to have passed through the strike zone. Players and managers in their dugouts on the field, closer to home plate than any spectators, are especially prone to this reaction. Many televised baseball games now display a computer-generated strike zone box next to the batter, allowing viewers to see for themselves where a pitched ball goes in relation to the strike zone. Slow-motion instant replay adds an additional complication: after the umpire makes their call, the pitch can be viewed at a much slower speed, placing television commentators and team officials and fans in the stands with smartphones[4] in a position to second-guess the umpire almost immediately.

In all of these cases, when someone disagrees with the umpire's call of "strike," the usual objection is something like, "that wasn't a strike." This is a disagreement about whether a descriptive claim is true or not, and it should be resolvable among competent speakers by simply using the agreed-on procedures and definitions. But the problem here is precisely that the speakers do *not* agree on the procedure, even though they agree on the definition. My disagreement with the umpire based on my viewing of the pitch in slow-motion replay is based on the notion that the correct procedure should rely less on the umpire and more on viewing the replay in slow motion; the umpire's call is based on the notion that the correct procedure should be his[5] determination in real time. *Neither one of these claims is any more "factual" than the other.* They are, instead, additional facts, operating somewhat in parallel, much like the chemist and the interior designer's facts about the candle on my desk. From each perspective, it is clear that the pitch was or was not a strike, and the claim can be evaluated in a relatively straightforward way. Arguments between umpires (or referees) and other viewers are actually disagreements about procedures, not about facts.

---

3 Lest anyone conclude that this is a problematic ambiguity specific to the game of baseball, consider the determination by a referee that a football player has been injured (and by "football" here I mean what U.S. readers will likely know as "soccer," unlike readers in the rest of the world). It is obviously in the footballer's interest to have sustained a minor injury, because that opens up the possibility of free kicks and even the expulsion of opposing players from the game. Here too the referee steps in and makes a determination that allows the game to proceed.

4 Fans without smartphones cannot watch almost-instantaneous slow-motion replays of pitches, because Major League Baseball prohibits such replays from being shown on the stadium monitors.

5 At the time of writing, all umpires in Major League Baseball are male.

Part of why the conceptual aspects of the argument are often obscured is that in this day and age we have a marked preference for ever-finer-grained measurement devices, especially when it comes to physical aspects of the world. We build laboratory instruments capable of detecting the slightest variations in physical quantity, we design and engineer devices and materials to a level of precision undreamed of by previous generations. We measure the outcomes of sporting events down to the millionth of a second (International Olympic Committee 2021) and we use artificial intelligence to track the course of play (White 2021). We have a tendency to confuse greater precision with increased factuality, as though facts were simply features of the world which we could more or less accurately measure, rather than true factic descriptive claims *about* the world that depend on a practical consensus regarding definitions and procedures. Increased precision is an impressive development of one class of observational procedures, but it would be misleading to reserve the label of "fact" exclusively for these kinds of measurements—especially as this would make it impossible to treat most of the claims we make in everyday life as if they were intended to be factually true unless they were supposed to be evaluated with the most precise means possible. Is someone correctly described as "late" if they walk through the door a tenth of a second after the specified meeting-time?[6] How much precision we need in ascertaining whether a claim is factually true or not depends on the context; additional precision is not always either necessary or desirable.

Baseball has traditionally been a sport in which even clocks were shunned; a game of baseball takes as long as it takes for one team to emerge victorious, based on a strict rotation of chances at the plate. Only very recently has Major League Baseball introduced a number of timed innovations designed to speed up the game, including a "pitch clock" which governs how long a pitcher has to throw the ball towards home plate; this came only after much strenuous resistance (King 2019). Baseball was also very late in embracing any form of instant-replay review, only allowing umpires to use this technology starting in 2008, and only giving teams the right to ask for such review starting in 2014—long after most other major sports had adopted sophisticated measurement technologies including instant replay. Even in adopting replay review, however, Major League Baseball carved out a class of things that are not reviewable, including the determination of whether a pitch is a ball or a strike. The technology certainly exists to determine, in a mechanical and consistent way, whether a pitched baseball passed through the strike zone or not, and although that procedure has not been adopted (as of this writing), the existence of that technology certainly exacerbates the tussle between umpires and other observers. But what it does *not* do is make the umpire's calls any less factual descriptions.

---

6 "It all depends on what we call 'the goal'. Is it inexact when I don't give the distance of the sun from us to the nearest meter, or tell a joiner the width of a table to the nearest thousandth of a millimeter?" (Wittgenstein 1958, para. 88) Although there *might* be contexts in which such exactness would be required, does that make more inexact claims factually false?

The point here is not that baseball is correct to resist ways of determining whether pitches are balls or strikes that rely on instruments other than trained real-time human observation unaided by anything more sophisticated than glasses or contact lenses. The point is that a decision to adopt different ways of determining whether a pitch has or has not passed through the strike zone is a decision about *how* to evaluate the truth of a claim—which procedure to use—and is therefore a decision about the kind of context the claim inhabits and what the sentence in which the claim is expressed actually *means* in that context. "That pitch was not a strike" means one thing if we are using slow-motion instant replay to determine balls and strikes, and another if we are using the umpire's call to determine balls and strikes. Wittgenstein once commented that "it is only the method of answering the question that tells you what the question was really about" (Waismann 1979, 79), and although he was likely not thinking of the question "was that pitch a strike?" at the time, the sentiment seems entirely appropriate. Deciding to change the procedure would change the meaning of the question and, almost certainly, the entire character of the game.

Types of Description

That said, there is clearly a difference between the kinds of descriptions that I discussed in the previous chapter, and the kind of description that relies on an umpire's or referee's judgment—or on the judgment of designated expert agencies. If we have a practical consensus about *both* definitions *and* procedures, the existence of such a consensus in practice makes possible the impersonal evaluation of whether a claim is true or not by any competent speaker of the relevant language. The evaluation of a factic descriptive claim in such circumstances is quite decentralized, as anyone can do it and everyone will inevitably reach the same conclusion. A true factic description can't be sensibly disagreed with by a competent speaker of the relevant language: either the book is on the shelf, or it is not. Adding in sophisticated procedures for evaluating claims doesn't change the logic of the resulting description, and it doesn't change the dependence of the truth of factic claims on a consensus about how to evaluate them. Within a particular descriptive practice, impersonally true facts can be generated by anyone competent to use its definition and procedure.

I will call those *simple descriptions*. They might be thought of as an idealized form of factic description, especially insofar as actual communities of speakers rarely have as clear and consistent a sense of the definitions and procedures, and as firm a consensus about competent language use, as the parties in stylized examples do! In practice, the sign of a simple description is less that everything goes as smoothly as expected, and more that disagreements are handled only in the four ways that I have outlined: an investigation into definitions, an investigation into procedures, a determination that one party has made a mistake, or a determination that a claimant is not a competent speaker of the relevant language. The two former investigations have the potential to dissolve an apparent disagreement by revealing that the parties are using different definitions or procedures: I claim that

King Crimson is a rock band, you claim that they are a jazz band, and after some conversation we either agree to adopt the same (mutually exclusive) definitions of "rock" and "jazz" and the same procedure for classifying a band as one or the other[7]—in which case we cannot sensibly disagree about which category King Crimson fits into—or we decide to retain our separate definitions and procedures. Either way, we remain in the realm of simple description, since the ideal for which we are striving is the kind of consensus with which a competent speaker cannot sensibly disagree.[8]

What makes a simple description *simple* is that a group of competent speakers applies a common set of definitions and procedures in order to—with intent to— bring an object before us, and this has no implications for the type of definition or procedure involved. As I pointed out in the previous chapter, descriptions need not be limited to the direct and unmediated observation of a physical object. The very notion that there can be such a thing as "direct and unmediated observation," and the kind of five-senses empiricism that such a notion gives rise to, does more harm than good when it comes to thinking through these issues, because it leads us to doubt whether a device-enabled way of perceiving is actually a description—as though there were something suspect about calling a measurement with a volt-ameter of the electrical voltage flowing through a wire a description of that wire. Given the multitude of changes over the centuries in the kinds of instruments that we use to perceive the world around us (Gifford 1991), and the ways that correct use of instruments forms part of the practice of competent language use both for communities of specialists (e.g., brewers determining the amount of sugar in wort by taking a specific gravity reading) and for ordinary people (e.g., determining how cold it is outside by looking at a thermometer, or at an electronic device that reports the results obtained from a thermometer), it is simply unstainable to limit observation to our unaided senses. We use devices and instruments—"prosthetics," we might call them (Shotter 1993b)—in our descriptions all the time, and doing so doesn't make the resulting descriptions any less simple.

There can even be arguments or controversies about whether a given instrument is a good one without interrupting the logically simple nature of a simple description. Consider a famous example: the controversy over Galileo's use of a telescope to observe the moons of Jupiter, which formed an important part of his case that the earth was not the center of the universe with the planets arranged around it in crystal spheres (Feyerabend 1993). While some of the case brought against Galileo involved the interpretation of passages of the Christian Bible, some of it also involved questions about the reliability of the telescope itself as a means of observation. Nowadays this looks strange to us, but only because we have accepted

---

7 Or, we might agree to include a third definition—"a jazz-rock hybrid" or "progressive rock"—into our descriptive vocabulary. This is almost certainly the best way to deal with a multifaceted band like King Crimson.

8 Of course, if we each retain separate definitions and procedures, we have in effect divided the community into separate parts, *within each of which* factic descriptions can be coherently evaluated. Recognizing that we have done this can potentially clear up a lot of apparent contradictions.

that the prosthetically enhanced sight afforded by a telescope is a perfectly reasonable extension of our senses into far distances. We do the same with microscopes for small phenomena, with instant replay with freeze-frames to capture events too quick for our eyes to see, and with detectors that show us evidence of subatomic particles and trace compounds in the air or on a variety of surfaces. We even do it with the sampling techniques used to make claims about a population without having to actually measure each individual member of that population: a properly composed sample frame permits a generalization to the wider population (within a margin of error), as with public opinion polls.[9] As long as the community accepts these prosthetics as part of its competent practice, the descriptions that result from using them are just as simple as descriptions we produce using our unaided senses.

The other two determinations—mistakes and competence—blur into one another, since someone who is not a competent speaker is of course going to make a lot of mistakes. They are also determinations that cannot be made in advance, but only at the time, by the members of the relevant linguistic community. Someone who uses words oddly, in a way that we do not expect, "acquires a 'burden of eccentricity'," such that they have to show "exactly how the new use or behavior is a legitimate extension of the prior consensus of action, and a continuation of the practice that is worth pursuing, a productive and rich way to go on" (Medina 2004, 367). If instead of looking at the label associated with a band's music in some online music service—if that were the previously accepted procedure for determining what category a band fits into—you apply some formal pieces of music theory to ascertain what kind of chord progressions and rhythmic structures a band's music uses, it is not determined in advance whether this is an innovation that will be accepted by the community going forward or whether you will be judged to have made a mistake and incorrectly used the labels (thus being not a competent speaker). Instead, how we engage one another makes the practical determination that *then* makes a simple description possible: either the innovation becomes the new background against which factic descriptions are evaluated, or the old consensus remains operative and serves as the relevant background.

Keep in mind that these determinations are not necessarily explicit or deliberate, and are certainly never matters of unconstrained free choice. Language, and what counts as the correct use of language, is certainly *conventional*, but it is not *arbitrary*, inasmuch as people use words in particular ways not on a whim, but because they find it practical to do so (Pitkin 1973, 138). Once, entering a classroom and introducing oneself by giving one's pronouns would have been looked at as odd or unusual, but with changing societal acceptance of the complexities of gender, pronouns have become a reasonable and even expected element of classroom introductions in many, perhaps most, academic institutions, at least in the United States. That change happened not by executive fiat, but not at random either: the practice of giving one's pronouns was introduced and spread through a complex

---

9 The actual mechanics of conducting such a poll can be quite complicated, of course. This is not the place to go into such mechanics, any more than it is the place to go into the optics of Galileo's telescope.

interplay of activism and acceptance, much like other innovations in the way we speak and act.[10] Once a novel practice has spread and become part of the practical background, it can serve as the basis for correcting someone's mistake or determining that someone is not a competent speaker. Either of those determinations supports a simple description—e.g., this person is nonbinary, as shown by their use of they/them pronouns—by maintaining the relevant practical consensus: someone who disagrees with the claim has made a mistake, or is not a competent speaker.

But not all descriptions are simple descriptions, and we can relax the requirement of a practical consensus that involves *both* procedures *and* definitions without thereby giving up on facts. In situations where different observers might reasonably come to different conclusions about the correct way to describe something, one way we sometimes proceed is to designate someone whose determination we agree to treat as authoritative: an arbiter, a referee, a neutral third party. The baseball umpire plays this role; so too does an appraiser, who ascertains the value of some object in a way that doesn't obviously advantage either the buyer (who obviously would like the value to be low, so they can pay a lower price) or the seller (who obviously would like the value to be high, so they can charge a higher price). I will call these *discretionary descriptions*, since they rely on the exercise of discretion on the part of some observer whose judgment all parties agree to accept. In a discretionary description, part of what it means to be a competent speaker is to accept that the procedure for applying a definition is not completely decentralized, but instead involves listening to an authority; their authority derives from their position in a socially sustained process, like appraising an object or umpiring a baseball game.

Some might object that this key role for discretion places discretionary descriptions outside of the realm of even potential factuality. But *within their appropriate context*, a discretionary description is just as solid a basis for going on as a simple description. The dimensions of a baseball infield are precisely specified in the official rules, and the accepted, ordinary procedure for using that definition to answer the question "Is this baseball field correctly sized?" involves no authority-related discretion at all. Anyone can measure the size of the field using the commonly-accepted procedures for measurement, and having determined that the field is correctly proportioned, the game can proceed.[11] Similarly, once a pitch is called a ball or a strike, according to a procedure that involves the umpire's discretion, the players and managers take that fact into account in making their next moves. Saying that a pitch was *called* a ball or a strike rather than that the pitch *was*

---

10   I am not at this point giving an *explanation* of how a change like this takes place; I am instead analyzing the *logic* that such a change gives rise to when it comes to factic descriptions. On the social processes by which such diffusion of novel practices and usages takes place, see, among others (Tilly 2002); on pronouns in particular, see Goldenberg and Brubaker (2024).

11   A decentralized factic description of this kind might in practice be *certified* by some authoritative agency, but the tacit promise here is that if *anyone* were to measure the field correctly, they would get the same results. Such certification is a matter of simple description, not discretionary description.

a ball or a strike is as pedantic as saying that the field's dimensions were *measured to be* correct rather than that they *are* correct, and there is no practical difference between these formulations when it comes to the playing of the game. Indeed, the only difference is that in a discretionary description, the authoritative arbiter's declaration is an indispensable part of the process of assessing whether a claim is true, and that discretion resolves what could otherwise be nothing but an unending disagreement.

This does not, however, mean that a discretionary description is nothing but one person's opinion, arbitrarily imposed on everyone else. A discretionary description is still a *description*, and as such is still attuned to the object being described. My description of a song as "rock" and your description of that same song as "country" both rely on aspects of the song, and in certain cases both are equally plausible descriptions of the piece. In order to determine which chart the song should be listed on—the rock chart or the country chart—we have to have a consensus about what kind of song it is. If a simple description is not possible, because each of us insist on our description as being correct, a discretionary description of the song can classify it as one or another kind of song for the purposes of tracking how popular it is, and the song's placement in one or the other category is a fact as surely as a pitch is either a ball or a strike once the umpire makes their call. In a discretionary description, the members of the community have agreed to abide by the arbiter's determination as long as it remains in that zone of ambiguity where competent speakers might reasonably disagree, and within that zone the arbiter's determination *is* the fact of the matter.[12]

In this way, discretionary descriptions address many situations where not just any competent speaker would arrive at the same conclusion about whether a statement intended to be factual were true or not. A book on the library shelves might be plausibly described as history *or* sociology, but since the book can only occupy one location, a classification decision has to be made so that the book can be found by people looking for it. Even a classification system as elaborate as the Library of Congress system used by most libraries in the United States cannot possibly eliminate all ambiguity, so there is discretion built into the system both at the point when a book is first classified, and in the process for re-classifying a book somewhere down the line.[13] As an example of the former, consider the novel whose U.S. title is *Harry Potter and the Sorcerer's Stone*.[14] This novel has the Library of Congress call number PZ7.R79835 Har 1999, where "PZ7" is a class number for

---

12 Here again, I am interested in the *logic* of claims relying on this kind of discretion. The dependence of certain factual determinations on the authoritative selection of an arbiter does not tell us anything about the concrete social and political processes through which such arbiters are established and maintained. On the latter issue see, inter alia, Kaczmarska (2020) and Hansen-Magnusson and Vetterlein (2023); on the WHO in particular, see Davies and Harman (2024).

13 The Library of Congress's policy office maintains the schedule used to classify books, entertaining suggestions from any librarian; professional groups like the American Library Association (https://www.ala.org) discuss broader issues relevant to different classification schemes.

14 For this example, and fascinating conversations about the nuances of library cataloging, I am indebted to Alayne Mundt and Gwendolyn Reece of the American University Library faculty.

young adult fiction 1870–2014, ".R79835" indicates the book's author, and "Har 1998" indicates the book's publication date and the first significant word of its title.[15] But the novel could also easily be given the call number PR6068.O93 H35 1998, where "PR6068" is for English literature 1961–2000 by authors whose last name begins with R, ".O93" refers to the author's specific name, and "H35 1998" is another way of relating the first word of the title and the publication year. It is up to individual libraries to determine where to shelve the book, so that its location works best for that library's collection and clientele. So whether we are aware of it or not, in using a library's classification system to locate a book, we are in much the same situation as the baseball player relying on the umpire's discretion about whether a pitch was a ball or a strike. It's just that the moment of discretion in library classification is less visible than the umpire's calls are.

We should therefore think of simple and discretionary descriptions as different types of factic description that can be equally factually true. Simple factic descriptions require no authoritative pronouncements because everyone using the agreed-on definitions and procedures in a competent way *necessarily* reaches the same conclusions about whether a claim is true or false. Here there can be no doubt about what the facts are. Discretion is introduced when we need to reach the same conclusions for some practical purpose but cannot do so in a decentralized way; the resulting facts are just as impersonally true as those resulting from a simple description. Disagreement in such cases means withdrawing consent from the discretionary procedure—refusing to abide by the arbiter's decision—and, perhaps, proposing an alternate procedure according to which the object would be factically described in a different way. So while there is more room for potential disagreement with a discretionary description, inasmuch as it relies on the ongoing acceptance of an arbiter's authority, that alone does not place us outside of the realm of fact.

With this in mind, return to the World Health Organization's 2020 pronouncement that COVID-19 was a pandemic. Although no explicit formal definition of "pandemic" was offered, the colloquial meaning of the term "pandemic," perhaps best exemplified by its use in films like *Outbreak* (1995) and *Contagion* (2011), involves not just a widespread disease, but a widespread *deadly* disease. Certainly Dr. Ghebreyesus' statement envisioned the future death rate potentially rising if governments did not take the necessary steps, and in making the pronouncement, the WHO was claiming the authority to determine that COVID-19 fit the criteria of making such a rise in the death rate likely. Such an assessment is more like a discretionary description than it is like a simple description, since it occupies a necessarily more speculative space. Simple descriptions work, in part, because the object being described is visible or otherwise perceivable, but potentials are a good deal trickier to become attuned to, with a lot more room for disagreement. As such, the abandoned 2009 definition of a pandemic relied on community-level outbreaks

---

15 I am deliberately using the *U.S.* version of the novel in this example, because the Library of Congress system is the accepted standard for most libraries in the United States, but not necessarily outside of it. *Harry Potter and the Philosopher's Stone*, the original novel, was published in the United Kingdom in 1997, the year before being published in the United States.

of a disease because such outbreaks are regarded by epidemiologists as reliable indicators that the disease-causing agent—the virus or bacterium—is in widespread circulation in the population. But while describing a person as infected with a virus or bacterium is a relatively straightforward instance of a factic descriptive claim, once we agree in practice on a definition of "infected" and on a procedure for determining who is infected, moving from the statement "Eliza is infected with the COVID-19 virus" to the statement "Eliza will potentially become ill" involves something else. The truth or falsity of the second statement cannot just be evaluated observationally; it depends on our extrapolation of a possible future world, and not just on the correct use of words to describe objects in this world. That in turn means that we are in the realm of judgment and discretion, and rather far from simple description.

Objections to the WHO's pronouncement are in important ways similar to that of objections to an umpire's call during a baseball game. If construed as factic descriptions, claims that the COVID-19 virus was no more serious than the flu, or that the disease could be effectively resisted by sufficient manly willpower and thus was not a pandemic but a moral failing, question the WHO's authority to determine whether something was or was not a pandemic.[16] Just like a fan or a commentator questioning an umpire's call, objectors are suggesting that the WHO got it wrong, and that a different call should have been made. That in turn either suggests that one moment of discretion ought to be reconsidered, or that the entire practical consensus about discretionary authority ought to be reconsidered—as when Donald Trump terminated financial support for the WHO in September 2020, and started a process to withdraw the United States from the organization (Kaiser Family Foundation 2023). And just as in the case of baseball umpiring, we draw the wrong lesson from these controversies if we conclude that discretionary descriptions are *arbitrary* or *subjective*; instead, the correct lesson to draw concerns the ways that true factic descriptions *depend on practical consensus*, whether that is a practical consensus about definitions and procedures and competence in the case of simple descriptions, or whether that practical consensus also includes recognition of a discretionary authority as in the case of discretionary descriptions.

This touches on an old issue within many philosophical traditions, including the European Enlightenment tradition on which so many of our contemporary institutions are based: the relationship between knowledge and authority. One side of that dispute would deny that authority plays any role in the determination of a valid knowledge-claim, in effect (and in the language I am developing here) saying that only simple factic descriptions are valid knowledge. The other side would collapse the distinction between valid knowledge and claims that are accepted as knowledge, placing authority at the center of any knowledge-claim and in effect denying that *any* factic descriptions are simple descriptions. Instead of choosing

---

16 I am making a deliberate decision not to cite any of the people making objections to the seriousness of the global outbreak of COVID-19, which the WHO reports as being responsible for almost 7 million deaths worldwide. On populist COVID denial generally, see Agius, Rosamond, and Kinnvall (2020).

either side, the position I am working through here is less dichotomous and more of a both/and stance. Yes, there are simple descriptions, in which no discretionary authority is involved; but there are also discretionary descriptions, which rely for their factic validity on a community consensus about leaving a determination up to an authorized party. A discretionary description is intrinsically more contestable than a simple description, because the community can reconsider or withdraw its consensus without thereby abandoning its shared definitions; we can still agree on what a "pandemic" is but move away from the notion that the WHO has the authority to determine whether something is or is not validly factically described as a pandemic. But it remains a description nonetheless.[17]

In this respect, the practice of asking someone for their pronouns looks both like an acknowledgment that a person's gender has *always* been a matter of discretionary description, and an emerging consensus that the authoritative agency for giving that description is the person themselves. Once it was commonly accepted that doctors and other medical professionals determined a person's gender at birth, and that this determination was fixed and irrevocable—even in cases of people whose physiology didn't clearly fall into either the category "male" or the category "female." Other authority figures—parents, relatives, religious officials—played a role here as well, policing the boundaries of what kinds of gender expressions were appropriate for which persons.[18] But the conceptual distinction between sex and gender, the fluidity of gender and sex categories, and the increased availability and publicity of procedures and practices for altering one's sex and one's gender have combined to disrupt that older consensus (Butler 1999; Beauvoir 2011). What has changed is the location of authority: away from a third-party arbiter who can pronounce what a person's gender is, and towards the person themselves. Objections to the practice of asking for pronouns are thus objections to a person having authority over their own gender identity, even and perhaps especially when they take the form of loud assertions that a person simply or really "is" X or Y gender. If it were the case that gender was a simple description—if we all agreed on definitions, procedures, and competent language use—then there would be no need for such loud assertions, because it would be as easy to adjudicate a factic descriptive claim about anyone's gender as it is to adjudicate a factic descriptive claim about anyone's height. But it never has been, and the only question is where the discretionary authority ought to lie: with the person themselves, or with someone else (Saguy and Williams 2022, 25).[19]

---

17 In this sense, opposition to the WHO on the grounds of "national sovereignty" or similar principles needs to be distinguished from a dispute about the facts. What is being opposed in such cases is the WHO's discretionary authority—and, as such, the opposition isn't introducing a different set of facts so much as a different procedure for making and assessing factic claims.

18 Indeed, up until the eighteenth century or so in Europe, the priest was the major source of such discretionary authority (Foucault 1980).

19 Readers familiar with the famous distinction drawn by John Searle (1995) between brute, social, and institutional facts might notice that in some ways the simple fact/discretionary fact distinction I am drawing here revisits these categories. Unlike Searle, though, I am emphasizing the logical dependence of *all* types of facts on shared definitions and procedures, and this means that, in

Different Descriptions

Up until this point in the discussion I have been deliberately silent about where definitions and procedures come from, so that I could focus on the roles that they play in acts of factic description. Competent speakers take definitions and procedures for granted when they are describing something factically; if they did not, then there could be no consensus either about the correct way to describe something or about the competent use of words. Determining whether the caffeinated beverage I have just been served is a "flat white" or a "latte" depends on the definition of each drink (flat whites are made with microfoam and with less milk overall than a latte) and on the procedure used to make the determination (watching the barista prepare the drink, tasting the beverage, estimating its volume since a latte will often be larger than a flat white, etc.). While describing, we cannot simultaneously question the definition or procedure involved in the description, as this shifts the focus from the object—the thing we are intending to bring before ourselves, in this example the drink on the table in front of me—to our linguistic and conceptual equipment. And that in turn takes us away from factic description, because *our definitions and procedures are not objects*. They are not things that we perceive; they are the means through which we perceive.

This is a subtle but crucial point, so I need to linger on it briefly. Certainly definitions can be found in dictionaries, and directions for carrying out procedures can be found in manuals or can be gleaned by watching someone perform them. In this sense, definitions and procedures *can* be treated as objects and factically described, as when we give a definition of a pandemic by citing a document or spell out the tacit procedure for determining that something is a pandemic by watching the WHO make that determination. But in so doing, we are removing ourselves from the process, so to speak, and treating the definitions and procedures in question *as though they belonged to someone else*. When we cite a document we are providing *the document's* definition of a pandemic; when we spell out how the WHO makes its determination we are providing *the WHO's procedure*. In so doing we are taking for granted *our own* definitions and procedures, the ones that we are using to describe what the document says or what the WHO does. Our definitions and procedures, and the practical consensus surrounding their competent use, are what enable us to make factic claims about objects, including about other people's definitions and procedures. It is simply not possible to treat the definitions and procedures we are using to produce factic descriptions as objects at the same time as we are using them.

That said, we sometimes *do* describe definitions and procedures that we ourselves use on other occasions. Often when we do this, we are comparatively or competitively assessing different ways of describing some object. We can talk about the benefits and drawbacks of measuring the length of a room with a ruler or a tape

---

Searle's terms, *all* facts are "social facts," whether they rely on distributed processes or on authoritative arbiters for their evaluation.

measure versus measuring the room's length by seeing how many steps it takes to cross from one wall to another; in so doing we have to describe the definitions and procedures involved in each form of measurement, temporarily freezing them in place as though they were not ongoingly maintained practices. We thus *abstract* our definitions and procedures from their practical contexts, bracketing the negotiations about competent use in which we are ordinarily engaged when actually using those definitions and procedures: we *arrest* what are, in actuality, ongoing transactions and processes.[20] In effect, we imagine that "measuring with a ruler or tape measure" and "measuring by taking steps" are unambiguously clear activities rather than the contingent results of our practical efforts to move boxes into a room or set up an office space or whatever. While this certainly can be a useful exercise—for instance, if we have to decide whether to instruct the movers to use a ruler or to walk across the room before they start loading boxes and furniture into it—it can lead to needless conceptual difficulties if we forget that what we are actually doing is temporarily and provisionally distancing ourselves from our definitions and procedures in order to evaluate them.

Chief among these conceptual difficulties is the notion that we can decide between different definitions and procedures by asking which is more accurate or correct, which in practice usually means which better *corresponds* to the objects being factically described. This in turn is often spun up into an overarching account of progress in factic—"scientific"—knowledge, in which our definitions and procedures get better over time at describing objects in the world as they actually are (e.g., Popper 1996). Once we thought that thunder was the noise made by angry gods, but now we know that it is a byproduct of lightning discharges, which are themselves products of electric charges in moving air masses. Or: once we thought that war was an expression of a human desire for power, but now we know that it is a recurrent aspect of an anarchic international system (Elman and Elman 2003). But this assessment—that one definition and procedure combination corresponds better to an object than another such combination does—presumes that it is sensible to describe the object *outside of those definitions and procedures*, and that in turn logically means a third set of definitions and procedures that we can use to generate a description of the object we can then compare to the descriptions generated by the first two combinations. We can only say that one way of measuring a room is a more accurate way of measuring the room than another way if we have a *third* way of measuring that presumably gives us the room's "actual" length. Demonstrating that that third way corresponds better to the object would then require a *fourth* way, and so on, and so on, ad infinitum.

The problem here can be traced back to the way that factic description itself works. Precisely because a true factic description is a claim with which a competent speaker of the relevant language cannot sensibly disagree, it seems to

---

20 Although some (e.g., Kaczmarska 2019; Pratt 2020) would call this kind of provisional analytical stabilization of an ongoing process "reification," I would prefer to reserve that word for the specific fallacy involved in mistaking our conceptual equipment for the world itself: confusing the map and the territory, treating the map as though it *were* the territory.

us—competent speakers of the relevant language—that the description just tells what and how some object *really is*. Other descriptive practices, utilizing different definitions and procedures from ours, generate descriptive claims that we are then tempted to evaluate in terms of whether they correspond to the object *as we have described it ourselves*. But when we do so, we are not comparing descriptions to "reality" as much as we are comparing combinations of definitions and procedures *to one another*. It is somewhat disingenuous to presume that *our* descriptions arising from *our* definitions and procedures are the appropriate baseline against which all others should be evaluated, when what we should instead be doing is explicitly making the case that one set of definitions and procedures is better than another. We can't, or at least we shouldn't, do this by claiming better correspondence with objects, so we need to build a case for a definition and a procedure in terms of the purpose for which we are describing in the first place—what in the previous chapter I called the "secondary intention" of an act of description. There is no overall best way to measure the length of a room, and describing the room in meters is no more or less true than describing it in paces—although each might be more or less useful depending on what we want the description *for*. Our practical purposes and dealings in the world toss up definitions and procedures, which demonstrate their value by being useful. But we go wrong if we attribute that usefulness to some kind of correspondence *of our definitions and procedures* to the objects we are describing.

Many scholarly controversies about definitions display this problem. Consider the sometimes interminable discussions about whether some group of armed dissidents is a "terrorist organization" or not. Bruce Hoffman's agenda-setting discussion canvasses hundreds of years of divergent definitions of "terrorism" before settling on a definition emphasizing "the deliberate creation and exploitation of fear through violence or the threat of violence in the pursuit of political change" (Hoffman 2006, 40). Other analysts look to the decentralized organizational form of a dissident group as the distinguishing characteristic of terrorism (Comas, Shrivastava, and Martin 2015); still others emphasize the characteristics of the ideology espoused by a group (Ackerman and Burnham 2019). For all of these authors, the proper procedure for describing a group as a terrorist organization involves a clear delineation of the appropriate characteristics and a scholarly determination whether a group possesses these characteristics or not. Clearly these different definitions will lead to different sets of organizations being described as "terrorist," and to controversies as to whether, for example, armed militia groups in the United States are terrorist organizations or not. The ongoing controversy has prompted some critical terrorism studies scholars to abandon the effort to define terrorism in advance—thus changing the descriptive procedure as well as the definition—and to focus instead on how different political actors label one another "terrorist" under different circumstances (Stump and Dixit 2013; Dixit 2016). This generates yet another set of organizations properly described as "terrorist" using a different descriptive practice.

Faced with this disagreement, we may be tempted to ask which set of definitions and procedures are *correct*. But in practice, because this can't mean which definitions and procedures better correspond to the object, this means asking ourselves which definitions and procedures most closely correspond to our own sensibilities, or which generates a set of terrorist organizations—political actors that are factically truly described as "terrorist" according to some definition and procedure—that most closely corresponds to our inchoate intuitions about which organizations *ought* to be on that list. There is nothing inherently wrong with doing this, and indeed a good way of refining a definition or a procedure is to look at the results it gives us and see whether those results make sense in terms of what we want to do with them. We could, to take a different example, define a political act as a public declaration of support for a candidate or a policy, but that definition would exclude what many if not most of us living in democracies regard as the most important political act—voting—because that can't be factically described using this definition as a political act because it's not a public statement of support. Something about the results of describing acts using that definition of a "political act" strikes us as problematic, and unless we have a good reason for excluding voting from our set of acts factically described as political, we may well seek a different definition.[21]

Making definitions and procedures explicit can therefore serve as an engine for adopting, abandoning, or altering those definitions and procedures. Explicit definitions and procedures help us to figure out the contours of our own sensibilities, and to organize our language and our practices in a way that "unravels the knots in our thinking" (Wittgenstein 1993, 183). Asking about the correctness of a definition or a procedure is actually asking whether that definition or procedure coheres with other aspects of our practical lives, especially the purposes for which we need the factic descriptions that result from competently using those definitions and procedures. *Within* a community of competent speakers using the same definitions and procedures, factic claims can be evaluated for their truth: a certain organization is or is not a terrorist organization, a certain disease is or is not a pandemic, a certain caffeinated beverage is or is not a flat white. But our definitions and procedures themselves "are not candidates for true/false" in the same way (Kuhn 2000, 104); they make factic claims possible, but are not themselves factic claims. Nor are they objects to be factically described, except as one moment in a process of clarifying our thinking.

Here the specter of relativism raises its head once again, because if definitions and procedures are anchored in practical consensus rather than in some independent feature of the objects described, what is to prevent different communities from arriving at different factic descriptions that are equally true? And more to the point, what is to prevent those different factic descriptions from contradicting one another? Is there no way to resolve such controversies without choosing a side, and declaring by fiat that some set of procedures and definitions is better than any

---

21 One such reason might be that we are treating politics as public controversy, and focusing more on the space of such controversy than on the determination of who is elected to public office. Discussions about what politics *is* take us out of the realm of factic claims altogether, and into political theory—a realm in which facts rarely if ever decide the answers to questions.

of the alternatives? In that case, we would be stuck with "one person's 'terrorist' is another person's 'freedom fighter'" as a denial that such claims are factic *at all*, but instead cannot be anything but emblems of political partisanship—just like the "alternative facts" from the previous chapter.

But as we have seen, this line of thinking rests on a philosophical confusion that ignores how definitions and procedures actually work in factic descriptions. My description of a political actor as a "terrorist organization" and your description of that actor as an "organization of freedom fighters" *might*, it is true, be nothing more than signals of our political commitments: if we agree with an organization's aims and believe that its use of violence is justified, we aren't going to describe it in ordinary speech as a "terrorist organization" as long as the conventional meaning of "terrorist" carries the kinds of negative connotations that it does in our contemporary discussions. But if we intend something other than a signal of our approval or disapproval with our description—if we intend our description to be *factually true*—then we are in a somewhat different situation. Faced with someone's description of what I would call "an organization of freedom fighters" as a "terrorist organization," there are only four logically possible options:

1) We are using different words for the same definitions. What I mean by "organization of freedom fighters" is what you mean by "terrorist organization." In this case there is no actual disagreement between us; there is only a difference of terminology. Any relativism here is only apparent.
2) One of us has made a mistake, and misunderstood the definitions or misused the procedures. I confused the names of two groups, or you mistakenly believed that a group had admitted responsibility for some civilian deaths where it had not. Once again, no relativism, just a fairly ordinary factic dispute—or a question of linguistic competence.
3) We are operating with the same definitions but different procedures. I say that a political actor is an "organization of freedom fighters" because the manifesto on their website makes reference to inequity and injustice suffered by the civilian population; you look at the frequency of their acts targeting civilians, and the number of civilian deaths for which they admit responsibility, and conclude that they are a "terrorist organization." Here we differ on whether the correct descriptive procedure involves reading programmatic public statements or examining the behavioral record. In this situation we can reach different descriptive conclusions—we can make different true factic claims—without any relativism being involved. Indeed, we might have a conversation about which procedure is better for determining whether some actor is a terrorist organization or not (maybe you say "talk is cheap, action is what counts," while I reply "we have to take actors' own meanings seriously if we want to make sense of social life"), and the positions we take in that conversation are almost certainly connected to our broader theories about political and social action. If we reach some agreement about procedures, then we can relatively easily come to a consensus about whether some actor is factically described as a "terrorist organization" or not.

4) We are operating with different definitions, or with different procedures, or with different definitions *and* different procedures. What I mean by "terrorist organization," a label I do not claim fits the object, is not what you mean by "terrorist organization," a label you claim does fit the object—either because we have different criteria or different ways of assessing whether those criteria are met, or perhaps both. (Or maybe our discussion of our different procedures did not lead to us adopting a common procedure, but instead to maintaining our different commitments insofar as they are revealed to be profoundly interwoven with our broader notions about political action: our theories, our overall worldview, etc.) This poses a problem of *translation*, inasmuch as we are quite literally saying *different things*. Even if we are using similar words, this is as accidental as when a word in German looks or sounds like a word in English, and assuming that the meaning of a word is somehow carried in its graphemes or phonemes produces no end of confusion. Different communities use words in different ways, and if you and I disagree about whether some factic claim is true, then we need to ask some questions about how your claim is being translated into my language, and vice versa.

This last case comes the closest to what most people—and many philosophers—mean by "relativism." But different languages divide up the world in different ways, and every speaker of more than one language knows of examples of words and phrases that "don't translate," and for which more elaborate explanations are required: the German term *Schadenfreude*,[22] for example, which doesn't have a direct English equivalent. These linguistic and cultural differences would only indicate "relativism" if it were the case that it was possible to make a true factic claim in one language and then correctly translate that claim into another language with a false factic claim. But imagine how that would work: I say, "this candle is cylindrical in shape," making a factic claim. Presume that the claim is factically true. If I translate that factically true claim into another language, I cannot do so with words that mean "this candle is rectangular in shape," because that's not the claim being made in the original language. Instead I have to look for a word or words that are used similarly to how we use the word "cylindrical," and once I have found them, the claim is factically true in both languages. If I don't or can't find such words—maybe I am translating into a language that doesn't have make a distinction between what we call "cylindrical" and what we call "rectangular"—then there simply is no way to make the claim in the target language into which I am translating. Either way, the specter of relativism dissolves, "like a lump of sugar in water" (Wittgenstein 1993, 183).

Some philosophers argue that this conservation of truth across translation points to a "disquotation" account of what it means for a claim to be true (e.g., Searle 1995, 200-203). According to this account, what it means for "this candle is cylindrical in shape" to be true is that this candle is cylindrical in shape: the

---

22 If you are not a German speaker, look it up.

claim expressed by the words in quotation marks is true if the claim expressed by the same words *not* in quotation marks is true. While not exactly wrong, the disquotation analysis of truth can be very misleading, in that it gives rise to the peculiar notion that, say, a candle's being cylindrical in shape or not is somehow independent of our descriptive vocabulary. On the one hand, this is quite silly, because "candle" and "cylindrical" are *our* words, not naturally occurring objects; whether they are a true description of this object or not depends on our competent use of language, and it's not clear what it would even mean to say that a candle would be cylindrical in shape if there was no language containing those words. At the same time, disquotation is a disingenuous sleight of hand, because the part of the sentence not in quotation marks is still *part of our language* and still a descriptive claim that we are making.[23] Hence it adds nothing of consequence beyond the original claim itself.

But disquotation does capture a key intuition about true factic descriptions, which is that they are *impersonally* true. For us, using our language, "this candle is cylindrical in shape" isn't true or false for us, but simply true or false: either it results from the correct and competent use of definitions and procedures or it does not, and that does not depend on any of us individually. The claim does inhabit a linguistic context, with shared standards of correct use, but that doesn't detract from its factic character:

> That two shekels plus two shekels make four shekels is just as true for us as for the Babylonians…If others have indeed asserted those claims that our form of words conveys, then they have asserted what is true—and true unqualifiedly rather than "true for us" or "true for them." The fact that the affirmation of a fact must proceed from within a historico-cultural setting does not mean that the correctness and appropriateness of what is said will be restricted to such a setting.
>
> (Rescher 1997, 61)

Whether a claim is *comprehensible* depends on shared standards of competent linguistic use, but those standards do not themselves determine whether a claim is factically true or not. After all, I can make perfectly comprehensible factic claims, like "the candle is on the floor," which are false; our mutual comprehension of the claim doesn't make it true, and the claim's truth or falsity is not a matter of personal preference. This impersonal quality of facts is what "disquotation" is picking up, but without acknowledging the importance of translation. It is not that a factically true claim is somehow true outside of all languages and contexts, since a claim can only be meaningfully stated in a linguistic context. But once the claim has been

---

23   Recall, in this connection, the third-party description (what we the viewers see on the screen) that made the scenario from the previous chapter involving Captain Picard and the Cardassian torturer work. Disquotation, I would argue, plays much the same role as the view on screen does, and like the view on the screen, disquotation is still a *view from somewhere* inside of a linguistic community.

stated, its truth or falsity isn't a matter of whim or decision, but of the correct use of definitions and procedures.

What, then, of situations in which some factic claim that we once held to be factual turns out not to be factual, either on the grounds of new evidence that we have found, or on the grounds of changed definitions and procedures? Almost inevitably, we regard our earlier views as a mistake, but we may also be tempted to say that what we claimed in the past was factual *then* but is not factual *now*. I factically described the object on my desk as a candle in virtue of its wick and composition, but then I learn (by reading the label on the bottom of the object, perhaps) that it is an art object never intended to be burned, so it's not a candle after all. But was it *ever* factually a candle?

Or, consider a different example: the common characterization of human forager societies in the distant past as characterized by "separate subsistence roles for females and males" (Anderson et al. 2023, 1), with the males engaged in the hunting of game while the females engaged in the gathering of plants. This description, and its associated descriptions of men as aggressive and women as nurturing, was until very recently taken for granted in much scholarly anthropological literature and among the general public. Evidence for this description—since it's not possible to observe societies in the distant past directly—came from ethnographic studies of contemporary forager societies, and worked by describing those societies in terms of the gender-divided hunter/gather dichotomy and then extrapolating into the past. But recent archaeological discoveries have called this description into question, revealing more evidence of female hunters in the past; in addition, a new examination of the ethnographic data from 63 contemporary foraging societies around the world indicates that 79 percent of them "demonstrated female hunting" and over 70 percent of the female hunting observed was "intentional, meaning that females play an active and important role in hunting—and the teaching of hunting" (ibid., 6). So have the facts changed? Or was the prior characterization of forager societies as divided between male hunters and female gathers *never* factual?

In analyzing such situations it is easy to be misled by the way that our factual claims logically admit no disagreement along competent speakers. Having been established, they serve as the basis on which to characterize other claims as something other than facts. As John Dewey once cogently observed, a claim

> which is growing in acceptance…gets logical or intellectual or objective force; that which is losing standing, which is increasingly doubtful, gets qualified as just a notion, a fancy, a prejudice, misconception—or finally just an error, a mental slip.…Evaluated as fanciful in *validity* it becomes a mere fancy in its existence.
>
> (Dewey 2007, 72)

This is not an argument about the power of mere acceptance to make some claim true or false; it is instead an argument about what happens when definitions and procedures change and when discrepant evidence comes to light. We used to think that forager societies had discrete male-hunter and female-gatherer roles, but now we are not so sure, and from *this* point of view—from our *current* perspective—our older thinking looks fanciful or erroneous.

Part of the complexity here is that whenever we are examining *someone else's* factual knowledge, we slip all too easily into the habit of evaluating their factic claims from *our* perspective, using *our* definitions and procedures. We even do this with our own past selves: I thought it was a candle but now I see that it is not. While this is a well-known problem in anthropological circles (e.g., Winch 1990)—when you are studying a society that believes in witchcraft, do you accept their terms or do you treat witchcraft as something false?—what is less appreciated is that whenever we are talking about *someone else's* claims, we have moved from the analysis of their claims as factic claims, to the analysis of their claims as matters of belief or of social institution. The question has shifted from "Is this factic claim true or false?" to "Do these people believe or accept this claim as true?" and we have accordingly moved from factic evaluation to questions of psychology and sociology. To treat a claim as factic and to evaluate it as such is to, in important ways, make it into *our* claim, translate it into *our* terms, and evaluate it using *our* definitions and procedures—just because those are the ways that we determine facts ourselves. Leaving the claim with other people, letting it stand as theirs rather than ours, means in a sense bracketing the issue of whether the claim is factically true or false, and merely noting—observing—the claim's status in that group.

As so often when thinking through these issues, we are (as Wittgenstein once put it) held captive by a picture that lies "in our language" (1958, sec. 115). That picture involves a separation between our language and "the facts," as though facts were part of some language-independent world to which our language merely refers, rather than arising from *within* our competently spoken language. Facts are true descriptive claims, not objects, and as long as we remember this then the apparent difficulty of something having once been a fact and then no longer being a fact simply dissolves. It is not true that forager societies were cleanly divided into male hunters and female gatherers; that claim, made in our language with our definitions and procedures, is a false factic claim.[24] And from our point of view, the fact that this claim was broadly accepted by past scholars and is still broadly accepted by many members of the general public thus becomes puzzling, and stands in need of further investigation...but that does not make the claim factically true. Facts are *impersonally* true, and as soon as we introduce a reference group *by whom* a claim is accepted as true, we aren't treating that claim as factic any longer. Instead we have moved to psychology, sociology, anthropology, perhaps even to political science, and we are talking not about the claim's epistemic status, but about its role and its function.

---

24 Even if it is possible for us to imagine how we might have arrived at the conclusion that forager societies were cleanly divided into these two gender-specific roles, it remains the case that we can't regard that conclusion as factically true in the light of current evidence and argument. Seeing how someone else arrived at a conclusion that is factically false when evaluated with our definitions, procedures, and standards of linguistic competence may be a useful exercise in developing empathy, but it has zero implications for the factic truth or falsity of the claim itself.

So to the question of whether some factically false claim might be "true for" some other group of people, even "true for" us in the past, there is only one proper response. To say that a claim is "true for" some specific group of people is to shift the terms of the discussion from the claim's factic truth and falsity to the claim's acceptance—whether as a matter of individual belief or as a matter of social consensus—by that group. Widespread acceptance does not in any way mean that a claim is factically true. The test of factic truth is that the claim cannot sensibly be disagreed with by competent speakers of the relevant language; this is not the same as observing that the claim is *not* disagreed with by members of a group. The latter requires empirical evidence about (other) people's behavior, while the former requires our own engaged participation in the community as a competent speaker.

Science, Religion, Poetry

It is critical to the preceding discussion that the claims in question be *factic* descriptions, descriptions that intend to be true in the sense of being claims with which competent speakers of the relevant language cannot sensibly disagree. Without this intention, even descriptive claims might well stand in opposition to one another without a possible resolution. After all, there are different kinds of descriptions, and many descriptions are not factic: they may be poetic, for instance, or they may be based in faith commitments. We wouldn't fault a description like Homer's "wine-dark sea"—used in both the *Iliad* and the *Odyssey* for rough waters—because the water described did not look to us like wine, any more than we would fault a comparison of the object of someone's affections with a red red rose by pointing out the different chemical composition of human beings and roses. Nor does it make much sense to treat a Christian declaration like "Jesus Christ was the Son of God" as a factic claim, even though it is certainly a description, and indeed, a description that would be agreed with by many, perhaps most, practicing Christians.

One easy way to ascertain that these poetic and religious descriptions are not factic is to consider what happens when someone disagrees with them. A poetic description may or may not move us, and may do so without calling into question either procedures, definitions, or competent language use; we would simply say, were someone unmoved by our poetry, that it did not resonate with them, or at most that they don't *appreciate* it. What we would not do is to investigate their definitions and procedures, or wonder about their linguistic competence. When we are talking about poetic language, it is entirely acceptable for different descriptions to coexist, because to compose poetry is not to aim at an account that all competent speakers of the relevant language would have to agree with. Individual expressiveness is built into the practice of poetry in a way that it simply is not when we are talking about factic claims.

As for religious descriptions, although there are certain similarities between how religious communities and scientific communities operate in politics—claiming specialized knowledge that allows them to serve as authorities delivering valuable advice (Sandal 2011)—there is a critical difference between the *kind* of knowledge that they claim. Religious claims depend on a commitment of faith, and outside of that commitment, there is no reason for someone to accept a claim as true. Disagreement with a claim that is broadly accepted in a religious community is not going to be met with questions about linguistic competence, inasmuch as religious discourse contains a category for unbelief. Citing a "sacred text" as evidence for a claim doesn't resolve the problem either, inasmuch as doing so presumes that the questioner already accepts the sacredness of the text, but this is precisely what is at issue when an unbeliever and a believer disagree about an issue. The only people who assent to religious claims are believers, and people who don't believe are offered testimony rather than definitions and procedures. Religious claims are thus not factic claims, and truth—even descriptive truth—in a religious context means something different than it does outside of that context.

Science, however, *is* a factic enterprise, dedicated to the production of claims that are systematic, susceptible to public criticism, and focused on objects in the world (Jackson 2016). As such, it does not contain a category like "unbelief"—or, for that matter, a category like the kind of "taste" that is invoked when we say that someone doesn't appreciate our poetry. If I claim that molecules of ordinary water are composed of two hydrogen atoms bonded to a single atom of oxygen, "I don't believe it" or "that doesn't speak to me" is simply not a sensible response. Instead, we have to look at definitions, procedures, and competent language use, and evaluate the claim in a way that asks whether it can be disagreed with, or whether given our presently established vocabulary the claim simply *cannot* be disagreed with—any more than it is possible to disagree with the factically true description of the candle on my desk as cylindrical. Changes in our vocabulary don't invalidate the factic character of the scientific enterprise, so long as we are clear about what it *means* for a claim to be a fact: "water molecules are composed of two hydrogen and one oxygen atom" is our claim about water's composition, and is a fact in that no one who uses those words competently will disagree. If we mistakenly tie the truth of our claim to some invariant characteristic of the world, we run into the sorts of philosophical and conceptual conundrums I have been discussing, and working to dissolve, throughout this chapter.

The position I have been outlining here also denies the coherence of a notion like "alternative facts." All that is required is an intent to generate claims with which no competent speaker of the relevant language can sensibly disagree, together with an awareness that our language is embedded in our practical lives and our ways of engaging with objects and with one another. Because it is useful to bring objects before ourselves in particular ways—the location of the candle, the severity of the disease, the number of people in a place—we have generated ways of using language to do so, and elaborated definitions and procedures that we can use in making our way in the world. Only in the idle imaginations of armchair philosophers are those competent uses of definitions and procedures strange or bizarre; our language, and our competent linguistic practice, is a record of what works, and definitions and procedures that do not serve a useful purpose are only going to remain part of our toolkit until someone notices that they aren't working.

Obviously, this process of linguistic adaptation and change is neither seamless nor instantaneous. Wittgenstein once suggested that we see our language as "an old city: a maze of little streets and squares, old and new houses, and houses with extensions from various periods; and all of this surrounded by a multitude of newer suburbs with straight and regular streets and uniform houses" (Wittgenstein 1958, sec. 18). Actual, living languages aren't complete or consistent, and they can easily contain a plethora of definitions and procedures which can be used in different ways. The point in highlighting the factic intent of certain kinds of descriptive claims is to point to a way that this multifaceted kaleidoscope might be brought into focus for certain specific purposes: when we need claims with which competent language-speakers cannot disagree—facts—to serve as a way of coordinating activities and choosing among courses of action. As long as we are operating with factic claims, it is always at least possible to teach people how to use the relevant language correctly, and then to demonstrate that a given factic claim expressed in that language is either impersonally true or impersonally false. In so doing, we explore a different part of the city, or shape it in ways that work better for us.

One important implication is that when confronted with a claim that we understand as factic, it is *always* appropriate to investigate the definitions and procedures involved in generating that claim. This is the case regardless of who is making the claim, and whether the claim is a simple or a discretionary description. The impersonally true character of facts means that what sustains them is not an arbitrary exercise of political or social authority; the truth and falsity of factic claims are determinable in a decentralized manner, by anyone who is a competent speaker of the relevant language. Facts can be "checked," and they can be checked by *anyone*. But checking the facts—evaluating the truth of a factic claim—never means just disagreeing. Instead, it means disclosing the definitions and procedures involved, and seeing whether they have been used competently. Sometimes this process reveals that someone has made a mistake, either the original claimant or we ourselves when we doubted that the claim was true. Sometimes this process shows that we are operating with different procedures, and perhaps the resulting conversation questioning one or the other procedure leads us to adopt a common procedure and thus leads us to a common set of facts. Sometimes this process reveals that the speaker is simply inhabiting a different community and speaking a different language than we ourselves are, in which case we can end up with different facts that point to different aspects of objects, but without contradicting one another. And sometimes the process reveals, contrary to our initial understanding, that what we thought was a factic claim is not, or at least can not be helpfully understood as, factic.

3   Causal Explanations

Diagnoses by academic researchers of the problems of higher education have become something of a hot commodity in the publishing world in recent years. One such book, written by a pair of economists, argues that the dysfunctions of colleges and universities in the United States are a result of the incentive structures confronting faculty, administrators, and students alike (Brennan and Magness 2019): students are motivated to put in minimal effort and even to cheat in order to obtain the credential of a degree; administrators are motivated to expand their bureaucratic domains and budgets; and faculty are motivated to maximize their earnings by devoting as much time to research and as little time to teaching or service as they can. The authors adduce a lot of data about the behavior of these constituencies in the aggregate, supplementing their general claims with colorful anecdotes and quantitative measurements of costs, earnings, employment patterns, and the like.

One particularly biting portion of the analysis involves the growth of general education (sometimes called "core," "distribution," or "liberal arts") requirements. The authors express skepticism that such requirements reflect a broad consensus about what students ought to learn as part of their undergraduate degrees, and suggest that the moralistic language used by advocates of such requirements masks a more mundane form of self-interest. The growth in composition or college writing courses, to take just one of their examples, can be accounted for not in terms of ethical conceptions of what makes for a learned person, but in terms of falling enrollments in literature courses and the interest this creates among the literature faculty for arrangements that force students into their classes. The behavior of literature departments in pursuing such curricular requirements can thus be characterized as a form of rent-seeking, using the word "rent" in the technical economics sense of unearned revenue generated by, in this case, the department's ownership of a resource (composition/writing classes) that student-consumers are *forced* to "purchase" (by enrolling in those classes) instead of spending their time elsewhere. The authors apply the same analysis to general education course requirements writ large, regardless of which department benefits from the resulting shifts in student enrollment.

DOI: 10.4324/9781003455912-3

Some of this account is descriptive in the sense that I have been discussing in the previous two chapters. In particular, the description of the process by which students enroll in classes as a series of market transactions—with the university faculty acting as suppliers of a commodity that students buy with their tuition dollars[1]—is much the same, logically speaking, as the descriptions of objects advanced by other communities of practice. Economists have a particular conceptual vocabulary that they deploy in describing patterns of social interaction, just the same way that chemists and interior designers have particular conceptual vocabularies that they deploy in describing the candle on my desk. Having described student enrollment in classes as a marketplace, economists can then bring the various tools of market analysis particular to their academic discipline to bear on the situation, and therefore factically describe *any* curricular requirements as something of a market distortion (because the student-consumers do not get to spend their money freely). Coupled with an ethical injunction like "markets should be completely free," which is a claim that cannot be plausibly understood as a factic description of anything, a description of such market distortions can serve as a powerful critique of existing arrangements.[2]

But some of this account is not descriptive, but *explanatory*—and in particular, *causally* explanatory. The authors want to do more than to describe patterns of student enrollment as market distortions; they want to explain why we have the arrangements and patterns that we do in fact have, as opposed to other arrangements or patterns that we do not in fact have. As is usual for economists, the explanations that the authors put forward are explanations revolving around rational self-interest, and much of the book is devoted to arguing that the peculiarities of higher education in the United States are causally explained by self-interest, incentive structures, and strategic behavioral tradeoffs: requirements and conditions of professorial employment are caused by rent-seeking, cheating is widespread because it is rational for students to cheat under certain circumstances, administrative offices grow because they look for new ways to justify their existences. But in the book's conclusion, the authors re-state some of their claims in a way that sounds less explanatory than descriptive:

Academics frequently use moral language to disguise their pursuit of their own self-interest. Certain forms of activism, including activism on behalf of tenure, appear to be little more than rent-seeking...Faculty exploit students by forcing them to take useless and ineffective courses that students don't want to.

---

1 This is oversimplifying, of course. Except in rare instances, students do not purchase classes directly from the faculty members teaching those classes, and many degree-seeking students do not pay by the class in any case, but instead pay for the right to enroll in a given number of classes. The "buying" and "selling" in the enrollment "marketplace" is thus considerably more mediated than the ideal-typical marketplace transaction would be.

2 The book's subtitle—"The Moral Mess of Higher Education"—should serve as a small clue as to the authors' ethical orientation.

The purpose of many gen[eral] ed[ucation classe]s is to transfer money from students to professors.

(Brennan and Magness 2019, 277)

Notice what has happened here. Notions like "rent-seeking," previously offered as part of a causal explanation, are now presented as though they described an object (in this case, faculty behavior). It is as though a causal explanation could become a fact, despite its very different logical structure: descriptions bring an object before us, but causal explanations deal with alternative possibilities and with questions like *why* and *how* rather than *what*. And in this instance, the slippage is especially worrying, because it appears to justify a description (e.g., "activism on behalf of tenure" is "little more than rent-seeking") with an appeal to a causal explanation (professorial behavior is explained by incentives that promote rent-seeking) that is in turn justified by the description of the activity itself in economic terms. A neat, and quite tautological, circle.

Exploring how this slippage becomes possible, and making the case that we need to keep causal explanations separate from facts, will require me to delve a bit into the history of the presently dominant philosophy of causal explanation across the Anglophone social sciences: *neopositivism*, which is a descendant of early twentieth-century logical positivism combined with an emphasis on systematic efforts to *falsify* factic claims as the living core of the scientific approach to knowledge-production.[3] On the neopositivist account, causal explanation becomes nothing other than first stating the relevant empirical generalizations, and then establishing that a particular case has the particular characteristics mentioned in the generalization.

Both the general pattern and the case-specific characteristics are *facts* in precisely the sense discussed in the preceding two chapters, and explanation means relating these facts to one another in a specific way: we subsume the individual case under the general pattern, so that the former becomes an instance of the latter rather than an idiosyncratic happening. The case then becomes an instance of the general pattern. Indeed, neopositivists claim that the success of the modern sciences is precisely due to their embrace of techniques designed to distinguish "systematic" from "accidental" variation, differentiating genuinely general patterns from spurious ones. The authors of one of the standard neopositivist methods manuals in Political Science bluntly declare that "*one of the fundamental goals of inference is to distinguish the systematic component from the nonsystematic component of the phenomena we study...*distinguishing between the two is an essential task of social science" (King, Keohane, and Verba 1994, 56, emphasis in original). Hence, the only truly secure knowledge we can have is knowledge of patterns that repeat across cases, and only those patterns of association (say, between incentives and behavior) indicate causality. If the claimed association doesn't show up generally and significantly across cases, then any connection between the two

---

3 The fuller story can be found in Bernstein (1978) and in Jackson (2016, especially Chapters 2 and 3).

elements—even one plausibly observed in a particular case—might not *really* be causal. We might instead have been deceived by an unrepresentative or atypical case, and made a too-hasty generalization.

But this "covering law" model of causality and causal explanation has been picked apart in numerous ways over the course of the second half of the twentieth century. Many of those critiques involve a separation of causal claims from causal explanations, on the grounds that evaluating or vetting a causal claim and constructing a causal explanation are two different operations (Waldner 2007, 145–46): the former rests on hypothetical inferences from causal claims that set up expectations about subsequent observations, while the latter uses presumptively valid causal claims, together with factic descriptions, to show why and how a particular outcome came about. According to the critics, a causal explanation is not likely to look anything like a linear combination of discrete variables, but will likely feature case-specific sequences and interactions in ways that are difficult to capture generally or formally. We work all the time with everyday causal explanations that rely on just such sequences and interactions—we regard my dropping of the glass onto the concrete floor as the cause of the glass breaking—without feeling a need to spell out a general law that could cover such occurrences, even though the covering law model mandates that we should.[4]

Beyond Nomothetic Generalization

Hence the challenge is to produce a more adequate account of causal explanation that does not conflate claims and explanations in this way, and which makes room for ways of conceptualizing causality that go beyond neopositivism. In order to do so, we need to go back to the roots of the neopositivist approach, and in particular to Carl Hempel's (1965, 235) classic account of causal explanation as "showing that the event in question was not 'a matter of chance,' but was to be expected in view of certain antecedent or simultaneous conditions," and thus as producing "rational scientific anticipation which rests on the assumption of general laws." On this account, to produce a causal explanation is to make inferences "from the conjunction of one or more hypotheses and one or more statements of initial conditions" (Waldner 2007, 150) and then to seek observational evidence that can confirm or refute those inferences. The point of the exercise is to generate valid nomothetic generalizations. Once we have those nomothetic generalizations, explanation, in the neopositivist account, becomes a simple matter of subsuming cases under the relevant covering laws, thus rendering the specific observed outcomes *rationally*— or *nomically—expectable* (Fetzer 2000, 120–21).

But there are a variety of difficulties here. For one thing, once nomothetic generalizations have been reconstructed in the neopositivist way as irreducibly *hypothetical*, it is very unclear just when we would ever be justified in regarding

---

4 For helpful comments on the originally published version of this chapter (Jackson 2017a), I am grateful to Hidemi Suganami, Adam Humphreys, Derek Beach, and Nick Onuf, and to two anonymous reviewers.

such a generalization as a covering law that could more or less unproblematically serve as the major premise in a Hempelian explanation. And the covering law in such an explanation *must* be at least provisionally treated as certain in order for the explanation to proceed. To use one of Hempel's own favorite examples, we explain the behavior of soap bubbles observed while washing dishes with reference to both the "particular facts" about the situation and "the gas laws and various other laws…concerning the exchange of heat between bodies of different temperature, the elastic behavior of soap bubbles, etc." by using the covering laws to logically connect the particular facts of the situation to the observed outcome (Hempel 2001, 277). In order to explain the observed outcome, the covering laws—which Hempel also calls "uniformities expressed by general laws"—can't simultaneously be subject to empirical evaluation. Seeing the expected soap-bubble behavior should not make us more confident that the covering laws are correct, because we already assumed that they *were* correct in constructing the explanation; conversely, *not* seeing the expected soap-bubble behavior and using that as a reason to doubt the covering laws means giving up on explaining what we did see, at least for the moment.[5]

In addition, it is quite unclear just how the invocation of a general covering law (even if presumptively valid) could *ever* suffice to explain any specific case. Abbott (1988, 181; 1992, 58) notes that statisticians drop out of their calculations and tell stories with proper names whenever they are asked to show how their general patterns explain any specific outcome. Suganami (1996, 124–25) points out that the most we can get from the invocation of a general law as a premise in a deductive argument about a specific case is a conclusion that a claim that the outcome occurred must be true; this is a far cry from showing that the outcome was somehow entailed by the antecedent conditions. And there are numerous other problems with this approach pointed out by philosophers of science over the years,[6] such as the fact that "nomic expectability" might obtain without contributing anything to an explanation (e.g., "whenever I ask my computer nicely before pressing the power button, it starts up without a hitch," even though my polite demeanor clearly contributes nothing to a causal explanation of the computer's starting up), and the fact that although regularities might be observed that have no place in any explanation (such as an observed covariation between sunspot activity and the fluctuation of stock prices), the covering law account does not have any easy way to dismiss such irrelevant but observed uniformities.[7]

5 This was not a problem for a member of the original Vienna Circle of logical positivists, for whom the growth of knowledge was fundamentally about the use of logic to construct valid statements on the secure ground of the physical sciences (nicely on display throughout Carnap 2012; see also Carus 2010, 155–58), but the neopositivist move to regarding scientific knowledge as *always* uncertain makes it much less clear when one should switch from explanation using a presumptively valid covering law to the empirical evaluation of that now-hypothetical covering law.
6 Nicely summarized in Achinstein (2010a) and Woodward (2005, 154–61).
7 James Fetzer's proposal (2000, 128) to modify the covering law account by replacing nomic expectability with nomic responsibility—"Explanations explain by citing all and only those properties whose presence made a difference to the occurrence of their explanandum events. And properties

Hempel himself was aware of these difficulties.[8] Because "subsumption under a covering law" exhausts explanation for a neopositivist, it frees neopositivist scholars to focus on the empirical/statistical evaluation of hypothetical covering laws, and to spend their time inferring and testing rather than explaining. On the contrary, for Hempel, explanation was the very essence of scientific activity, and he offered the covering law model as a reconstruction of the basic way "in which empirical science answers the question as to the Why? of empirical phenomena" (Hempel 2001, 69). Hempel's extension of this model to the analysis of human action, whether in history or in psychology, was intended to show that *any* explanation relies, even if only implicitly, on general claims of either a categorical or a probabilistic character, with appropriate scope and domain conditions.[9]

Thus, when Hempel asks what distinguishes a recounting of a sequence of events from an explanation of an outcome, or what distinguishes the determination of a correct course of action from an explanation of the action actually undertaken, he answers by sketching the general notions that an author has at least implicitly drawn on. Commenting on Frederick Jackson Turner's account of the American frontier, and in particular on Turner's argument that farmers moved west to take advantage of cheap land and the possibility of more productive agriculture, Hempel notes:

> This passage is clearly intended to do more than describe a sequence of particular events: it is meant to afford an understanding of the farmers' westward advance by pointing to their interests and needs and by calling attention to the facts and the opportunities facing them. Again, this explanation takes it for granted that under such conditions normal human beings will tend to seize new opportunities in the manner in which the pioneer farmers did.
>
> (Ibid., 286)

Similarly, when discussing the difference between an argument that a particular action was "rational" and an explanation of why a particular person acted in the expected rational way, Hempel notes that such an explanation typically features a tacit premise to the effect that "in a situation of type C any rational agent will do x,"

whose presence made no difference to their occurrence must be excluded as explanatorily irrelevant."—is intriguing, but only displaces the problem, because now we need additional laws about what "makes a difference" in what circumstances, and those laws are subject to the same problems as the first set of laws.

8 Despite often being *cited* as authorization for the covering-law model of causal explanation, Hempel is too little actually *read* on this point. The problem is compounded by the way that "Hempel" has become a caricature from which most contemporary accounts of causal explanation seek to distance themselves—usually without noting the powerful continuities between their views and what Hempel *actually* said.

9 The covering law model of explanation encompasses *both* deductive-nomothetic and inductive-statistical explanations (Hempel 2001, 297). For Hempel, both categorical and probabilistic claims figure into an explanation in *exactly the same way*: by providing the justification for connecting empirical observations to one another. And there is nothing anti-Hempelian about specifying a more restricted domain within which a covering law is valid; Hempel never argues that all categorical claims have to be *universally* valid.

and that this premise is what makes it possible to connect the situation to the action observed (ibid., 316–17). If Hempel is correct—and on this point, I think he is—then in the very *grammar* of the notion of explanation is an assumption that some general claim will be at least implicitly invoked. To say that the relative balance of military capabilities explains a state's decision to go to war relies on some general claim connecting relative military capabilities with such decisions; if it did not, we would be looking at factic descriptions of military capabilities rather than at explanations of decisions. The same reasoning holds for arguments about academic administrators expanding their domains, or arguments about students cheating.

Of course, Hempel's argument goes further than this, specifying the *character* of the general claims in question as being lawlike as well as empirical. But one need not agree with his specific characterization of general claims in order to accept the broader point: that there is a difference between general claims and the specific explanations that invoke them, and hence that general claims play a different role when they are being evaluated than they do when they are being used in an explanation. As something to be evaluated, a lawlike empirical generalization can be treated as a factic claim that intends to *describe* a relationship between distinct data points; but as something to ground an explanation, that general claim is being treated not as factic (and hence fallible), but as presumptively true. This difference is even more pronounced when we are talking about *causal* explanation in particular, because causal explanations are always explanations of particular events or outcomes, while general causal claims are by definition not about particular events or outcomes (Dray 2000, 230).[10] And from this richer Hempelian perspective, it is immediately clear that simply quoting general findings, no matter how important those findings may be, is *not an explanation*. Not yet, at any rate.

Acts of Explanation

One difficulty with turning from the evaluation of causal claims to the construction of causal explanations is that it is not only the neopositivist practice of social science that eclipses the latter to focus on the former; discussions in the philosophy

---

10   But here a neopositivist might object: in a model in which some independent variable is statistically significant, isn't that variable then a "general explanation" for the outcome in the various cases, exerting a definite causal effect in those cases which is, on average, the value of the coefficient assigned to that variable in the model? I think this is mistaken, for two reasons: a) what does the "explaining" in such a situation is not any individual variable, but *the model as a whole*, and b) what the model explains is *not* the outcome in any individual case, but the *distribution* of outcomes across the population—and "the distribution" is a particular outcome rather than a general one. The neopositivist's misleading way of speaking draws on precisely the same conceptual slippage that I am trying to highlight in this chapter, namely, the conflation of causal claims and causal explanations, to the detriment of the latter. The reliance on measures of statistical significance in a model, instead of paying more attention to the overall "goodness of fit" or even to the actual *values* of the coefficients estimated for independent variables in the model, means that the whole operation is ultimately about evaluating various hypothetical generalizations instead of being about *explaining* anything in particular. For a similar critique, see Ziliak and McCloskey (2008). I discuss "average causal effect" more directly in the next chapter.

of causation do so as well. In Nancy Cartwright's helpful terminology, most con-temporary philosophical discussions of causation are aimed at "hunting causes" rather than "using" them: "They provide an elaborate procedure for deciding when we can attach the label 'cause.' But then what? There is nothing more in the account that allows us to move anywhere from that, nothing that licenses any inferences for use" (2007, 49). Much ink has been spilled discussing the problem of identifying and evaluating general causal claims, and even though much of this work disagrees with Hempel's strict insistence on nomothetic generalizations as the necessary form of a causal claim, there seems to be broad agreement with the idea that once one *has* valid causal claims, causal explanation is a relatively unproblematic and subordinate step.

As an alternative, I believe, we should actually do what Hempel himself did: start with explanation—Cartwright's "use" of causes—and see what this might tell us about the role played by general claims in the explanation of par-ticular outcomes. But where Hempel tried to rationally reconstruct the logic of physical-scientific explanation and then to extend that to the analysis of human social action, I will do what I have done in previous chapters and begin with the everyday language-games that we play. After all, our philosophical and technical notions of explanation are not radical contrasts with our quotidian notions, but are instead refinements of everyday usage for specialized purposes. What we *do* when we explain in a social-scientific context is not fundamentally different from what we do in everyday explanation.

I find Peter Achinstein's pragmatic-illocutionary approach (initially presented in Achinstein 1985; with subsequent developments collected in 2010b) to be an especially compelling place to begin. As I did in my analysis of factic claims, Achinstein's account starts with the *intention* of an act of explanation: what are we trying to do when we explain something? In the first instance, he argues, we are trying to answer a question, which is to say, we are trying to bring about a "state of understanding" in the person to whom the explanation is offered, where a state of understanding means that the person not only knows a correct answer to the question, but knows that it *is* a correct answer to the question (Achinstein 2010b, 106–8). Thus, the kind of understanding that an explanation is intended to produce is different from a simple command of the facts; unlike a simple information request, the kind of question that calls for an explanation involves an abstract noun like "reason" that stands in need of further specification (ibid.: 26–28). Achinstein's example of this is the question "For what reason did Nero fiddle?" which calls for an explanation that can give specific content to the abstract noun "reason."

Achinstein's broad account of explanation has space for both causal and non-causal explanations: questions about functions, purposes, methods, and implications fit his semantic model, alongside questions about reasons, causes, and outcomes. These are all nouns that are sufficiently abstract, at least from the agent's point of view (Achinstein 1985, 32–34). But this breadth comes at a price, and that price is the limitation of the "state of understanding" to *propositional* knowledge about the meaning of an abstract noun. It is as though in asking for an explanation of how to ride a bicycle ("What procedure should I follow in order to ride a bicycle?") I were concerned with the ambiguity of the word "procedure," when it is manifestly clear that in asking the question what I am actually concerned with is a problem of a different sort: the *practical* problem of how to actually ride a bicycle.

Hence I think we need to push Achinstein's pragmatism a bit further, past the semantics of particular questions, and into what John Dewey (1910, 109–10) would call the *problem-situation* out of which the need for an explanation arises in the first place. The sorts of questions with which Achinstein is concerned strike me as more likely to appear in a final examination for a course than in the course of everyday living. If on a final exam I ask the question "What are the causes of the First World War?" I am probably asking for an enumeration of the causes of the First World War, likely derived from the readings and lectures from earlier in the semester. The test here is a test of factual recall, and the student demonstrates her competence by providing the correct answer. So the practical problem-situation is the student's need to sit for the exam, and the grader's need to assess the student's propositional knowledge; the problem is resolved by the student's giving an answer, and the grader's determination whether or not the answer is correct. But even though the student is arguably in what Achinstein would regard as a "state of understanding" regarding the exam question,[11] what is provided by the student is *not*, I think, an explanation of the First World War—especially since to do well on the exam, the student need not know anything about the First World War beyond being able to recall those few facts she crammed into her short-term memory at the study session the previous evening.

Hence: contra Achinstein, bringing about a "state of understanding" is not a sufficient definition of the intention of an explanation; but, following Achinstein, the way to grasp the distinctiveness of an act of explanation is indeed to focus on the intention to affect the recipient of the explanation in some way. What if the problem-situation is that the questioner *does not know how to do something*? If instead of asking which answers to put on the exam they ask how to take an exam, they are no longer just requesting information, because they are asking out of a different problem-situation, and more than information is needed to help them resolve their perplexity (Dewey 2007, 182). Instead, the solution to the problem involves them acquiring not propositional knowledge, but practical capacities: they have to *learn* how to competently sit for an exam. In answer to questions like these, information is insufficient; what is required instead is an *explanation.*

To bring this back to international studies, consider what is often regarded as the founding question of the field: why is there inter-state war, and is there any-thing we can do about it? Since the field came into being in part as a way of trying to come to terms with the horrors of the First World War, it is not improbable that "What are the causes of the First World War?" was a question asked fairly often during those early days.[12] Although this is verbally identical to the exam question considered above, because the problem-situation is different, giving an answer to

---

11 Unless, of course, they have cheated on the exam.
12 And even into the present, e.g., Lebow (2014).

the question on the exam is not going to be accompanied by the same intention as giving an answer to the question in a social-scientific journal or a scholarly book. Instead, the scholarly answer to the question, precisely because it arises in a problem-situation in which we do not know how to accomplish what we want to accomplish—how to avoid the horrors of major inter-state war—is an explanation intended to augment or enhance our practical capacity, and thus to make it possible for us to *do* something to resolve our predicament. In this sense, explanation is connected to "procedural learning, where what is learned is how to do something or how to act properly or effectively" (Machamer 2004, 32). Explaining is thus one form of *teaching*, and a form specifically germane to human beings in linguistically infused social relations: one might explain to a puppy over and over again that they should not urinate in the house or chase the cats, emphasizing the inappropriateness of his behavior, but this is not likely to accomplish anything. But with human beings, explaining something using language at least has the possibility of affecting the practical capacity of the recipient of the explanation.

In other words, an explanation is *not*, in the first instance, oriented towards objects in the world the way that descriptions are. Instead, it is oriented towards *other people*, aiming to resolve their practical perplexities. To borrow terminology from the philosopher Martin Buber (1971), a description is an "I–it" relationship, marking a connection between a subject ("I") and an object ("it"). This is not an individual matter, however, insofar as the language we use to describe objects is not a personal possession but a shared social enterprise. Nonetheless, Buber's label picks up the way that descriptions, especially factic descriptions, are attuned to an object in an impersonal way: my factic description, if true, is shared by other competent speakers of the relevant language, allowing the "I" in the "I–it" relationship to become interchangeable with other people. Thus my true factic description ceases to be *my* description, and becomes just *a* true factic description of the object.

Buber goes on to argue that relationships between people aren't, or shouldn't be thought of as, I–it relationships. Instead, they are "I–Thou" relationships, based on a mutual recognition of the speaker and listener as subjects rather than as objects.[13] When "I" explain something to a "Thou,"[14] I am orienting myself towards you in a rather different way than, say, the way that I orient myself towards the candle on my desk. I expect my words to be able to *move* you, and I expect that you, like

13 Unfortunately, in English "thou" sounds archaic, because we have collapsed the difference between the second person singular and the second-person plural, as well as eliminating the distinctions between various forms of the second person pronoun. With first- and third-person forms, we still distinguish between "I" and "me" as well as between (e.g.) "they" and "them," but for the second person whether singular, plural, subject, or object, we nowadays just use "you." Other languages—including the German in which Buber wrote—do not do this.

14 Technically, the objective form of the second person singular in English would be "thee." But the contrast Buber is making is between a relationship between a subject and another subject on one hand, and a subject and an object on the other. When "I" explain to "thee" I am treating you as a "Thou" and not as an "it"—even though "thee/Thou" cannot function as the subject of the sentence, and remains an object, albeit distinct from an "it." Thanks to Cathy Elliott for the careful grammatical reading and discussion here.

me, are a conversational interlocutor whose concerns and perplexities are comprehensible to me.[15] If I don't make those assumptions, then I can't explain anything *to you*, and that is the point of the distinction: acts of explanations are always acts directed at other people, intending to enhance their practical capacities and resolve their difficulties. The act of describing aims to get the person out of the way and bring the object into view, but explaining is always explaining *to* someone, and in so doing working on *their* capacities for subsequent action.

Note that whether a particular explanation *succeeds* in affecting the capacity of the recipient or not is not the issue. Instead, what matters is that the *intention* that accompanies an act of explanation aims to affect the capacity of the recipient of the explanation: the future state that my explanation points towards, which is only explicable in light of the problem-situation from which your question arose (Anscombe 1963, 34–35). Prompted by a question stemming from your inability to ride your bicycle, my explanation is intended to help you ride your bicycle; whether or not it *actually* helps you ride your bicycle is a secondary matter, because even a bad explanation is still, logically speaking, an explanation. For inter-state war in the context of the field of international studies, my explanation is intended to resolve the problem by giving you concrete action steps, not to simply re-state established facts. Explanations are intended to solve problems and resolve problem-situations, and to do so by shaping the practical capacity of the recipient; they do not simply provide information.

Causal Explanation

The pragmatic account of explanation above is still too broad to serve as the foundation for a reconstruction of causal explanation, since what I have said about enhancing practical capacities applies equally to causal explanations and to other kinds of explanations. We therefore need to understand what is distinctive about causality per se. Contra neopositivist doctrine, what is most distinctive about a causal claim is neither its lawlikeness nor its empirical generality. Nancy Cartwright (2007, 44) points out that in the contemporary philosophical literature "there are a variety of different kind of relations picked out by the abstract term 'causes' and a variety of different—correct—uses of the term for a variety of different purposes," including probabilistic, invariance, modularity, and causal-process accounts, and that these accounts often disagree on whether a given relation is properly characterized as "causal." But it is not as though these different uses are incommensurately or radically different from one another. Anscombe (1993, 92) suggests that "the core, the common feature, of causality in its various kinds" is simply that "effects derive from, arise out of, come of, their causes." Various diverse accounts of causality share a family resemblance, which Wittgenstein (1993, 387–89) insightfully characterized as a "prototype" involving looking around for the thing producing an

---

15   "My attitude towards him is an attitude towards a soul. I am not of the opinion that he has a soul" (Wittgenstein 1990, volume One, sec. 324).

outcome: a person pulling on a string as the cause of the tug I feel on the string, or the food eaten by some goats as the cause for their decreased milk production. In all these cases, we look around for whatever makes a difference: "Calling something 'the cause' is like pointing and saying: '*He's* to blame!' We instinctively get rid of the cause if we don't want the effect. We instinctively look from what has been hit to what hit it" (ibid., 373). To identify a cause, then, is basically to identify whatever made a difference to the outcome.[16]

We have encountered this notion of causal explanation in the previous chapter, albeit briefly. The WHO's discretionary description of COVID-19 as a pandemic involved a judgment that the disease was sufficiently deadly as to warrant that description; that judgment, in turn, relied on explanations of individual deaths that identified COVID-19 as the cause. Determining that an individual person has died is a reasonably straightforward factic descriptive process, despite some ambiguous borderline cases in which, for a time, it may be impossible to say with certainty whether someone is dead or alive. A death rate is a relatively straightforward computation from those descriptions: take the number of people who died in a given period of time, and divide that by the total population at the beginning of that period of time. That gives you a simple description of what percentage of the population died during that time-period. But the characterization of a person's death as resulting *from* something specific, like a disease, is much more complicated. Suppose someone tested positive for COVID-19, but was hit by a bus while crossing the street, and subsequently died. We would probably not characterize that person's death as resulting from the disease. But what if that person was unable to get out of the way of the bus because they were suffering from shortness of breath, an established symptom of this disease? Now things become murkier. And what if someone who had not tested positive for COVID-19 went to the hospital with chest pains, but all of the available emergency room beds were occupied with COVID patients, and by the time the person's heart attack was diagnosed, it was too late to treat them?

Ambiguities like this permeate *every* quantitative account of COVID deaths, and slightly different protocols for how a "death from COVID" is to be counted can produce quite different numerical results. For instance, prior to 5 April 2020, the U.S. Centers for Disease Control and Prevention (CDC) guidelines only recorded "confirmed" cases of COVID-related deaths, requiring laboratory evidence that a deceased person was infected with the virus. After this date, CDC guidelines changed to include both confirmed and "probable" cases in the official numbers, with probable cases being determined by several criteria that do not necessitate a laboratory test, but which rely on clinical and epidemiological criteria: a person who exhibited symptoms of the disease, in an area where the disease was widely prevalent, is a probable case. Insisting on laboratory tests as the sole criterion of a death from COVID would result in a far lower number of deaths being characterized

---

16 Along these lines, see also Ruggie's (1998) Polkinghorne-inspired notion of causation as involving anything that is significant in bringing about an outcome.

in this way, so the new guidance unsurprisingly resulted in numbers being adjusted upwards. This was a certainly a good decision from a public heath point of view, as it eliminated some of the undercounting of deaths due to COVID: deaths of people who would not otherwise have died, had they not been infected with the disease. But even these revised numbers did not capture every death that might have resulted from COVID-19, and other ambiguities persisted: different jurisdictions report deaths in different ways and at different times, and not every person who died from COVID died in medical care, so their deaths might not be reported as resulting from COVID at all.

Confronting these ambiguities in how a death is reported and recorded is, in many parts of the world, the responsibility of medical examiners, coroners, and others charged with the official recording of the manner of death. In the United States, a professional association—the National Association of Medical Examiners—provides a set of standards and trainings that are linked to the National Vital Statistics System, the official repository of information about causes of death for the country. Collecting this data depends on the responsible authorities in each locale filling out the cause and manner of death sections of the death certificate, and doing so in a consistent way that allows information to be aggregated from those individual forms. As an aid to doing so, the person filling out the death certificate has at their disposal a number of principles and precepts, including the International Classification of Diseases (ICD) document maintained by the WHO, along with a series of guidance documents that the association has produced.[17] Key to the guidance is the notion that the person filling out the form should distinguish between underlying, intermediate, and immediate causes of death, and record them on the form in such a way that they display "a sequential cause and effect relationship when read from bottom to top." The form also includes a section for "conditions contributing to death but not resulting in the underlying cause of death" (Hanzlick 1997, 3). Everything entered on the form should use the standard language and coding specified in the ICD, so specifying the cause of death becomes a matter of determining a chain of conditions and events and describing it in a standardized way.

The inherent limitations to this process of standardization are explicitly recognized in the guidance documents themselves.

The recommendations contained herein are not standards and should not be used to evaluate the performance of a given certifier in a given case. Death certification and manner-of-death classification require judgment, and room must be allowed for discretion on a case by case basis…The "arguments," principles, and foundations used to support certain recommendations in this Guide cannot be applied uniformly to every conceivable death scenario because issues sometimes vary with the manner of death being discussed.

(Hanzlick, Hunsacker III, and Davis 2002, 2)

---

17   Yes, there is even an app for that: the Cause of Death Reference Guide.

The process of death certification cannot be separated from the exercise of judgment on the part of the person filling out the form. The ICD, and the list of acceptable manners of death (natural, accident, suicide, homicide, and undetermined) valid in most U.S. states, provide a background set of terms from which the person may draw, but they do not exhaustively determine how those terms should be used. Hence:

> Judgment should be used when writing a cause-of-death statement. A good rule is to include sufficient information to tell a story about the sequence of diseases (conditions), nonspecific processes, and complications leading to death, being sure not to omit an underlying cause of death that is stated as etiologically specific [*sic*] as possible.
>
> (Hanzlick 1997, 7)

Asking someone to certify a death is asking someone to draw on an intricate vocabulary to construct a plausible account, supported by appropriate evidence, of how a life ended. In constructing that account, the "but-for" principle is commonly suggested, especially when determining underlying causes and the manner of a death: but-for the factor in question, "would the person have died when [they] did?" (Hanzlick, Hunsacker III, and Davis 2002, 7). And this in turn requires the certifier to speculate about what might have happened "but-for" the thing that *actually* happened.[18] Doing so allows the medical examiner to zero in on the cause of death as the factor that made a difference: in this case, the difference between death and life.

Combining this broad notion of causality with the account of explanation I developed above, it would appear that the distinctive mark of a *causal* explanation would have to be the specific kind of capacity it aims to enhance. Now, logically speaking, identifying a factor that made a difference to an outcome is equivalent to providing instructions for achieving, or preventing, that outcome. If I know that a death occurred because of poison, that also means that I know that administering that poison can produce death—and that avoiding that poison can prevent that kind of death. Hence, the capacity that a causal explanation aims to enhance must be about *making something happen* (as in Woodward 2005). A causal explanation, as opposed to other forms of explanation, responds to a problem-situation in which the problem involves getting something done, and responds by telling the recipient how to do it. I am driving a car, and I want to know how to make the car go faster, or keep the engine from stalling, or drive on the highway. Or suppose you become enthralled by the game of baseball, and want to know how to actually throw a curveball yourself, or to hit one. In both cases, the central problem is that we do not know how to bring about a desired result. The kind of practical capacity that is needed here involves some sort of recipe or plan intended to produce the

---

18 This speculative aspect is what distinguishes the judgment exercised by medical examiners from the judgment exercised by authorized describers in a discretionary description. Umpires *determine* whether a pitch was a ball or a strike; medical examiners *explain* a death.

outcome—a set of instructions, where instructions are the imperative form of a causal explanation.[19]

But the generic form of a question arising from such a problem-situation—"How do I do this?"—obscures an important point, which is that asking how to do something always implies "…as opposed to something else." "How do I ride a bicycle"…as opposed to falling off of it? "How do I hit a curveball"…as opposed to swinging over it? It also obscures the fundamental similarity between this form of question and a question-form that is more common in the social sciences, namely "Why do we have/observe X"? Here again there is an implied "…as opposed to something else," as in: "Why do we have poverty"…as opposed to an equality of means? "Why do we have inter-state war"…as opposed to peace among states?[20] Both "why" and "how" questions seek answers that will explain the presence of something as opposed to something else, and in so doing will supply a recipe for making something happen: changing whatever the inputs are will, in principle, change the outcome. If we know why we have inter-state war as opposed to peace among states, we can look for ways to alter whatever produces inter-state war, just the way that if I know how I am missing the curveball, I can look for ways to alter my swing and increase my chances of connecting the bat with the ball.

The WHRT Formula

Questions that call for a causal explanation seem, much of the time, to follow a reasonably standard formula: "why/how…rather than…" or WHRT for short. The WHRT formula aims at the basic core of what it means to say that something "causes" something else: that the cause *brings about* the outcome, and does so in such a way that we get the outcome that we (factually) get and not some other outcome. The adjustments I make to my swing cause me to hit the baseball regularly rather than infrequently. The democratic character of inter-state dyads causes them to be peaceful dyads, rather than warlike dyads. And so on. Precisely *what kind of connection* has to exist between the causal input and the outcome is something that is left deliberately unspecified in the formula, making this a matter of scholarly debate and discussion rather than a categorical pronouncement *ex cathedra*. Regardless of the particular flavor of causation one chooses, a causal explanation—in international studies, and arguably in general—will be offered in response to a WHRT-question.

---

19 A causal explanation for why we have X is logically equivalent to a set of instructions for producing X, even if the practical challenges to *following* that set of instructions are quite insurmountable given the irreversibility of historical time. (I would be remiss in not acknowledging Hidemi Suganami's probing questions about the relationship between instructions and explanations as starting my thinking down this path.)

20 Note that specifying that "something else" does not imply that causal explanations are, in any strong sense, necessarily symmetrical. Explaining why we have war rather than peace in some specific case does not require us to adduce both causes of war *and* causes of peace; instead, what we are seeking is an explanation of what *made the difference* in this case, and gave us war rather than peace. Thanks to Derek Beach for productive disagreements on this issue.

The "WH" part of the formula is not even the most important part. The "RT" part of the formula suggests that any causal explanation is always, *necessarily*, a "contrastive" explanation (Grynaviski 2013). If we don't have a sense of what the "rather than" consists of, we have no way to evaluate whether an explanation is a good one, or whether it actually answers the question asked. Suganami (1996, 131–32) points out that depending on the shared background assumptions of the questioner and the responder, certain explanations might "count" as causal explanations while others do not; I would suggest that this is because we usually do not precisely and explicitly spell out the "rather than"[21] that we are thinking of, but leave it implicit. If I ask you for an explanation of inter-state war it is sometimes clear from the context whether I am asking "Why inter-state war rather than peace among states?" or "Why inter-state war rather than wars between civilizations?" but more often, I would submit, it is *not* especially clear, and we would all be well-advised to make the "rather than" part of our research questions as explicit as we can make them.

To show the utility of the "why/how…rather than…" (or WHRT) formula, look briefly at the research articles in a randomly selected (May 2014) issue of the journal *International Organization*.[22] Not all of the articles in this issue conform to the neopositivist model of evaluating hypothetical nomothetic generalizations across multiple cases, but they *do* all ask, and then try to answer, WHRT-questions. The lead article (Goldstein and Gulotty 2014) suggests that the U.S. president's ability to target potential economic dislocations explains why, between 1928 and 1964, certain products had their tariffs reduced while others did not. This is evidently answering a WHRT-question about each individual product (why a tariff reduction rather than no tariff reduction, or why no tariff reduction rather than a tariff reduction?) although the form of the analysis tends to obscure this, focusing instead on the systematic relationship between an input (presidential ability) and an output (the tariff level on a particular product). But this is mere semantics yet again, because the only way that the presidential ability to target potential economic dislocations can explain variations in the tariff level between products is if, in the case of *each specific product*, presidential ability can explain why the tariff was or was not reduced.[23] A similar kind of analysis covers other articles in the issue. Why do we see different kinds of post-election protests across cases? Because of the reporting practices of international election observers (Hyde and Marinov 2014). Why do some industries adopt protectionist responses to exchange-rate changes?

---

21 Bas Van Fraassen (1977; 2004) would likely call this the "contrast class."
22 I am not going to discuss the two "research notes" that also appear in the issue. I selected *IO* only because it is, by common consensus, the top U.S. IR journal at present.
23 Compare Suganami's (1996, 33–35) discussion of the difference between "the causes of war" and "the causes of a particular war." Inasmuch as the object of explanation in the article is the tariff level for *each specific product*, the aggregate explanation supervenes on case-specific explanations. If, on the contrary, the object of explanation were the *distribution of tariff levels*, the whole study would be a single-case study (explaining a systemic outcome) despite using data about a variety of products. And that in turn would make the Goldstein and Gulotty article very much like the Nelson article I discuss in the next paragraph.

Because of the effects of those changes on the competitiveness of the particular industry (Broz and Werfel 2014). Why do different financial actors adopt more or less risky strategies in times of uncertainty? Because of the social conventions present in different domains (Nelson and Katzenstein 2014).[24]

The other articles in the issue ask and attempt to answer WHRT-questions more directly. Why are IMF lending practices systematically biased rather than being more similar across countries? Because of the ideological affinities between IMF staff and some, but not other, country officials (Nelson 2014). Why do we now see individual accountability norms, rather than other norms, at the global level? Because of the dominance of a modernist world culture (Kim and Sharman 2014). Some of the directness here can be attributed to the fact that these two articles, unlike the other research articles in the issue, are efforts to explain *single cases* instead of offering explanations for outcomes in multiple cases. The article on the IMF, despite examining multiple IMF loans and country partnerships, has only one case-specific outcome (IMF lending practices) that it is seeking to explain; the article on individual accountability norms, despite looking at a variety of institutional settings and norm entrepreneurs, likewise has only one case-specific outcome (norms at the global level) that it is seeking to explain. But regardless of their single-case focus, these articles—no less than the statistical-comparative articles discussed above—take as their central question a puzzle involving the presence of some outcome rather than another.

General Claims and Specific Explanations

Useful though I find it to be, the WHRT formula doesn't quite suffice to define a causal explanation. There is no such thing as an unambiguously causal question; it is the *explanation* that can be causal, by responding to a WHRT-question in a particular way.

So what makes an explanation causal? As I suggested above, if the intention of a causal explanation is to enable effective practice, then the distinctive quality of a causal explanation cannot be its invocation of or reference to nomothetic generalizations. But at the same time, it is difficult to imagine a causal explanation intended to affect practical capacity that did *not* reference, invoke, or at any rate somehow draw on general causal claims. You ask me how to hit a curveball, and my explanation will make use of general claims about better anticipating where the ball will end up when it gets to you, claims that are unique neither to you nor to any particular instance of you trying to hit the ball. Similarly, if we ask why there is inter-state war or economic inequality in any particular instance, an explanation that answers the question actually asked will be an explanation that adduces those

---

24 Note that while the first three articles discussed in this paragraph use quantitative data and techniques, the Nelson and Katzenstein article is through and through "qualitative" (by which I simply mean "not quantitative," i.e., doesn't use numbers). Despite that, the overall form of the explanations offered is the same: here is some input that varies across cases, and connects to an output that also varies across those same cases.

factors that produced what we actually have as opposed to something else that we don't have—and logically speaking there is no way for that to happen *unless* there is some general statement connecting factors with the outcome. An explanation for a dysfunctional international organization that points to the "generic cultural form" of bureaucracy (as in Barnett and Finnemore 2004) relies, even if only implicitly, on a general claim about the connection between this cultural form and a set of outcomes. While the form of the explanation may be a case-specific narrative about how the input led to the outcome in this instance—here is this international organization, here it is bureaucratizing its operations, here are the dysfunctions that followed from that bureaucratization—that does not change the fact that the explanation will rely on general notions in order not to be simply a description of sequential happenings.

This dependence of causal explanation on general causal claims is perhaps easier to see in a causal explanation more directly connected to the production of an outcome. If you want to ride a bicycle but are unable to do so, and you ask me how to alter that outcome and produce another one, any explanation or set of instructions I give you will have to contain certain general claims about keeping your feet on the pedals, holding the handlebars steady, and the like. These claims are general in the first place in that they transfer from instance to instance (otherwise they wouldn't make very good advice), and then in that they transfer from rider to rider and bicycle to bicycle.[25] If it were *not* the case that keeping one's feet on the pedals and depressing them in sequence tended to produce forward motion of the bicycle, I wouldn't give you that advice, or I wouldn't explain the bicycle not moving forward by pointing out that you took your feet off of the pedals or weren't depressing them in sequence fast enough. Causal explanation depends on general causal claims; that generality is what bridges the gap between individual instances, and makes the explanation *useful*.

To put this another way: causal explanations are ultimately about *manipulability*.

> One ought to be able to associate with any successful explanation a hypothetical or counterfactual experiment that shows us that and how manipulation of the factors mentioned in the explanation…would be a way of manipulating or altering the phenomenon explained.
>
> (Woodward 2005, 11)

If one can actually carry out that experiment, so much the better: I don't have to simply imagine what would happen if I stopped pedaling the bicycle, I can go and try it out for myself, and see if alternative results are produced. When it comes to the general cultural form of bureaucracy, or the ideological proclivities of officials at the World Bank, or incentives facing academic departments debating a set of

---

25 But perhaps imperfectly so: a different bicycle might require slightly different degrees of pressure to move the pedals or steer the handlebars. This is, I submit, no different than the localization of other general lessons into specific contexts (e.g., the lessons international aid and conflict-resolution workers have acquired through multi-sited experiences, analyzed in Autesserre 2014).

curricular requirements, concretely manipulating those factors to see what might result might be impractical or even impossible. But it is sufficient that we be able to spell out what that counterfactual world might look like *if* we were able to manipulate those factors (Lebow 2010). Whether we can concretely manipulate the factors or not, what makes this elaboration of alternative outcomes possible is the use of general causal claims in specific causal explanations.

Because of their manipulationist form, causal explanations at least implicitly inhabit "a space of alternative possibilities" and let us see how "if these initial conditions had been different or had changed in various ways, various of these alternative possibilities would have been realized instead" (Woodward 2005, 191). Manipulability provides a useful way to distinguish between mere correlational association (even sequential association) and a causal connection: if I can't change the outcome by manipulating the inputs, the way I might adjust the volume of my speakers by turning a knob on the receiver, then the inputs aren't causally connected to the outcome. Likewise, if I can't spin out a plausible counterfactual world in which an organization had a different bureaucratic culture and acted differently—an exercise which amounts to "manipulating" the claimed causal factor *imaginatively* (Weber 1999a, 275)—I am not dealing with a causal connection.

The manipulability criterion does not, however, require that causal claims inevitably issue forth in the form of lawlike *empirical* generalizations. Instead, the causal connection between the volume control-knob and the volume of my speakers depends on the observation that I can normally or routinely alter the volume by turning the knob, even if that "normal" or "routine" connection isn't infallible, and even if it doesn't rise to a statistically significant 95 percent level of confidence. Causal claims begin in *practical* activities; through investigation we find some ways of manipulating objects in order to achieve desired ends, and the most generally useful of those become part of our common stock of knowledge, serving as a baseline for our expectations (Dewey 1910, 93–94. 133–34; Cartwright 2007, 28). Once a claim becomes such a baseline, we are surprised when something doesn't work the way it is "supposed" to—for instance, if turning the knob *fails to* produce the expected effect on speaker volume, my reaction is to look for the reason why it didn't (Anscombe 1993, 94). The generality of a causal claim is not, therefore, a simple matter of observed—factual—covariation between inputs and outputs, but is more *ideal-typical*:

> This construction brings together certain relationships and events of historical life into an internally coherent *conceptual* cosmos....It is formed by a one-sided *accentuation* of one or *several* perspectives, and through the synthesis of diffuse, discrete, *individual* phenomena, present sometimes more, sometimes less, sometimes not at all; subsumed by such one-sided, emphatic viewpoints so that they form a uniform construction *in thought*. In its conceptual purity this construction can never be found in reality, it is a *utopia*.
>
> (Weber 2003, 388)

The categorical expression of a causal claim as a general connection between a factor and an outcome[26] thus plays a different role than the observation of an empirical regularity would. The *logical* or *formal* generality of the former does not mean that we should always expect to see the latter. Given the "hurly-burly of many crossing contingencies" (Anscombe 1993, 100) characteristic of the open system of the actually existing world, and the important differences between that world and the artificial purity of the laboratory within which causal relations may be induced to show themselves as empirical generalizations (Bhaskar 1975), the connections we observe in the world may have little resemblance to the idealized statements that structure and summarize our expectations. My expectation that I can propel a bicycle forward by applying pressure to the pedals in sequence, or change the volume by turning the knob, or generate peaceful relations by joining states into a "security community" (as in Adler and Barnett 1998), might be foiled and frustrated by all kinds of situational contingencies. But this does not mean that we are immediately justified in tossing out the causal claim, as the claim might *still* have a role to play in the causal explanation of why the situation looks the way that it does, helping to set a normal expectation against which to appreciate the difference that some other factor made to the outcome.

However, a good causal explanation can't just use *any* causal claims. General causal claims can play a role in causal explanations of specific outcomes just as long as the relevant community of questioners and explainers understands them to be *in some sense valid*. That "in some sense" covers a lot of ground, because there are *many* ways to establish and evaluate the validity of a general causal claim. Definitionally, the important thing is that a causal claim be both logically general and relevant to the practical manipulation of an outcome: changing X produces changes in Y. There are a variety of ways to create and evaluate such causal claims. The most straightforward is simply to abstract from experience: we find that we can manipulate some outcome by altering some input, and we sum up that experience in a logically general claim.[27] In attempting to bake a pie, we learn that overworking the dough produces a tough crust, while being gentler with the dough produces a nicely flaky crust; that becomes a lesson we can transmit to others in the form of a general causal claim. If we did not have that experience, we would not have produced that summary in the first place, and if our experience changes, we will probably stop using that summary because it will no longer speak to any experiences that we have. Indeed, this might be the paradigm case for the

---

26 The core form of a causal claim is simply: X causes Y. Adding scope and domain conditions, weakening the claim so that it becomes "X sometimes causes Y" (or "X makes Y more likely"), adding a bunch of intervening variables between X and Y...none of these changes the basic point I am making here, which is that the claim of a causal connection between X and Y *is not necessarily an empirical generalization*. Nor does it *require* that we observe an empirical generalization in practice.

27 Or: a detached observer can abstractly summarize the experiences of people who *do* have direct experience manipulating some outcome by altering some input. Dewey (1920, 150–51) called this the liberating function of abstraction, and noted that practitioners themselves may not always be in the best position to abstractly "reconstruct" their experiences and make them available to others.

manipulability account of causal claims, and the most directly related to the practical problem of bringing about a result.

But there are other ways to go about creating and evaluating causal claims, without having to manipulate the relevant factors under controlled conditions. One might have practical experience of a connection between some input and some outcome—say, between being a third-party mediator and facilitating or brokering a cease-fire—and on that basis construct a plausible causal claim connecting the two. Or, reading across *multiple* events and situations, one might start to develop a conceptual vocabulary of mechanisms and processes useful for organizing different cases and showing how in each case there was a unique configuration of mechanisms and processes leading to a specific outcome. Instead of the manipulation of inputs, logical elaboration with myriad examples establishes the plausibility of each causal claim.[28] Or one might—as the economists whose argument I began this chapter with did—start off with a broad theory shared by a professional community of researchers about human behavior as rationally responding to incentives, and derive expectations about particular behaviors under particular conditions from that theory.[29] The point is that all of these causal claims emerge, in one way or another, from the experience of the analyst; to the extent that others share or recognize those experiences, the claim summarizes something more than an individual's idiosyncratic point of view, and can serve as part of a causal explanation.

What, then, of the neopositivist strategy of evaluating hypothetical causal claims against real-world, open-system data, and only retaining as unfalsified those claims corresponding to statistically significant correlations across cases? In other words, treating a claim that X causes Y as *only* being valid if X and Y statistically co-vary in a significant way? This is certainly *a* way of trying to evaluate causal claims. If we look at a statistically significant correlation as comparing different values of some input factors across cases to see if the outcome in question "changes" as they "change,"[30] we might conclude that a robust correlation indicates the presence of a causal connection that could support manipulationist explanations. A neopositivist

28   This is Charles Tilly's strategy in most of his later works—for example, Tilly (1998).
29   Despite their use of quantitative data, it is important to remember that the arguments made by economists are not typically based on *empirical* generalizations, but on general *theoretical* claims. The data does not do the explaining in an economic argument; the theory does. Note in this respect that the authors of *Cracks in the Ivory Tower* never seek to *test* the proposition that individuals respond rationally to incentives—and this is a perfectly fine way for them to proceed, methodologically speaking, as long as we do not mistake their explanation for evidence that the theoretical proposition is valid.
30   Scare-quotes here because, of course, the values of the inputs and the outcome *don't* actually change in any given case. Instead, each case is treated as though it were an independent trial in an experiment, and as though the value of the inputs had been set through an "intervention" (Woodward 2005, 98–99) rather than simply *occurring*, perhaps for a variety of distinct reasons. The danger in this procedure is that the causes of the values of the inputs in the different cases might not satisfy the "Causal Markov condition" (Hausman and Woodward 1999, 535) and hence not be "screened off" from the observed outcome. In a laboratory setting, we can artificially induce such situations (Cartwright 2007, 186–87); in the actual world, we need to be considerably more careful before pronouncing *anything* a "natural experiment."

evaluation of a general causal claim treats that claim as, in effect, a factic description of patterns that might or might not be found in observational data, and thus operationally *defines* "causality" as a pattern of systematic association between variables. What is being described in the general claim is the pattern, and like any factic description, the resulting statement is fallible and can be fact-checked.

But even if we accept this, it is still the case that *the statistical evaluation of causal claims is not a form of causal explanation*, any more than the other techniques for crafting and evaluating causal claims are forms of causal explanation. Causal explanations utilize causal claims, but they are not identical with causal claims. "Democracies don't go to war with one another" is *not an explanation* of why any given set of democracies don't or didn't go to war with one another, and it is *not a recipe* for producing more peaceful relations between countries by making them all democracies—it is, if anything, a piece of evidence in support of a causal claim connecting democratic regime-types with non-war outcomes. In order to move from a set of causal claims to a causal explanation, it is necessary that we move from logical generality to something more specific, and spell out just how we got from an initial situation to an outcome: precisely where things could have gone differently, what counterfactual trajectories might have happened that did not in fact happen, and which manipulations of which factors might have produced those alternative outcomes. The logical generality of causal claims is what makes such counterfactual construals possible in the first place, and therefore underpins an explanation of an outcome (we have Y rather than Z because of A, B, and C) that is also a set of directions for someone trying to bring about an outcome (if you do A, B, and C, Y rather than Z will result). Even if the causal claim in question is *also* empirically general, assessing that empirical generality remains distinct from using the causal claim to explain any specific outcome.

Case-Specific Explanations

To craft a causal explanation, we need to dive into the specifics of a particular case (Saylor 2020, 996–9). We need to talk, at a minimum, about the specific *sequence* in which things unfolded, because we need to know "how the previous stage or situation produces this certain result rather than some other. In other words, among all the changes that might have occurred at the next stage, this one did occur because of the activity that produced it" (Machamer 2004, 31). We also need to talk about tensions between different causal pathways and how they are mediated in any specific situation, as when the logic of bureaucratic rationality in conjunction with the logic of charismatic authority produces the particular organizational structure of the Catholic Church.[31] In this way, causal explanations are invariably case-specific and involve factic descriptions of the particulars of that case, while the causal claims on which they draw are *not* case-specific, but logically general.

---

31 This is, in summary form, Weber's (1976) argument.

There is a potentially tricky sematic issue here involving the word "case." Despite broad agreement in principle across the methodological spectrum that a case is not a natural unity but instead an artifact of the analysis, we tend to fall back in practice into the habit of thinking that certain kinds of things just *are* "cases," and other things are composed of multiple cases. For example, in international studies we traditionally read Kenneth Waltz (1979) as offering a "general" theory of inter-state behavior, because his account emphasizes anarchy at the international level as being a "permissive" cause of *all* inter-state wars, with *all* states therefore having to take the possibility of war into account as they formulate their policies. But this is a misreading, inasmuch as Waltz is not offering an account that spans multiple cases (be these particular states or particular inter-state interactions), but an account that relates one set of inputs (describing the structure of the inter-national system) to one outcome (the *possible recurrence* of inter-state war, and the consequent need for states to look after their own security). So it would make little sense to "test" Waltz's account by looking at multiple states or multiple interactions or even at individual state behaviors, because in Waltz's account there is only one case: the international system as a whole.[32]

Further, a theory like Waltz's is *not an explanation* in the terms I have outlined here. The connection between anarchy and war is, rather, a causal *claim*: a logically general distillation or ideal-typification (Goddard and Nexon 2005; Wæver 2009) of a set of experiences—in this instance, a set of experiences of inter-state politics that suggest a causal connection between international anarchy and state behavior, rather than a set of experiences involving the actual manipulation of international anarchy—that can be used in causal explanations only by putting it into the context of specific states and the specific interactions between them. In all such cases, Waltz suggests, there will be systemic pressure on states to balance power against one another, but this does *not* mean that in all inter-state interactions we should expect to see balancing behavior! As with any causal claim, its concrete manifest-ation in the actual world is far more contingent than it would be in a controlled laboratory setting; other processes could interfere, and in many instances the *deviation* from the expected balancing behavior might be the genuinely interesting thing.[33] The power of the explanation depends not on the statistical validation of the causal claims used within it, but on whether the explanation gives us a plausible counterfactual: if international anarchy were mitigated in this instance, would we see the same kind of state behavior?[34]

---

32 Suganami (2008) does not appear to take account of this possibility.

33 Variation from the baseline might be understood as pointing towards case-specific factors that interact with the general causal claim so as to produce a deviant outcome. A state that didn't balance power would be a significant anomaly in a Waltzian world, and we might want to know just why and how it managed not to do what we expected that international anarchy would pressure it to do.

34 This is not to downplay the significant ambiguity of "anarchy" and what it might mean to "miti-gate" it (to manipulate it, in the language I have been using here) in Waltz, which has been inci-sively analyzed by Buzan, Jones, and Little (1993) and Suganami (1996), among others.

In order to relate a general causal claim to a specific outcome, and thereby construct a causal explanation of why we see that outcome and not another, it is necessary to make reference to case-specific factors that are, by definition, absent from the general causal claims invoked in the explanation. If I aim to explain why you fell off of your bicycle, I might do so with reference to general claims about the speed of one's pedaling or the angle of the handlebars, but in order to construct this explanation, I need to talk not just about the general relationships, but about the specific connections that obtain in *this* case. You did not fall off of your bicycle because *one* has to be moving at a specific speed to stay upright, but because *you* were pedaling too slowly. The general causal claim supports the counterfactual that had you been pedaling faster, you would have remained balanced, and this allows the explanation of the observed outcome—your slow pedaling caused you to fall—as well giving rise to the instruction to pedal faster next time if you want to stay on the bicycle.

To return to the example with which I started this chapter, the same is true of the course requirements at a particular university. If it were the case that those requirements could be causally explained as resulting from rent-seeking behavior by that university's departments, then altering the behavior would produce different course requirements. Indeed, one way of evaluating that explanation would be to do just this, practically or imaginatively, either by changing the incentives that lead self-interested rational actors to look for economic rents, or by changing the way that those actors act (possibly by changing the actors into a different kind of actor, perhaps one that is simply not economically rational). Something similar is true of student cheating: if it is rational to cheat, one possible solution—albeit one that is ruled out in theory by the kinds of presumptions that economists typically make about human behavior—is to socialize students into a culture in which cheating is just not a feasible option, perhaps because of an honor code that has become a point of pride for everyone to uphold.[35] So if the causal explanation is a good one, then it provides instructions for generating outcomes, much the same way that a recipe for red velvet cake allows a baker to generate a tasty dessert. The general causal claims involved in such an explanation need not be themselves evaluated as factic descriptions of patterns of data; there are other sources of confidence in a general causal claim, including practical experience and established theory sustained by an intellectual community. And the causal explanation itself, while it needs to take account of the facts of the situation at hand (a department that doesn't exist at a particular university cannot engage in rent-seeking behavior, after all), is not itself a fact, but a recipe for generating outcomes. Such recipes cannot simply be evaluated factically, but have an irreducibly practical aspect to them.

---

35 Such socialization would be more dramatic than giving students an incentive to adhere to the honor code; it would involve helping students approach the world less as rational actors and more as moral agents. For some experimental evidence along these lines, see Gerlach (2017).

4   Explaining Outcomes Causally

After the U.S.-led invasion of Iraq in 2003, a minor controversy erupted which uncharacteristically propelled U.S. International Relations scholarship, at least momentarily, into the limelight.[1] Increasingly, official spokespersons for the United States deployed language strikingly similar to that deployed by researchers working on the "democratic peace," suggesting that the promotion of democracy was justified, in part, by the finding that democracies don't go to war with other democracies. President George W. Bush put the claim in typically grandiose terms in his second inaugural address (2005):

> We are led, by events and common sense, to one conclusion: The survival of liberty in our land increasingly depends on the success of liberty in other lands. The best hope for peace in our world is the expansion of freedom in all the world.

But the language of the democratic peace had been making its way into U.S. policy-making circles at least since the early 1990s, characterizing and perhaps coloring policy debates since long before Bush took office (Ish-Shalom 2008). Was democratic peace research responsible for the U.S. invasion of Iraq?

The leading exponent of the democratic peace, Bruce Russett, vigorously denied that it was. Indeed, Russett argued, "most of us who helped formulate and test the theory of democratic peace have consistently argued" that military intervention to democratize states was a problematic basis for state action. "Our creation has been perverted," Russett lamented (2005, 395–96). Russett also offered a variety of statistical evidence in support of his claim that non-military means of intervention are more likely to lead to successful democratization. But the matter is not so simple, because the claim upheld *throughout* the democratic peace literature rests on the notion that the democratic character of a regime exercises an independent and significant effect on observed outcomes: "it is the *level* of democracy that influences the likelihood of conflict, not how recently these political institutions

1 For helpful comments on previous drafts and discussion of the issues raised in this chapter I would like to thank Ned Lebow, Stefano Guzzini, Glauco Peres de Silva, Cathy Elliott, Mark Shirk, Ludvig Norman, and Kasia Kaczmarska.

DOI: 10.4324/9781003455912-4

were established" or any other ancillary factor (Oneal and Russett 2000, 276). If "being a democracy" is causally linked to the desired set of outcomes (in this case, not going to war with other democracies), then the policy of forced regime change appears to make some sense: whatever else is going on, the "democracyness" of the new democracy should start making itself felt in the state's post-intervention behavior.

Parts of this controversy involve confusion between general causal claims (democracies *in general* don't fight one another) and specific causal explanations (these countries don't fight one another because they are democracies) of the sort I discussed in the previous chapter. There is simply no warrant for presuming that a general causal claim—even one that is based on a statistically significant correlation between factors—can serve in a direct and immediate way as an instruction for bringing about an outcome. Rather, it is specific causal explanations that are recipes for generating outcomes in specific cases, and although those explanations rely on general causal claims, they are not simple restatements of the general claims. Relying on a general causal claim without taking the specific complexities of the situation into account is often a poor way to proceed.

But other parts of this controversy involve a slightly different issue, albeit one that is equally related to the neopositivist strategy of explaining an outcome by subsuming a specific case under a general empirical law. This procedure raises an immediate problem: we can only observe actual outcomes, and not the outcomes that *would have occurred* but for the causal factor in question. Factically speaking, either a country went to war or it did not, and we can only observe the world in which one or the other of these claims is true. Similarly, we can only observe the actual presence of causal factors, and not the counterfactual situation in which, say, a country that is factually described as a "democracy" was not a democracy. So we can't directly evaluate whether something specific happened *because* of a general pattern (Torigian 2021). The neopositivist answer to this conundrum is the notion of "average causal effect," which provides a way of moving from observations of particular instances of potential causes and effects, to broader accounts of the relationship between causes and effects—and then moving back to the explanation of specific outcomes, armed with that broad sense of how much some cause contributes to an effect. As such, neopositivist explanation by subsumption under a general law and average causal effect are intimately linked.

This pair of notions—subsumption and average causal effect—is not, however, exhaustive of what we mean when we say that we are explaining something, and in my view it misses the most distinctive thing about the act of explanation. As I argued in the previous chapter, when we explain something to someone, we are attempting to develop in them some novel capacity: *to explain* is to put an end to a perplexity, to resolve a problem of some sort. With causal explanations, the problem, and the associated capacity, involves *making something happen*: to explain some outcome causally is to equip the recipient of the explanation with the capacity, should they so choose, to bring about that outcome, at least in principle. Building on this broader sense of explanation, in this chapter I elaborate a configurational alternative to average causal effect, arguing that we can abandon the effort—modeled on the laboratory sciences—to empirically isolate individual causal factors so as to estimate their *individual* and *independent* effects on an outcome, in favor of a style of explanation that focuses on combinations of factors in specific arrangements and sequences. We do not abandon causation in doing so, although we do move beyond neopositivism, and with it explanation by subsumption as well as the notion of an average causal effect.

Focusing on these methodological issues is also critical if we want to make any coherent sense of the contemporary discussion about "mechanisms" in causal explanation (e.g., Machamer 2004; Illari 2011; Bennett and Checkel 2014). *If* one is a neopositivist committed to the epistemic project of nomothetic generalization, then mechanism-based causal explanations must of necessity be bounded by that goal: a mechanism can only be causal to the extent that it too can be reformulated as an empirical generalization and subjected to evaluation with cross-case evidence before functioning as the grounds on which subsume a specific instance under a general pattern. But if there were a methodological alternative to nomothetic generalization—some way of relating general causal claims to specific causal explanations that did not involve the logic of subsumption—then it might instead be the case that causal mechanisms did something other than provide case-specific details that *localized*, so to speak, general causal connections. Neopositivists acknowledge *only* the singular goal of explaining via subsumption under a nomothetic generalization, but if we look more broadly at instances of actual causal explanation especially in the social sciences, we can identify a *configurational* style of causal explanation that relates general causal claims to specific causal explanations in a quite distinct way. Making this configurational logic explicit, and contrasting it with the nomothetic subsumption logic prized and privileged by neopositivists, can only make these efforts clearer. And doing so will also produce a richer understanding of what it means to offer a causal explanation.

Nomothetic Generalization and Average Causal Effects

For the classic statement of the neopositivist approach to explanation, we have to return once more to Carl Hempel's 1942 article "The Function of General Laws in History." Coming out of the Vienna Circle tradition of logical positivism which was centrally concerned with the demarcation of science from non-science (Richardson 2006, 14), it is no surprise that Hempel spends considerable time in the piece setting out criteria by which to distinguish "genuine from pseudo-explanation." The key factor here is whether an account incorporates scientifically respectable notions, or instead deploys "pictorial and emotional appeals…vague analogies and intuitive 'plausibility'" (Hempel 1942, 37–38). As examples of the latter, Hempel lists "predestined fate" along with "'historic destination of a race'" and "'self-unfolding of absolute reason' in history" (ibid., 41). These are hardly politically neutral notions, especially for an article written in the midst of the Second World War, and Hempel's scathing dismissal of them shows some of what he thought was at stake in the effort to define the boundaries of correct scientific reason. The opposite of these "mere metaphors without cognitive content" is a general law, which Hempel defines as "a statement of universal conditional form which is capable of being confirmed or disconfirmed by suitable empirical findings" (ibid., 35). The takeaway message of the article is that history and psychology—and by implication all of the social sciences, even though Hempel like most philosophers of science isn't explicitly concerned with social science per se—rely on such empirically general laws every bit as much as the physical and natural sciences do.

One of the striking aspects of Hempel's argument is how *unproblematic* he takes the notion of a "general law" to be. Since Hempel is not trying to give precise operational instructions to researchers, this is perhaps not surprising, but it does raise some peculiar challenges for anyone looking not simply to *use* a general law in an explanation, but to *evaluate* whether a general law is actually valid. As I argued in the previous chapter, Hempel's concern is with the logic of explanation using general laws, and this procedure necessarily presumes that we have valid general laws available to us; otherwise, subsuming a particular case under a general law would not generate a properly scientific explanation. So the endeavor of evaluating a hypothetical general law must, in Hempel's framing, be separate from the endeavor of explaining an outcome. A general law used in an explanation is, so to speak, *presumptively valid* at the time it is used—perhaps it has been validated previously?—and this allows it to fulfill its scientific function of showing "that the event in question was not 'a matter of chance,' but was to be expected in view of certain antecedent or simultaneous conditions" (Hempel 1942, 39).

In his essay Hempel gives us pointers on when to throw out a putatively general law because it utilizes unverifiable nonsense-terms, but basically no guidance on how to *empirically* assess a proposed general law.[2] But one key practical problem in developing and evaluating general laws involving causal connections between antecedents and consequents is that the simple observation of correlations between factors is insufficient to determine whether some cause C is actually responsible for the effect E. In a famous paper, Paul Holland argued that this insufficiency was due to what he called the Fundamental Problem of Causal Inference. Given a causal factor (*t* for "treatment" in Holland's notation) and a default state of the world in which the casual factor is not present (*c* for "control"), the causal effect of applying *t* to a unit *u* is

$$Y_t(u) - Y_c(u)$$

which is the difference between the value of the outcome with the treatment applied to the unit, $Y_t(u)$, and the value of the outcome with the treatment not applied to the unit, $Y_c(u)$. The problem is that "it is impossible to *observe* the value of $Y_t(u)$ and $Y_c(u)$ on the same unit and, therefore, it is impossible to *observe* the effect of

---

2 I am focusing on this essay and not the broader corpus of Hempel's work because it is this essay that is the go-to citation for neopositivists in the field—and because even those who regard the field as having gotten beyond Hempel still make arguments about causation that are anticipated in this essay. On the more complicated question of Hempel's own thinking on scientific explanation more broadly, see Dray (2000).

t on *u*" (Holland 1986, 947). I can light a piece of paper on fire and observe as it blackens and turns to ash, but having lit the paper on fire, I cannot now observe the same piece of paper *without* my having lit it on fire; hence I cannot really observe the effect of my having lit the paper on fire. The connection between lighting the paper on fire and its turning to ash might be an accident, or a coincidence, or the result of random chance.

This would seem to pose a serious problem for the empirical identification and evaluation of Hempelian covering laws, as even the observation of a repeated association would fall victim to the skepticism voiced by David Hume: no number of observations can suffice to give us confidence that the next observation will follow the same pattern. The well-known "solution" to Hume's skepticism advanced by Karl Popper (1979)—convert *every* claim into a hypothetical claim, and stop worrying about whether we have gathered enough observations to make a hypothetical claim into a certain law—doesn't suffice here, because if we are faced with evidence that seems contrary to the general law, it is not clear whether we should toss out the hypothetical general law or whether we should look for additional factors in the situation that can account for why the expected outcome did not occur.[3] For Hempelian explanation to take place, we require some way to do what Holland argues is impossible to do observationally: we need to *know with certainty* that a casual factor produces an outcome. Simply *presuming* that a statement of universal conditional form ("if a piece of paper is lit on fire, it will turn to ash") is valid is obviously insufficient, but Hempel offers no way around the necessity to do just this when explaining any particular outcome.

Holland's discussion of the Fundamental Problem of Causal Inference doesn't end with a dismissal of the idea of causal covering laws, of course. Instead, Holland suggests that the way around the Fundamental Problem of Causal Inference is to shift from observations of *one* unit to observations of *many* similar units, and to replace $Y_t(u)$ and $Y_c(u)$ with $E(Y_t)$ and $E(Y_c)$: the expected value of the outcome with the treatment applied and not applied, respectively. This "statistical solution," Holland argues, "replaces the impossible-to-observe causal effect of *t* on a specific unit with the possible-to-estimate *average* causal effect of *t* over a population of units" (Holland 1986, 947). For a given unit we can only observe *either* the value of the outcome with the treatment applied *or* the value of the outcome with the treatment not applied, but across a number of units we can observe the average value of the outcome with the treatment applied or not applied, and then conclude that the *average causal effect* across units is $E(Y_t) - E(Y_c)$.

While it is certainly important to distinguish between Holland's definition of a causal effect for an individual unit and his statistical reformulation of causal effect in terms of population-level averages (Norman 2021, 943), it is equally important to note that Holland's definition of causal effect is itself not methodologically neutral. By defining a causal effect in terms of the difference that a single factor makes to an observed outcome, Holland has already made the crucial move that aligns

---

3 Imre Lakatos (1970) provides an insightful and influential discussion of the attendant difficulties.

his analysis with Hempel's: the *empirical independence* of a causal factor from other aspects of a unit. The causal factor, the treatment t, is essentially separate from—and therefore cleanly separable from—the unit in question, even if it takes sophisticated practical techniques to actually accomplish that separation. Indeed, Holland's statistical isolation of a causal factor through the random assignment of similar units to the treatment or the control group, which is absolutely essential to his analysis,[4] depends on the prior assumption of empirical independence, since researchers couldn't distinguish between treatment and control groups unless they could observe—factically—whether a unit belonged in one or the other group to begin with. Similarly, the unit homogeneity that his statistical argument also presumes—the units are alike in every relevant way *except for* the causal factor of interest—rests on an observational differentiation between the causal factor of interest and everything else of potential relevance. In order for me to say, using Holland's formula, that the difference between a piece of paper being solid and firm—$Y_c(u)$—and that same piece of paper being a pile of ash—$Y_t(u)$—is due to the application of the treatment t (the application of a lit match to the paper), I have to be able to somehow occupy an observational position from which I can see the treatment being applied and not being applied simultaneously, with everything else being held constant. Thus Holland's Fundamental Problem of Causality is due to his very *definition* of a causal effect in the first place.

Indeed, Holland's statistical procedure is nothing but the elaboration of this definition and its reliance on empirical independence and observational differentiation. To assess whether framing a problem in a particular way causes a person to display different levels of risk tolerance, for example, we empirically distinguish between different framings, and then randomly expose people to different frames in order to see how risk-tolerant people in the different groups are; this allows us to calculate an average causal effect across those populations (Druckman 2001). None of this makes any sense unless we can empirically distinguish between "exposure to a frame" and other aspects of people in the study. A claim like "framing an issue as a loss makes people more risk-averse" presumes that we can observationally—again, factically—divide the way that a particular issue is framed from, say, the more general attitude towards risk that a person displays, so that we can somehow "control for" that context.[5] Ordinarily we would do this by asking a person questions designed to measure their overall attitude towards risk, so that we could make sure that the observed outcomes were not simply a function of the attitudes that

---

4 Random assignment is so key to Holland's argument that he concludes the piece with the all-caps motto "NO CAUSATION WITHOUT MANIPULATION" (Holland 1986, 959), by which he means that it is impossible to estimate an average causal effect without the experimentalists' ability to randomly assign units to groups. Whether "natural experiments" or "field experiments" resolve this philosophical difficulty is a matter of some controversy, which I will not enter into here.

5 Random assignment of individuals is a way of "controlling for" such attitudes, by allowing any possible associations between the hypothesized causal factor and the other aspects of the individual context to vary at random across the whole population of the study (Holland 1986, 948–49). But this strategy also presumes that causal connections only show up in the data as systematic cross-case associations, so it merely pushes the problem down a level, so to speak.

the participants in the study already possessed—perhaps by placing people with similar attitudes towards risk on either side of the treatment/control divide. This in turn presumes that if a frame is causal then it exerts its effects independently of a person's attitude: that it is meaningful to speak of a frame's effects *in isolation*. And this is a more or less direct consequence of defining a causal effect in terms of the difference that a factor makes *independently*, an effect that can only show up empirically as a systematic connection between an input and an output. The resulting nomothetic generalization operates at the level of the population, since it contains average causal effects across units rather than unit-level effects, and it can then be applied to other members of the population in the way required by Hempel's procedure of explanation-by-subsumption.

To illustrate, consider this claim advanced by two prominent scholars of the "liberal international order" about why this order persists. "As long as interdependence—economic, security-related, and environmental—continues to grow, peoples and governments everywhere will be compelled to work together to solve problems or suffer grievous harm" (Deudney and Ikenberry 2018, 16). If we read this as a causal claim of the sort advanced by Hempel and Holland, we have to understand it as treating "interdependence" as separate and observationally separable from every other potential factor that might incline states to support institutionalized cooperation. Once we have done so, perhaps by introducing a sophisticated measurement of how much interdependence there is in a system of states at a given time, all of the consequences that Holland outlines become possible, including potential estimates of the average causal effect of the level of interdependence on institutionalized interstate cooperation that we might generate by looking across cases with different levels of interdependence.[6] The resulting general law can then be used in standard Hempelian fashion to explain the level of institutionalized cooperation in a given system of states at a given time—and to predict the consequences of either a changing or constant level of interdependence, since explanation and prediction are formally similar in this approach (Hempel 1942, 38).

But note all that has to happen in order for this explanation to make sense. Levels of interdependence have to be calculated separately from institutionalized cooperation, which is especially tricky for theoretical approaches that regard institutions as ways to manage and deal with the consequences of interdependence; this means that observed interdependence might depend on institutions, instead of the other way around. But interdependence also has to be calculated separately

---

6 Strictly speaking, Holland would not agree that we could generate a reliable estimate of an average causal effect through this kind of observational study. I am setting this issue aside for the moment, because there are almost no robust examples of random assignment studies in our field, and most everyone who relies on the Holland analysis (or its popularization in King, Keohane, and Verba 1994) works with observational data rather than experimental data. Indeed, many studies in this idiom work with data about the *attributes* of entities, which Holland himself (1986, 955) explicitly prohibits.

from any other factor that might incline a system of states towards institutionalized cooperation, including beliefs held by citizens and leaders of states about whether institutionalized cooperation is the best way to deal with the challenges that they are confronting. And then we have to treat different systems of states as though they only differed from one another in their levels of interdependence (however ascertained), so that an average causal effect can be calculated and we can reach a general statement about what levels of interdependence do to institutionalized cooperation.[7] Finally, we have to assume that the average causal effect, which is only visible at the level of the population, somehow also operates at the level of each individual unit—as though the general notion "level of interdependence" acted as a causal factor *in a specific case*, which, as Andrew Abbott reminds us, is a metaphysics "last taken seriously in the age of Aquinas" (Abbott 2001, 135). Surely in a *particular* system of states at a *particular* time, what does the causing is a *particular* level of interdependence, and not the level of interdependence in general?

Shifting to "mechanisms" at this point, while leaving the remainder of the methodological commitments of the neopositivist approach in place, would not do anything to solve the problem. Suppose that we were to "process-trace" (Beach and Pedersen 2013) interdependence and its consequences for institutionalized interstate cooperation, either by looking at how key decision-makers perceived the level of interdependence at a given point in time and drawing on their words and actions to show the connections between their perception and their actions, or by connecting levels of interdependence with incentive-structures for cooperative vs. conflictual actions. Implicit in taking this road are precisely the same assumptions as previously: interdependence can be identified and empirically isolated, and the effect that it exercises on the outcome is, logically speaking, dependent on a general claim about what interdependence does to institutionalized cooperation *not merely in this instance, but in general*. Making this claim more detailed by introducing a mechanism does not alter the basic logic of inference; it only makes it more difficult to empirically identify the causal factor as being present, because now the researcher needs not just the level of interdependence, but some process evidence about thinking or incentives. A causal explanation of the outcome still requires subsumption to a covering-law in precisely the same way; that law is now, however, something like "level of interdependence causes institutionalized cooperation by shaping beliefs/incentives." This is nothing but an average causal effect applied to a specific instance.

---

7 Multiple regression analysis does not solve this problem, but works around it: calculating the coefficients for multiple causal factors presumes that each causal factor exercises an *independent* influence on the dependent variable, even though those effects happen simultaneously (so to speak) and work together to produce the observed pattern of outcomes. Statistical significance tests tell us whether a particular factor exercises an effect net of all other factors, against a background presumption of a normal distribution (Ziliak and McCloskey 2008).

A Configurational Alternative

The core of a neopositivist notion of causal explanation is the notion that we can empirically and observationally distinguish a potential causal factor from its context, lifting it into some more general plane so that it can be transported from unit to unit and case to case. The laboratory-experimental procedures on which Holland bases his analysis, and the physical-science claims that Hempel uses as his paradigm cases of explanation by subsumption under a general law, have the distinct advantage of resting on practical techniques designed to do just this: to *actually*, insofar as possible, control the population under investigation in order to isolate the casual factor of interest, and to do so in a way that empirically generalizes to other members of the population. This kind of idealized Galilean experiment (Cartwright 2007, 48) does in practice what observational research techniques can only metaphorically emulate, and ensures (as much as possible) that potential causal factors are independent of one another and that they connect independently to the outcome in question.[8] In consequence, laboratory-experimental techniques, and the observational separation of individual causal factors from their contexts that they make possible, seem to underpin and make possible general causal knowledge of the sort often sought by scholars, even in the social sciences.

But it is unclear that when we *use* causal explanations in everyday life, we are drawing on the entire elaborate metaphysical architecture that Hempel and Holland elucidate. Indeed, as Elizabeth Anscombe points out, we are more often looking for a causal explanation when an outcome does *not* happen as expected. Instead, the problem is not so much to show that something was to be expected, as to show why things got derailed and perhaps how they might be put back on track (Anscombe 1993, 94). I turn the key in my car's ignition and the engine does not start; this is unexpected against the background of my general notion (derived from past experience) that turning the key starts the car's engine, regardless of whether that general notion fits the strictures of a nomothetic covering law or not. In fact, I likely only notice the turning of the key as a separate causal factor when the equipment doesn't work as it is "supposed" to, and the apparent separateness of the act of turning the key isn't due to laboratory-experimental procedures as much as to *practical concerns*: I need to get someplace, and the failure of the engine to start presents an impediment to my plans.[9] In this situation, which is more useful, a set of covering-laws or skilled mechanic? Even if the mechanic proceeds by testing various components of the car, looking for whatever is out of conformity with the way it is supposed be, only by a strained exercise of philosophical imagination are nomothetic generalizations playing any important role here—especially since the

---

8 In technical terms, this is the "Causal Markov condition" (Hausman and Woodward 1999) presumed by virtually every technique for estimating how a particular x affects the probability of the outcome Y.

9 Compare Heidegger's (1927, sec. 18) claim that we only notice the materiality of the hammer in our hand when for whatever reason the hammer *stops* functioning as expected, or when we stop using it *as a hammer*.

mechanic is working on *one* car, not a population of similar cars with randomly assigned component faults.

In addition, notice that the turning of the key in the ignition is only a causal factor if the rest of the car's systems are intact. It strains our language to say that the turning of the key is in any sense an *independent* causal factor, particularly since any observed connections between the turning of the key and the starting of the engine only come about because of a number of other elements in combination. It is simply meaningless to treat the turning of the key as an autonomous causal factor that could exercise an independent impact on the outcome...but this is *precisely* what the neopositivist approach to causal explanation would insist that we do! Indeed, we would have to generate an average causal effect for key-turning by comparing the results of turning vs. not turning an ignition key, and that would allow us to explain the engine starting in a given instance as somehow resulting from that average causal effect. It is unclear that we are doing this either when we explain why the engine started (or didn't start) or when we—correctly—claim that turning the key in the ignition has something to do with the engine starting.

What we therefore need is an account of causal explanation that operates without the neopositivist apparatus of nomothetic generalization, average causal effects, and explanation by subsumption. A first step in this direction might be to recognize that an explanation, as I argued in the previous chapter, is first and foremost a kind of action intended to bring about a state of understanding in the part of the target to whom it is addressed (Achinstein 2010b, 106–08). To explain something to someone is to help them understand the reasons for that something, whether we are talking about explaining to someone why some animal is (properly described as) a duck, or why some conflict is (properly described as) a war, or why the next number in the series {1, 2, 3,...} is 4 and not 5. As Wittgenstein pointed out, explanations understood in their everyday sense *can't* be reduced to a set of rules, and the result of an explanation *can't* be a mental picture; instead, it has to be a practical capacity to *do* something, like playing a game or solving an equation (Wittgenstein 1958, secs. 73–75). This in turn means that explanations are not reducible to the kinds of representational pictures of general empirical patterns prized by neopositivists. Indeed, we go wrong if we think of explanations as factic descriptions of things in the world. The (speech) act of explanation is something that takes place between people, and exemplifies an intersubjective relation *between* subjects rather than the kind of subject–object distinction exemplified in representational claims: an I–Thou relationship, rather than an I–it relationship (using terminology from Buber 1971). Everyday explanations are thus a good deal broader than the nomothetic-subsumption logic would suggest.

Causal explanations are a subset of this more general notion of explanation as a process of giving someone a *capacity to do something*, but this subset doesn't correspond to nomothetic generalizations either. An explanation of a piece of paper's turning to ash is logically equivalent to a set of instructions for transforming paper into ash, and that set of instructions can also be used negatively as a way of avoiding that outcome (if you don't want the piece of paper to crumble to ash, don't light it on fire). Exactly the same is true of causal explanations for wars, or international institutions, or policies designed to address climate change: a causal explanation of how and why we got a particular outcome rather than another one is logically equivalent to a set of instructions for producing that outcome. It matters not at all that for these large-scale outcomes we may not be practically able to accomplish the appropriate manipulation of the input factors. What makes a causal explanation work is that it supports counterfactual inferences, and not whether we can actually produce counterfactual outcomes. A conditional claim about what would happen if we were able to hold the average temperature increase of the planet under 2° C is far from a claim that we can actually accomplish such a thing—and whether we can accomplish it or not makes no difference to the validity of the claim itself.

It is worth lingering on this point briefly, because the neopositivist protocol for causal explanation *does* depend on the practical manipulation of input factors— ideally, in a laboratory, and otherwise, quasi-experimentally through sophisticated statistical techniques. In a controlled experimental setting, a researcher can apply a treatment to a randomly selected set of units, while *not* applying that treatment to a set of units that are as indistinguishable as possible from those in the treatment group. That practical manipulation of the input factor—whether a particular unit does or does not receive the treatment—means that we can generate data about the outcomes in each group. Because of the controlled experimental setting, including random assignment and unit homogeneity, we can therefore treat the outcome in each group as, in practice, the counterfactual outcome for the other group: the per- fect comparative case, so to speak, in which *only* the hypothesized causal factor varies between the groups. We can then confidently conclude that this factor is what produced the outcome. In the absence of a laboratory setting, we cannot con- cretely produce this kind of a pairing of outcomes such that each serves as the counterfactual for the other, but we can approximate this through the careful selec- tion and matching of units, reliance on the mean value theorem and the law of large numbers, and related technical procedures. The point of all these techniques, though, is to compensate for the researcher's inability to practically manipulate the input factor and generate the set of conceptually conjoined outcomes that a labora- tory experiment provides.

But the *logic* of causal explanation does not depend on these empirically observ- able pairs of outcomes varying across groups. If it did, then it would be literally impossible to causally explain outcomes that appear to have only happened once, like the formation of the contemporary international system, the globalization of industrial production and distribution, and the recent dramatic changes to the planet's climate. Certainly there is a neopositivist answer to this—find a broader population from which these outcomes can be drawn, such that they become cases *of* something appropriately general—but this is not the only answer. Although others have recognized this, I still find Max Weber's discussion of the issue in his 1904 methodological essay to be among the most trenchant and insightful. In part this is because Weber explicitly tackles the notion of causal-explanation-by-subsumption *in general*, and not just in the social sciences, although that is certainly where the bulk of his discussion takes place. But he begins by pointing out that astronomy, sometimes taken as a paradigm case of general laws covering specific outcomes, is actually concerned with the issue of "what *individual* result is created by the effect of these laws on an *individual constellation*, for it is these individually formed constellations that are of *significance* to us." By "constellation" here Weber does not mean the somewhat arbitrary groupings of visible stars that constitute the signs of the Zodiac, but instead the particular set of factors and conditions that characterize an individual situation of interest. His point is that as far back as we choose to go, we find only concrete sets of conditions that cannot themselves be somehow derived from general principles, and this in turn suggests a need to avoid styles of reasoning that do not take particularity seriously (Weber 2003, 375).

This is true in the case of the exact physical sciences, Weber notes, but it is even more important in the social sciences:

> Where the *individuality* of a phenomenon is concerned the question of causality does not concern *laws*, but rather concrete causal *relationships*; not a question in which the event simply becomes an exemplar of something else, but instead a question of to which individual constellation it should be attributed as a result: it is a question of attribution, of *imputation*. Wherever causal explanation of a "cultural phenomenon" is considered—of a "*historical individual*," to use a term occasionally used in the methodology of our discipline...knowledge of the *laws* of causation can never be the *objective* of investigation, but only a *means*.
> (Ibid., 379)

Weber's point is not that general laws are irrelevant to the causal explanation of a concrete event, but that general laws do something quite different than serving as headings under which to subsume individual instances. Concrete situations always exceed laws, precisely because they consist of multiple factors that can't be teased apart in anything like a laboratory-like way; what does the causing in a *specific* instance is not a general law or a generic factor, and not a sum of average causal effects, but instead the whole complex set of factors found in the situation. So general notions of all sorts can function only as adjuncts—as conceptual instruments or prosthetics—for allowing us to make sense of concrete situations. They do so in virtue of their *ideal-typical* character (ibid., 388), where ideal-types can be thought of as a conceptual grid or lens through which the concrete specificity of an individual situation becomes visible. Having the general notion of a "market economy" in mind is helpful for making sense of particular economic arrangements involving markets, despite the fact that no perfect market economy has ever existed or will exist—and despite the fact that the same arrangements that we apprehend (and factically describe as) as a "market economy" can be apprehended by other observers in different ways if they use different ideal-types than ours.

The gap between the ideal-typical characterization of a situation and the causal explanation of observed outcomes is filled, for Weber, by two insights. First is the recognition that in any actual situation, there are almost certainly multiple ideal-types that can afford us conceptual purchase on the situation, and that tensions between these ideal-types can allow us to hone in on precisely what is responsible for a particular observed outcome. This is the procedure that allows Weber to account for the specific blend of charismatic and rational-legal elements present in the institutionalized Roman Catholic church; the empirical situation displays not one or the other type of authority, but a mediated combination of both that only makes sense in light of the concrete historical trajectory of the "routinization of charisma" *in this instance*. Precisely because what we actually have available to us is a single situation, in which myriad elements occur in ways that cannot be cleanly—which is to say, *empirically*—separated from one another, an ideal-type plays a heuristic function in allowing us to sort out what is going on (ibid., 396–397).

In this way, part of what is being offered to the recipient in an explanation is the ideal-types themselves, as a kind of invitation to think about things in a certain way and thus to notice particular aspects of a concrete situation, and how they relate to one another. We thus offer someone our language, and encourage them to adopt it. Since causal explanation is a process of giving someone a capacity to do something, the relevant ideal-types are part of that capacity, much the way that my instructions to my daughter about how to ride a bicycle involve a particular orientation towards the task and a particular attunement to the equipment. An account of the rise of capitalism that emphasizes a changed ethical orientation towards the world of work (as we see in Weber's own treatment of the "Protestant ethic"), or an account of globalization that emphasizes communications infrastructures (e.g., Tworek 2021), directs our attention to aspects of situations without requiring us to be able to empirically and practically separate those aspects out from every other aspect. Instead, we find ourselves in the realm of counterfactual thought-experiments: what would have happened if something about this situation had been different? Unlike in the neopositivist account, counterfactuals here are not empirical instances of anything, but imagined scenarios that are plausible in light of the rest of our knowledge, and which allow researchers to puzzle out the importance of individual factors without having to empirically isolate them.

As an illustration, consider work on international norms that pays attention to the moment of decision-making ("Which norms should we adopt?") and not much attention the subsequent implementation of adopted norms ("How should we assess whether we are meeting the normative standard?"). An argument that implementation should be taken seriously involves both a demonstration that decision-making alone does not explain observed outcomes—perhaps because other ways of proceeding can be envisioned which would equally fall under the norm, but which would point to different courses of action—and the elaboration of an ideal-type of an implementation process (say, one based in Foucauldian notions of governmentality) that allows specific outcomes to be explained (as in Huelss 2017). The argument thus rests on the detailed examination of case-specific constellations of factors, plus the logical elaboration of unrealized-but-plausible counterfactuals; the conclusion is that apprehending things in this way helps explain the observed outcomes. As such, we can simply side-step the impossibility of empirically separating decision-making from implementation, and focus instead on how these factors in combination bring about outcomes.

Weber's second insight is that when we work with general ideal-typical notions to ascertain whether some aspect of a situation was or was not causally relevant to the outcome, we use the ideal-types as ways to discipline our empirical imaginations: we vary aspects of situations in thought, and see if an alternate outcome is something we can plausibly imagine—and we evaluate our claims by sharing them with others (Weber 1999a, 275). The important point here is that the relevant value-commitments, and the intuitions to which they give rise when developed into logically precise ideal-types, are not personal, but *common*, possessions. Ideal-types are rooted in a set of value-orientations characteristic of a group of researchers, and therefore also of the societies to which they belong. Those value-orientations themselves need not be consistent or coherent—this is, after all, why they need to be elaborated into ideal-types before they can serve a useful explanatory function—but take the form of weakly shared commonplaces in a living tradition which can be specified and developed in different and distinct ways (Shotter 1993b, 170–71). Think of a cultural commitment to individual liberty, existing in the morass of everyday life in the post-industrial "western"[10] world alongside a commitment to governmental efficiency and transparency. That value-commitment might underpin a libertarian/utilitarian account of human action, but it might also underpin something like Dewey's "new individualism" that prioritizes "personal participation in the development of a shared culture" that can solve pressing practical problems (Dewey 1999, 17). The very process of articulating an ideal-type is a situated intervention into a cultural context, and not just a neutral reflection of it, precisely because other reconstructions and elaborations are always possible.[11]

This insight both relativizes knowledge-claims and, paradoxically, secures their objectivity. Knowledge for Weber is necessarily bounded by cultural value-orientations, but can still be valid causal knowledge to the extent that scholars are clear in their procedures (Weber 2003, 399–400). Scholarship using ideal-types is certainly going to be focused on those elements of a concrete situation that have some kind of cultural significance for the research community, but

> it does *not* of course follow from this that cultural scientific *research* itself can only have *results* that are "subjective" in the sense of being valid for *one* person and not for another. What changes is rather the degree to which such results *interest* one person, but not another.

> (Ibid., 383)

---

10   There is no really appropriate term for what I mean here, but I suspect that most readers will understand what I am saying regardless.

11   I am setting aside the hypothetical scenario in which everyone, either in a group of researchers or in a whole society, has *exactly* the same set of value-commitments elucidated in *exactly* the same way. That might be a limit case for what I am describing here, but the experience of cults, militaries, and other "total institutions" (Goffman 1990) shows just how much effort has to be put into producing that level of uniformity—and how fragile uniformity is once that effort ceases.

The reliability of results comes from scholarly researchers elucidating ideal-types from their shared cultural values, and refining them by using them to explain concrete outcomes as a function of whether the research community can conceive of that outcome being different if some element of the particular case had been different. Expanding the circle to include wider publics beyond the researchers themselves does not alter the epistemic conditions of the process: causal explanation, whether to specialists or to a wider audience, involves equipping the target recipients to envision how outcomes would be different if aspects of a situation were changed. Here again, the implicated ideal-types are part of that capacity I offer to a recipient as part of my explanation, much the way that the instructions I follow about how to brew beer involve a particular orientation towards the task and a particular attunement to the equipment. That orientation and that attunement directs our attention to aspects of situations without requiring us to be able to empirically and practically separate those aspects out. It is sufficient that we be able to speculate, in a disciplined and refined way, about different ways in which things might have happened.

But it does not follow that just any factor can serve as part of a valid causal explanation. Key to the process is the logical refinement and *vetting* of the particular conceptual elements to be subsequently used in explaining an outcome. Value-orientations cannot simply be applied to produce a causal explanation of any merit, because causal explanation is not about simply *wanting* to generate an outcome, but about how to actually generate it. The main difference between neopositivists and others on this point is that the former would *only* regard general propositions as sufficiently well-vetted when they survive sufficiently rigorous empirical testing—empirical testing that relies on the whole apparatus of average causal effect, and produces not merely a distinction between factors that play a role and factors that do not, but a more or less precise estimate of what contribution each factor considered independently makes to the outcome. To the contrary, Weber's ideal-typification procedure depends on the disciplined imaginations of scholars to sort through potential causal elements, arriving at an approximate consensus on the basis of detailed empirical study and extensive debate. Yes, this means that our explanations are first and foremost *our* explanations, and in no way can be thought to simply emanate from the way that the world is in and of itself. While this might pose a problem for those who regard knowledge as ultimately representational, it is a more *pragmatic* starting-point, treating our concrete involvements with and in the world (rather than our observations of the world) as the source of our knowledge. As such, thought-experiments rather than (quasi-)laboratory experiments are more than sufficient.

In fact, configurational researchers can *also* incorporate laboratory results into their explanations; they are just not constrained to subject *every* general claim to laboratory (or laboratory-like) evaluation. Neopositivist researchers put like units in a laboratory and estimate an average causal effect that generalizes to the population as a whole, because they can observe both outcomes (treatment and control) at the same time, albeit in different portions of the population. Because neopositivist causation *is* the statistically significant association of a cause and an effect—the observed difference between treatment and control groups—what generalizes to other entities beyond those in the laboratory is that statistical relationship, an average causal effect that is assumed to operate outside of the laboratory just the way it did inside of the laboratory. But for researchers who treat the laboratory as one among other tools of investigation, the gap between the lab and the wider world can only be bridged by a "transfactual" assumption (Bhaskar 1998) that what has been revealed in the lab is a real-but-not-merely-empirical tendency, or *causal power* (Harré and Madden 1975), which may *or may not* show itself in the wider world in the form of a statistically significant association with an outcome. The laboratory environment is artificially pure, but in the messy actual world, different factors might interfere with one another's operations. Hence there can be no explanation by subsumption under a covering law, but only explanation by showing how vetted causal factors combine in case-specific ways to generate particular outcomes. Instead of an average causal effect, laboratory results—including the results of observational studies that use sophisticated statistical techniques to approximate a laboratory setting—are understood to tell us something about how a causal factor works, which in turn helps to fuel our disciplined imaginations as we generate explanations and counterfactual speculations.

The point here is that both neopositivist and configurational researchers agree that potential causal factors have to be vetted before they can be used to construct valid causal explanations. Configurational researchers simply have a wider palette of options for doing so, because they are not constrained by the notion of an average causal effect.[12] Scientific realists, especially, emphasize the need for the laboratory vetting of causal factors, but to disclose causal powers rather than to generate estimates of independent effect sizes; critical realists, although equally insistent that causal factors are mind-independently real, are more inclined to accept the existence of an ongoing tradition of inquiry and some transcendental reasoning about conditions of possibility as sufficient for grounding causal factors in something other than subjective whim (Wight 2006; Kurki 2008). "Relational realists" in the mode of Charles Tilly (e.g., Tilly 1998; McAdam, Tarrow, and Tilly 2001), meanwhile, advocate the formation of sets of abstract causal mechanisms from deep historical knowledge across cases and across time; the resulting heuristics direct our attention to various points of similarity and difference between situations, making possible rich explanatory narratives that are nonetheless rooted in broader generalities (Krinsky and Mische 2013, 16–17; see also Demetriou 2009). Andrew Abbott (2001, 189), on the other hand, calls for a "narrative positivism" that utilizes abstract categories derived from a number of different kind of

12 Indeed, configurational researchers are more comfortable than neopositivists with the realization that sometimes causal factors vanish from our explanations simply because we no longer find them culturally plausible. It is unclear that notions like sin and virtue and honor were ever *falsified*, but it is undeniable that they have been more or less prominent in our explanations at different times throughout history (along these lines, see Lebow 2003 on the role of "tragedy" in our accounts). I wonder whether future generations will think much the same about the currently prominent notion of "material interests."

modeling procedures, and shows how they combine in particular situations; what underwrites the validity of the categories is the role that they play in the various models (including, but not limited to, statistical models) on which the researcher— and the research community—draws. And Weber's procedure of ideal-typification, as discussed above (see also Jackson 2017), uses the dialogue of the situated scholarly community as a process of sifting through claims and potential causal factors.[13] But regardless of the precise details, the basic commitment to vetting causal factors remains constant, and serves as a check on scholars' capacities to simply dream up explanations that they wish were valid.

Configurational vs. Neopositivist Explanation

All of that said, the really crucial distinction between neopositivist and configurational researchers comes about not when vetting potential causal factors, but when determining what to do with them after they have been vetted. Indeed, neopositivists often downplay or neglect this part of the operation entirely, since explanation-by-subsumption gives a clear directive: if we know that X increases the likelihood of Y by some definite amount—the average causal effect—then we can explain the occurrence of Y by simply pointing to the presence of X. But configurational researchers proceed not by subsumption, but by a careful and comprehensive tracing of how factors combined in a specific instance to produce a specific outcome. Hence a configurational explanation gives something like a recipe for the production of the outcome, where a neopositivist explanation gives more of a checklist about the presence and absence of particular causal factors. This is equally the case whether those causal factors are taken to be variable attributes, mechanisms, factors, or whatever else; the important methodological issues involving research design and the logic of inference happen at a level of abstraction somewhat above mere vocabulary.

By way of illustration, consider two recent qualitative studies[14] that draw on archival evidence about decision-making, but do so in methodologically quite distinct ways. Rosemary Kelanic (2016) argues that states pursue anticipatory strategies intended to secure their control of key resources based on their vulnerability to coercion if another power controlled those resources, and uses a comparison between Britain at the end of the First World War and Germany during the Second World War to illustrate a connection between high levels of vulnerability and strategies of direct control of key resources (in this instance, oil). Her theory associates

---

13   The importance of the consensus of the research community to the production of valid explanations is also a cornerstone of Pierre Duhem's approach to scientific knowledge (see the discussion in Chernoff 2014), and is actually central to Imre Lakatos's thinking about progressive problemshifts, despite the neopositivist (mis)construal of Lakatos that remains sadly dominant in the field (on the problems of the neopositivist reading of Lakatos, see Jackson and Nexon 2009). John Dewey would obviously agree, as would—broadly speaking—other "constructivists" in the strong epistemic sense (e.g., Onuf 1998).

14   Using the term "qualitative" here in its *method* sense, i.e., as involving at least in part empirical data that is not quantified and presented numerically.

two components of vulnerability—a state's petroleum deficit and the threat that the state's oil supply will be interrupted—with particular anticipatory strategies, working abstractly and drawing on other scholarship to generate a model (Figure 1 on p. 193) and a series of predicted consequences for various types of vulnerability (Figure 2 on p. 195). Because the logic of the argument involves the condition of vulnerability imposing itself on decision-makers' minds, she can then look for evidence in the deliberations of those decision-makers, as recorded in documents and speeches—process evidence, evidence of the mechanism through which the condition of vulnerability is translated into specific courses of action.

When we get to the case evidence, it quickly becomes abundantly clear that the explanation on offer here is one of subsumption: the overall argumentative frame is about evaluating the validity of the general theory, and the article is framed as an exercise in the potential falsification of the general claim. The key take-away point is that "leaders feared oil coercion and chose anticipatory strategies based on the petroleum deficit and the susceptibility of imports to disruption" (ibid., 196), and *not* that the strategies pursued by British and German leaders are explained by their respective states' vulnerability to coercion. Explanation of any state's *particular* strategy takes a back seat to the task of ascertaining whether or not the hypothesized causal factor (vulnerability) and attendant mechanism (fear of coercion) are present in the documentary record. The operative question throughout is not why a given state pursued the strategy that it pursued, but whether a perception of vulnerability was part of the deliberative process. This leads Kelanic, for example, to simply note that the British strategy of direct control of oil reserves took advantage of British colonial possessions in the Middle East, rather than explaining British strategy as emerging from a combination—a configuration—of imperialism and vulnerability. And although Kelanic notes that a state's petroleum deficit is in part a function of its military strategy—*blitzkrieg* presented Germany with less of an oil deficit than a prolonged period of attrition warfare did—the methodological necessity to treat causal factors as independent of one another prevents a consideration of how military doctrine and resource availability might have conditioned one another in a causal complex bringing about different state actions at different times.

Contrast this style of argument and explanation with that on display in Paul Musgrave and Daniel H. Nexon's account (2018) of why China and the United States pursued costly projects (the Ming treasure fleets and the Apollo moon landings, respectively) that were not expected to yield significant military or economic benefits. Like Kelanic, they lay out an abstract theory of state action; theirs is about the symbolic importance of such projects to the drive for legitimacy, and the importance of legitimacy in the broader, hierarchically structured field of international affairs. But when diving into the case narratives, they pursue a rather different approach than Kelanic does, more concerned with showing that a valid explanation of the observed outcome in each case needs to incorporate the causal factor that they highlight than with simply documenting the presence of the causal factor in the case. The goal here is not to test the symbolic/legitimacy argument against economic and military-security alternatives, and more to illustrate that an account that does *not* take the search for legitimacy seriously cannot explain the outcome. Particularly in the U.S. case, they acknowledge that the Apollo project had some military and economic benefits, but that either of those grounds alone are insufficient to explain both why the moon landings were pursued in the first place and why the program was terminated when it was. Instead, the configuration of symbolic and legitimation concerns with military and economic considerations is what explains the outcome in each case.

Mechanisms—mechanisms of decision-making, mechanisms that leave traces in the documentary archival record—are central to both of these studies. But at a methodological level, what is *done* with those mechanisms is quite different. The neopositivist approach to causal mechanisms treats a mechanism as nothing but a finer-grained intervening variable (as in George and Bennett 2005), and seeks to circumscribe whatever effect a mechanism might display by statistically significant evidence of connections between inputs and outputs that holds across cases. Hence the importance for Kelanic of comparing across cases in order to isolate, to the extent possible, the role of the fear of petroleum vulnerability in strategic decision-making, and in documenting the presence of the mechanism in connecting the independent variable (vulnerability itself) with the dependent variable (state oil strategy)—as well as the insistence on treating vulnerability as independent from strategy instead of as part of a complex causal configuration with it. By contrast, Musgrave and Nexon (2018, 603) pursue the analytical approach of "uncommon foundations," exploring different concrete instances in which their theorized causal mechanism—itself explicitly understood as an ideal-type—manifests and operates. There is thus no attempt in their account to make *any* general conclusion about state action; the generality of their theorized mechanism is logical, not empirical, and its explanatory value can only be demonstrated in specific cases, complementing the insufficiency of rival explanations.[15] Legitimation concerns do not function in their explanations as independent causal factors, but as parts of broader causal complexes that generate outcomes. Hence we might say that the final and perhaps most important difference between neopositivist and configurational approaches to causal explanation is that for neopositivists, what does the causing in any specific instance is a *sum of average causal effects* associated with each of the causal factors involved, while what does the causing in a configurational account is *the entire causal complex* that is specific to that case—a causal complex composed of elements that might recur elsewhere, but in different combinations, and hence might be involved in the production of very different outcomes.[16]

---

15 That said, there are also traces of pseudomorphosis—in this instance, a distortion of the presentation of the argument resulting from the dominance of neopositivism in the field—in Musgrave and Nexon's piece, as they write carefully enough that a neopositivist might mistake what they are doing for a hypothesis-test using evidence from two dissimilar cases. Of course, if that were what they were *actually* up to, then their logic of case selection would make little sense, and their dismissal of economic and military-security factors in the U.S. case would have to be more definitive.

16 Fritz Ringer's (1997) otherwise very insightful explication of Max Weber's methodology elides this distinction, unfortunately, and treats Weber as holding a summative rather than a configurational notion of causation. I have advanced a contrary account in Jackson (2017b).

In presenting this contrast between neopositivist and configurational explanatory strategies, I have quite deliberately overdrawn the distinction, so as to disclose the *logic* of these approaches in ways that are all too often obscured in practice—especially in a field as dominated by neopositivism as ours has traditionally been. Bare terms like "mechanism" are insufficient, as there are at least these two very different ways of *using* causal mechanisms in explanations. And while I suspect that many people appealing to mechanisms in their scholarship are tacitly advocating something like a configurational logic of explanation, and expressing dissatisfaction with the dominant neopositivist canon, teasing this out of the unavoidably ambiguous writing on display in pieces that are published in leading social science journals—many of which are themselves largely dominated by an unreflective neopositivism when it comes to these conceptual and philosophical issues—is a necessarily fraught endeavor. My hope is that explicit articulations of a configurational logic of explanation will promote greater methodological clarity going forward. Perhaps one day, configurationally-inclined scholars will not need to defend themselves against charges that they have failed to produce sufficient variation in their independent variables, or that they have neglected to specify the empirical generality of their theorized causal processes and factors. Asking them to do so is like expecting a gardener to be able to fix your sink, instead of appreciating the complementarity of distinct ways of proceeding, and the *diversity* of modes of causal explanation.

Evaluating Causal Explanations

While it is important to recognize the diversity of modes of causal explanation, this is insufficient for the task of determining whether any given causal explanation is a good one or not. Vetting a causal claim is one part of the story, and certainly there is a factic question to be answered about whether any particular causal factor mentioned in that causal claim is *in fact* present in the case at hand. For neopositivists, this looks like enough to determine whether a causal explanation is valid, because "X makes it Z more likely that Y outcome will result" (which is a statement of average causal effect Z, or how much difference X makes *independently* to the outcome Y) combined with "X is present in this case" seems to warrant the conclusion "Y is Z more likely." But note the slippage from causal explanation understood as answering a WHRT-question about the outcome in this *specific* case, and back to the kind of general "expectability" of subsumption: knowing that an outcome was more likely to occur doesn't necessarily tell us why the outcome actually occurred. (Toss a six-sided die and it will land on one of six faces, and a precise probability forecast of how often the die will land on any one face—one-sixth of the tosses—doesn't tell us why it landed on *this* face on *this* toss.) Someone interested in configurational explanation would say that knowing that Y was Z more likely to have occurred doesn't actually *explain* why, *in this case*, we got Y rather than some other outcome.

To illustrate: our dog was experiencing stomach troubles, waking up from a sound sleep in the middle of the night and needing to go outside, which was a departure from their previous behavior of sleeping through the night just fine. My wife and I investigated, and found that the only recent change in their diet had been a new kind of dog chew made from yak cheese. On the basis of previous pet allergies we had dealt with, we speculated that these chews might be responsible for the dog's upset stomach, and some online searching combined with a conversation with a veterinarian lent some credibility to that speculation. We thus hypothesized that the change in diet was causing the problem, and we removed the yak cheese chews from daily circulation. Within a day or two the dog's sleeping habits returned to normal.

Note what this investigation did and did not do. We did not test a general causal claim about the relationship between yak cheese chews and upset stomachs by looking at aggregated data, although we did evaluate the general causal claim on the basis of experience and through conversations with a competent authority. Nor did we treat our dog's upset stomach as an occasion to test a general hypothesis; what we did instead was to draw on presumptively valid general causal claims to construct a case-specific explanation of the outcome. What does the explaining in this case is not the mere presence of yak cheese chews in our dog's diet; nor does the average effect of yak cheese chews on dog digestive systems enter the picture, even implicitly. Instead, it is the dog's diet overall that explains their stomach issues, and does so in a manipulationist form: had the diet been different, the issues would not have resulted. We then actually manipulated the situation (by taking the yak cheese chews out of their diet) in order to see whether we could generate the outcome we desired, and the success of that manipulation is what indicates that the explanation was a good one.

The point is that the standards for what makes a causal explanation a good one vary considerably between the two approaches that I have discussed in this chapter. There is room for a consideration of facts in both, since a causal factor cannot either exercise an average causal effect or contribute to an overall causal configuration if it is not *in fact* present in a given case: yak cheese cannot in any sense cause a dog's upset stomach if the dog didn't eat any, and "being a democracy" cannot in any sense cause a country to act peacefully if a country isn't a democracy. But then the standards diverge, because the neopositivist evaluation of a casual explanation looks at the average causal effect that a given factor exercises *in general*, while a configurational explanation looks to integrate that factor into a plausible account of how an outcome was produced, and if possible looks to manipulate the situation in order to see if the plausible explanation stands up. While there is a great deal of technical discussion about precisely how to do any of these things in practice—how to calculate an average causal effect, how to tell a plausible causal story, how to determine whether a given manipulation of a situation "counts" as a demonstration that a causal explanation works—I want to keep the focus here on the *conceptual* issues that we all too often lose sight of under the barrage of technical detail.

It is especially important to do so because much if not most of the existing discussions of these issues across the social sciences is concerned with the question "How do we know if X is really a, or the, cause of Y?"—and in answering that question more or less exclusively by treating general causal claims as hypothetical empirical generalizations to be evaluated against (preferably quantitative) data, which in turn allows us to determine average causal effects and then to causally explain outcomes by showing that they were to be expected. A lot of very creative solutions have been developed for doing just this. But contrary to the position adopted by advocates of a "unified framework" for causality (e.g., Gerring 2005), this procedure does not exhaust causal explanation, and it does not achieve the tacit neopositivist aim of making a valid causal explanation into a fact. Causal explanations invariably rely on general causal claims, but those claims need not give us average causal effects of elements in isolation than can then be more or less mechanically applied to particular cases and particular outcomes.

Indeed, that kind of mechanical application is precisely what democratic peace researchers objected to in the use by policymakers of their conclusions, or something suspiciously like those conclusions, as justifications for military invasion and forced regime change. If it were actually—factually—the case that "being a democracy" was a separate causal factor that made it Z more likely that a given regime would be peaceful, then the logic of *imposing* democracy in order to get more peace would make a certain amount of sense. But there is a necessary and inevitable gap between a general causal claim and a case-specific causal explanation that can only be filled by a notion like average causal effect if we accept that it is sufficient to raise the likelihood of an outcome in order to explain it, and in order to do something about it. But when my dog was ill, our goal was to make them well, not to merely raise the likelihood that they would be well. A configurational explanation of what was making them sick was thus more helpful than a statistical finding about an average causal effect. A policymaker considering forcing regime change through invasion might be similarly advised to look less at the statistically vetted general causal claims about democracy and peace, and the average causal effect of "being a democracy" that such analysis reveals, and more at the configurational explanation of why *this* regime is acting in a warlike manner and how we might alter that. The whole story, rather than the estimate of the average causal effect, is what is useful here, particularly as causal stories involving forced regime change rarely end well.[17]

17 On the insufficiency of forced regime change to explain the often-cited examples of Germany and Japan after the Second World War, see, respectively, Jackson (2006) and Katzenstein and Sil (2008). On the more general issue of military defeat and subsequent state action, see Zarakol (2010).

5   Interpretive Explanation

Charles Anthony Woodward Manning is not a scholar whose work is read much these days, either in international studies or beyond it.[1] This may seem an odd fate for the second, and to date the longest, occupant of the world's second-oldest professorship in International Relations (the Montague Burton professorship)[2] and the person who "put the concept of 'international society' on the intellectual map" of Anglophone international studies scholarship (Navari 2013, 210). Part of the explanation may be Manning's exclusion from the British Committee on the Theory of International Relations, the founding core group of what is often called "the English School" by many contemporary scholars (e.g., Dunne 1998). Another part may be Manning's relatively sparse published output; Hidemi Suganami's exhaustive list of Manning's publications (Suganami 2001, 106–7) contains just 38 items, not a lot for an academic career lasting over 40 years—and of those published items, only one was a book, a few were articles in academic journals, and the rest contained "a number of radio talks and short articles in relatively obscure places" (ibid., 92). Manning's influence was, rather, through his teaching (a good number of the second generation of British international studies scholars were his students) and his general intellectual influence on his colleagues, which went hand

1 Earlier versions of this chapter (sometimes with a different title) were presented at: the workshop "Interpreting the English School," University of California at Berkeley, October 2016; the ISA-Northeast annual meeting, November 2016; Aberystwyth University, December 2016; McGill University, January 2017; the ISA annual meeting, February 2017; and the University of Oslo, May 2017. Thanks to the participants in these events for helpful feedback—I have especially benefitted from comments by Mark Bevir, Ian Hall, Cornelia Navari, Vincent Pouliot, Catherine Lu, Kacper Szulecki, and Einar Wigen, plus an anonymous reviewer, as well as general and ongoing discussions about the relation between explanation and meaning with Simon Pratt, Harry Gould, Dvora Yanow, and Xymena Kurowska.
2 The Montague Burton Professorship at the London School of Economics was originally the Ernest Cassel Professorship at the University of London, and was founded in 1919 (but not occupied until 1924) shortly after the endowment of the world's first professorship in international relations, the Woodrow Wilson professorship at Aberystwyth University. Manning held the post from 1930 until 1962.

DOI: 10.4324/9781003455912-5

in hand with his sustained efforts to establish the study of international affairs as a separate academic endeavor in the U.K.[3]

But I cannot help but think that another important part of the explanation for Manning's general absence from the pantheon of foundational thinkers in Anglophone international studies might have to do with his late-in-life defense of his home country South Africa's apartheid system. In 1964 he published an article in *Foreign Affairs* entitled "In Defense of Apartheid" in which he argued that because "within the confines of geographical South Africa there are more than one or two societies," and because those societies were at different levels of development, the apartheid system was therefore a justified way to preserve the autonomy and existence of those separate societies (Manning 1964, 148). And on October 14, 1965 he appeared before the International Court of Justice at The Hague, which was hearing a case concerning South Africa's imposition of the apartheid system in its "mandatory" territory[4] of what was then called South West Africa; during his testimony, Manning argued that:

> It makes a difference, and this not merely in philosophical analysis but in administrative practice and in constitutional planning, whether one thinks of the individual as the only reality, or, of the group as equally real, or, whether one is prepared to accommodate and embrace within one's social picture both the primordial reality of the individual and the social reality, or *quasi*-reality, of the group: for you find two competing dispositions or tendencies, the one stressing, the other seeking to minimize, the differences between various ethnic groups—the one accepting and paying respect to the diversity of cultures within the confines of a given territory, the other tending to disregard the multiplicity of lesser communities within the totality of a country as a whole.
>
> (Manning 1966, 5–6)

Here Manning extends the approach he generally took towards international affairs into the question of the relations between ethnic groups. Overall, his intellectual project might be justly characterized as "an 'interpretive' approach that

---

3 Indeed, Manning would not have liked my use of the term "international studies" to refer to this academic endeavor, as he spent a not inconsiderable part of his life working to establish "a subject whose subject-matter is the relationships between the members of a society…known conventionally as the family of nations" whose "natural name is international relations" (Manning 1954, 84). He was also adamant that International Relations be understood as a separate academic discipline, although he also sometimes characterized it as a branch of political sociology. On Manning's efforts in this regard, see Long (2005).

4 South Africa had received the authority and responsibility to govern the former German colony under the League of Nations Mandate system established after the First World War. South Africa refused to transfer the territory to U.N. authority and jurisdiction after the Second World War, leading to a prolonged legal and armed struggle over the territory's status. The U.N. General Assembly terminated the mandate in 1966, but the territory only became the independent Republic of Namibia in 1990, after decades of conflict. The ICJ case in which Manning testified involved charges that South Africa's imposition of apartheid in the territory violated the terms of its mandate.

concentrated on the beliefs of individual actors in international relations, assuming that explaining and evaluating their actions depends on interpreting the meaning they had for the actors who performed them" (Hall 2015, 34). This interpretive approach was widely shared by Manning's contemporaries in the English School, none of whom would have found much to disagree with in Manning's declaration that in order to make sense of international affairs, it was necessary to start with "international society" just because the actors themselves started with such a notion:

> there already exists a scheme, a sorry one perhaps, but given, and a going concern. We might like to re-mould it, but its existence we can scarcely doubt ....The "scheme" at any given stage derives its character from that composite prevailing image of it which lives in the collective psyche of the given generation.
>
> (Manning 1962, 8–9)

So the goal of studying international affairs was to properly depict the meaningful "scheme" that underpinned the "going concern" of how things were presently organized.

Applied to inter-*state* relations, Manning's approach yielded a rich delineation of the legal and institutional arrangements that provided the architecture for international affairs—including the notion that although state action was notionally affixed to a collective entity, "responsibility for it, existentially, can only lie where it belongs," with biological individuals as the only *real* actors (ibid., 74). In this way Manning's interpretive approach produced, from what Wittgenstein (1958) might have called the "form of life" of inter-state dealings, a conceptually sparer depiction of the principles that organized these myriad activities. The way that such principles organized activity was by serving as the theoretical presuppositions and normative commitments of the theories-in-use that led people to produce and reproduce a particular "socially constructed social reality" (Suganami 2001, 102); the organizing principles worked by being *believed*, or at least *accepted*, by the individuals involved. While this does not make those presuppositions and principles valid or compelling in any transcendental sense, it does suggest that they have to be in effect *treated as valid* in order for a sensible analysis to be produced, as the social arrangements in question would literally make no sense without them. To understand how the game is played, one has to treat its rules as at least provisionally given. This is more or less the classical English School approach to the analysis of international affairs.

Applied to arrangements under apartheid, this kind of approach yielded more or less the same thing: a delineation of the principles and presuppositions of the apartheid system, including the notion of an ethnic group as an irreducible foundation for social order, and the related notion that an ethnic group's level of "development" vis-à-vis other ethnic groups was a more or less easily measurable quantity. Transplanted from the classroom to the courtroom, however, the *delineation* of organizing principles easily becomes, and became, *advocacy* of those principles against alternatives. Without delving too deeply into Manning's motives—we can *guess*, of course, that he took it upon himself to appear in court and to write for *Foreign Affairs* just because he wanted to publicly defend those principles[5]—we can notice the particular stance of his interpretive approach: a certain passive receptiveness of the scholar when facing a "going concern," such that what speaks thorough the scholar are the basic organizing principles of the domain under investigation. Having settled on a domain to analyze, the scholar is subsequently bound by the ways that that domain is in fact organized. *Criticizing* those principles would seem difficult, if not impossible—at least from within Manning's interpretive approach.

In this chapter I want to more carefully distinguish between an interpretive approach per se, in which the goal is to sensibly depict a social setting in such a way that the reader or listener would be able to participate appropriately in that setting, and Manning's particular take on intergroup relations including inter*ethnic* relations. In order to do so, I will start off delineating the contours of an *interpretive explanation*, and the key importance for such an explanation of clearly specifying where the scholar and her audience are standing relative to the social setting being explained. This in turn will enable me to identify the particular slippage that connects Manning's account of international society with his advocacy of particular ways of managing ethnic diversity: a slippage between a set of organizing principles, or what Nick Onuf (1989) would call an "operative paradigm," and a description of a putatively "real" state of affairs. The potential for this slippage inheres in the interpretivist commitments exemplified by Manning: precisely because the interpretive approach depends on the recovery of operative, practical meanings and rules, the danger looms that an analyst can fall into naturalizing and reproducing those meanings and rules. This slippage, relatively unproblematic in the case of international society to the extent that the assumptions of international society as a "going concern" are widely shared, is more troubling precisely because the racist assumptions of apartheid are both less widely shared and, even at the time that Manning was writing, more actively contested.

Manning's tale is thus a cautionary one, disclosing both the promises and the pitfalls of an interpretive stance. By extending the analysis I have developed in the previous chapters, and treating interpretation as a kind of *explanation* rather than as a simple *description* of how a social arrangement is organized, I hope to both avoid the pitfalls and redeem the promises. I will argue that interpretive explanation is like causal explanation in being explanatory and not descriptive, in aiming to give a novel capacity to its recipients, and also in enjoying a similar relationship to factic descriptions in virtue of its incorporation of general claims—although those general claims are not involved with the production of outcomes. They are instead *rules for "going on" appropriately in context*. Interpretation is thus just as explanatory as causal explanation is, albeit responding to a different kind of problem-situation and seeking to develop a different kind of capacity in its recipient. And

---

5 Here I would disagree with Peter Wilson's (2004, 757) somewhat more charitable account of Manning as having a naively idealistic, "highly abstract," and "literal" notion of apartheid, but my reading does not turn on any precise specification of Manning's motives.

taking seriously the relative positions of the explainer, the recipient, and the social group whose arrangements are being interpretively explained turns out to be crucial to a clear account of what makes a good interpretive explanation.

"Interpretive" as a Methodological Commitment

Manning's work is a useful place to "cut in" to the question of whether the interpretivist approach to knowledge-production is intrinsically, for lack of a better word, *conservative* when it comes to laying out the principles of a given, ongoing social order. This is so not only for historical reasons—Manning's influence on successive generations of English School scholarship is hardly open to question, despite the fact that his work is rarely cited any longer—but also because Manning is unusually philosophically explicit about his position and his approach. To construct a proper diagnosis of Manning's position, we first have to come to terms with Manning's *methodology*, which is to say with the question of what makes his explanation an interpretive one, and what kind of knowledge such an explanation aims to provide. Manning's own somewhat scattered reflections on this issue are nonetheless a great help in the enterprise, and allow us to glimpse what lies behind or beneath interpretivist scholarship, especially interpretive scholarship on international affairs writ large.

That said, coming to terms with what makes for an interpretive explanation is made quite challenging by the fact that "interpretive" often functions in the field nowadays as a *theoretical* claim rather than as a methodological one. So when Stefano Guzzini (2011, 338) introduces "interpretivist process-tracing" as an alternative to neopositivist notions of causality that might allow us to appreciate, for example, the role played by securitization moves in bringing about outcomes, the term "interpretivist" seems to signal only that the causal mechanisms in question involve meaning and meaning-making practices. But this locution would not allow us to talk about a distinctly interpretivist stance on knowledge-production per se, because it focuses our attention on *what* is studied rather than on *how* it is studied. There are plenty of approaches across the sciences with a similarly mechanistic and processual understanding of causation, but basically no concern with meaningful practices. Guzzini's approach has a lot to recommend it, but providing a clear operational definition of "interpretive" as a methodology distinct from other methodologies is not one of its benefits.

The challenge is made even more acute by the all-too-common juxtaposition of "interpretivist" to "positivist" in a broad-brush contrast that I think especially unhelpful. Although the contrast does in part foreground methodological commitments, the category "positivist" is far broader than any rigorous philosophical definition of logical positivism or logical empiricism would be,[6] and often makes quantification—a clear issue of *method* rather than of *methodology*—into a core feature of the approach, thus making "non-positivist" roughly equivalent

---

6 On logical positivism and its evolution and variants, see Galison (1990) and Reisch (2005).

to "qualitative." Typically, the positivist-interpretivist distinction (as in Schwartz-Shea and Yanow 2012, and Schaffer 2015) juxtaposes the former's (theoretical) concern with behavior to the latter's concern with meaning; the former's use of formal and quantitative methods and techniques with the latter's preference for texts and interviews and participant-observation; and the former's celebration of hypothesis-testing and covering-laws with...well, this is where matters become less clear, because beyond rejecting the neopositivist project of successively refining nomothetic generalizations, is it not apparent what all of the scholarship gathered up into the "interpretivist" camp actually has in common, methodologic-ally speaking. Just what is distinctive about knowledge that is produced by taking the self-understanding of actors as a starting-point? Why would such knowledge have to adhere to different procedures of validation, or contribute something distinctive to the overall catalog of valid explanations?

One possibility is to argue that knowledge of human beings produced by other human beings just *is* constitutively distinct, by virtue of the necessary internality of the observer to the thing observed: when humans observe other humans, we are observing ourselves. Such an "anti-naturalist" position (Bevir and Kedar 2008) has ample precedents in the nineteenth-century distinction between "explaining" and "understanding" that underpinned and informed the turn to hermeneutics by Dilthey, Heidegger, and Gadamer. It is also similar to Peter Winch's (1990) notion that social science can and should be concerned with the kind of explic-ation and analysis of social rules pioneered by Ludwig Wittgenstein, which is in turn connected with Clifford Geertz's (1973, 5) call for "not an experimental science in search of law but an interpretative one in search of meaning." But while going down this road would provide some grounds for defining a distinct inter-pretive approach, it begs a particularly thorny *methodological* question by effect-ively side-stepping the whole issue of *how we know* that human beings and human social activity are fundamentally different from the activity of non-human objects of investigation—and what the *status* of that knowledge is. Either we don't *know*, in which case the anti-naturalist position becomes a political stance or an ethical commitment; or we know *the way we know other natural facts*—factually[7]—which contradicts the basic notion that we can only have internal participatory knowledge of human beings and their activities; or we know in some distinctly humanist way, which tautologically assumes what we were trying to prove, namely, the existence of a distinctly humanist way of knowing in the first place. In any case, all such delineations of an interpretive approach seem less solid and secure than their advocates would like them to be.

The root problem with all of these efforts to place the study of human social activity on a distinct basis is that they confuse and conflate theory and method-ology. As Roy Bhaskar (1998) pointed out, there is absolutely no reason why

---

7 If it were a fact that human beings and human social activity were different from non-human objects of investigation, then—as per the analysis in Chapters 1 and 2 above—it would have to be the case that this claim was *impersonally* true. It is difficult if not impossible to reconcile such impersonality with the notion that human beings have a necessarily internal relationship to other human beings.

one can't simultaneously maintain that human beings and human societies are ontologically distinct from natural objects, *and* that both kinds of entities can be studied in similar ways, with appropriate adjustments being made for the particular characteristics of human beings (such as their capacity for self-reflection). The apparent successes in the social sciences of a number of research traditions explicitly modeled on the natural sciences, particularly the use of statistical techniques to explore systematic relationships between demographic factors (including race and gender) and patterns of global inequality and conflict, would seem to underscore the point: human beings and their societies *can* be studied in ways that don't look much like the explication of social rules and patterns of meaning. Methodology just isn't the same as theory, and the firm *theoretical* insistence that human beings are distinct in virtue of their meaning-making activities provides precisely no *methodological* guidance as to how we ought to study those activities. It is entirely too hasty to move from studies of rhetorical deployment and symbolic reframing to a notion of "constitutive causality that seeks to explain events in terms of actors' understandings of their own contexts," and in so doing reject "a more mechanistic causality" (Schwartz-Shea and Yanow 2012, 52), as though the nature of the object of study—known in some *ex ante* or perhaps even *a priori* way?—determined the kind of explanation that can be sensibly made of it.[8]

All of that said, there *is* a methodologically compelling way to distinguish between interpretive and other approaches, resting not on the character of the object of study so much as on the *intention* of the study. As in previous chapters, by intention here I do not mean a motive, or a subjective reason held by the researcher for engaging in a study; I mean instead the goal or outcome *envisioned* by the study itself, the purpose for the study without which the study itself would make no sense. In Elizabeth Anscombe's (1963, 24–25) terms, an intention answers the question "why?" but in a specific sense: an intention provides the meaningful unity in terms of which an action makes sense in the first place, by disclosing the "future state of affairs" (ibid., 35) which the action aims at bringing about. In this instance, when the action in question is a study that generates knowledge of some object, we are in effect talking about what Max Weber (1999b, 161) would call the "knowledge-interest" (*Erkenntnisinteresse*) served by the study, the kind of knowledge it seeks to produce. Thinking along those lines, interpretive knowledge might be distinguished not merely by being knowledge of human beings and their social relations, but by being knowledge that aims to convey to the recipient some sense of the appropriate way of participating in the activity or arrangement under investigation. Clarifying the rules, and placing actions in their appropriate social and meaningful context, would therefore not be an end in itself, but a *means* to the end of explaining just what is going on.

---

8 It is also striking that many authors who insist on the distinctiveness of human beings as an object of study also attempt to claim the label "causal" for their proposed way of studying human beings and their societies. The analysis of causal explanations I have presented in the previous two chapters runs in the other direction: specifying causal explanation more precisely so as to open up space for genuine methodological alternatives.

Such a methodological construal of "interpretive" fits nicely with what Manning thought the point of writing and teaching about international affairs was. The student of international affairs, he once declared, was a "connoisseur-in-the-making of international relationships," someone seeking to develop a feel for how the going concern actually worked (Manning 1962, 182).[9] He went on to compare this with the kind of feel for the game that a spectator develops in a sport like cricket:

> Connoisseurship at a cricket match is not simply the knowledge of what at any moment is the score...there is a difference between casual alertness to the course and state of a particular match, and knowledge of the *kind* of game of which it is merely an instance—knowledge, namely, of its principle, its possibilities, its spirit and traditions, its ethos even—knowledge, in short, of the understandings, the assumptions, the anxieties, the expectations and the hopes, with which, as well as the context and conditions in which, so many specimens of man the player come together on such occasions on such a field.
>
> (Ibid., 195)

Therefore, he argued, what students needed from their teachers, and what the readers of scholarship in international affairs more generally needed from those producing such scholarship, was "an awareness of not just the current course of the game, but of the nature of the game as such" (ibid., 196). While such an awareness might be effectively produced in part through telling someone what the rules are, it would be a mistake to confuse the capacity to appreciate the game with the merely factual knowledge of the rules (which might allow one to calculate the score, but not to figure out what move to make next...or whether that last move was a valid one). Appreciating the game is similar to playing it in that both are *practical* capacities, connected to a flow of activity rather than to a static logical or cognitive framework (Tanney 2000). As Wittgenstein once commented, there must be "a way of grasping a rule that is *not* an *interpretation*, but is expressed in actual cases of what we call 'following the rule' and 'going against it'" (Wittgenstein 1958, sec. 201); that "way of grasping" is the practical capacity for what he would elsewhere call "going on" in an appropriate manner.[10]

Developing this capacity is the goal—the intention—of what might be called *interpretive explanation*: interpretive because it requires drawing out the rules in order to derive more or less compelling implications from them, and explanation because it seeks to resolve a particular perplexity that the recipient has: the perplexity of "going on" appropriately. The resulting practical knowledge of how to

---

9   On the centrality of "connoisseurship" to Manning's thinking and pedagogy, see the excellent discussion in Wilson (2004, 764–66).

10   The resemblance here is not merely accidental, inasmuch as Manning read a good deal of Wittgenstein and adopted some of his terminology, albeit not in a dedicated or systematic way, e.g., his use of phrases like "'language games', 'forms of life', or, simply, fields of social experience" (Manning 1962, 11) and his explicit reference to "Wittgensteinian jargon" (ibid., 99). For a further exploration of Manning's basically Wittgensteinian take on "games," see Aalberts (2010, 254–56).

"go on" goes by many names, depending on how one conceptualizes the social arrangement in question: "competence" (Adler and Pouliot 2011), the ability to "pass" as a member of a social or cultural group (Greenblatt 2007), a "practical-moral" grasp of situationally appropriate possibilities (Bernstein 1983; Shotter 1993b). While it might be easier to imagine how such knowledge could be produced when studying human beings embedded in human societies, there is no philosophically compelling reason why such knowledge might not be produced when studying other objects: animals (Horowitz 2010), forests (Kohn 2013), even physical things more generally (Bogost 2012). We can develop connoisseurship, to return to Manning's term, of a plethora of objects and arrangements, and what distinguishes this way of knowing and this way of producing knowledge from other ways is the *epistemic* goal, rather than some essential *ontological* characteristic of the thing known.

So when we use a word like "meaning" to mark the distinctive character of an interpretive explanation—which we often do—we are making a *methodological* claim about how to explain, rather than a *theoretical* or *ontological* claim about what we are explaining.[11] To say with Clifford Geertz (1973, 5) that we are "in search of meaning" when we engage in interpretation is to say that we are seeking to clarify what it is like to be a part of a group, an organization, an institution, and to explicate the "shared way of life" (Deutsch 1957, 46) characteristic of that setting or social arrangement.[12] "Meaning" here indicates that we are looking for the self-understanding of the actors involved, and investigating the sense that those actors make of the world. It also indicates that we are engaged in explanation rather than description, inasmuch as meaning isn't an object in the world so much as a set of instructions for "going on" in the world. To say what something—a word, a gesture, a symbol—*means* is to participate in the process of determining rules for appropriate use, offering a construal that stands or falls based on the ways that others respond to it: acceptance, rejection, negotiation, or some combination. I tell you that this piece of colored cloth is a "flag" that *means* "the nation," and that it is therefore deserving of respect; if you agree (explicitly in words, or implicitly by acting in the respectful manner I have insisted on), you have helped to stabilize the meaning of the object, and if you disagree, the meaning remains ongoingly contested. Interpreting an object is explaining to someone what they ought to do and how they ought to act with regard to it. And interpreting a setting or a social arrangement is explaining to someone what they ought to do and how they ought to

---

11 Klein Schaarsberg's (2023) call to treat "the pluriverse" as a methodological principle has some family resemblance with my point here, although her approach seems to sometimes lean towards an attempt to deny that true factic claims translate across meaningful worlds.

12 I am borrowing the term "social arrangement" from Nicholas Onuf (1989, 157–58), who suggests it as an alternative to the notion of "order": "my metaphorical move from order to arrangement shifts the normative weight invested in the term 'problem' [as in 'the problem of order'] away from stability and toward the facticity of 'arrangements' as having been arranged." See also Onuf (1998).

act in order to fit into it: explicating the meanings (instructions and rules for appropriate use) held by the community of actors in that setting.[13]

Interpretation as a Form of Explanation

We can get a clearer understanding of the distinctiveness of an interpretive approach understood methodologically by contrasting it to the mode of explanation most commonly on display in the contemporary social *and* natural sciences, which has been the topic of the preceding two chapters: causal explanation. Both causal and interpretive explanations differ from description, but they do so in different ways, and those differences are methodologically consequential. So in order to get a handle on what an interpretive explanation is, we have to once again start with description—especially inasmuch as interpretive explanation is sometimes called "thick description" by those contemporary social scientists whose first introduction to this kind of scholarship was Clifford Geertz's 1973 classic *The Interpretation of Cultures*.[14] And as always, we have to start not with the formal characteristics of written words, but with the concrete, practical situations out of which questions come, questions to which *acts of explanation* (as in Achinstein 1985) as well as acts of description come, since ultimately methodology is about different ways of approaching the asking and answering of questions.

So, to recap: factic description, as I argued in Chapters 1 and 2, is a kind of speech act that aims to put the interlocutors into the same knowing relationship with a common object. As such, a factic description always implicitly answers a question like "What is that?" and does so by making a determination about what something is, a determination which is comprehensible to (and perhaps contestable by) both speaker and listener precisely in virtue of their shared conceptual vocabulary. "That's a mallard," said in reference to a particular waterfowl, only makes sense to the extent that both parties share a set of criteria according to which the word "mallard" is properly applied to the bird in question. Description is declarative and propositional, "not essentially indexed to any particular speaker or audience" beyond the basic situation of belonging to the community of speakers of the

---

13 When Ian Bogost (2012, 109) suggests that one approach to an object-oriented ontology involves "constructing artifacts that illustrate the perspectives of objects," he is in effect suggesting that we make efforts to enter into the meaningful world of those objects. That would make philosophical carpentry of the sort that Bogost recommends into a form of interpretive explanation—albeit one that remains tenuous insofar as it "seeks to capture and characterize an experience it can never fully understand, offering a rendering satisfactory enough to allow the artifact's operator to gain some insight into an alien thing's experience" (ibid., 100). I mention this only to underscore the point that interpretive explanation is *not*, in any fundamental or constitutive sense, limited to the investigation of human social relations. Ursula Le Guin's remarkable short story "Direction of the Road" is exemplary here.

14 Geertz's use of the term "description" owes a lot more to Wittgenstein than is usually acknowledged or sufficiently appreciated, and as such what Geertz had in mind by appending the modifier "thick" is quite a bit different from the ordinary-language meaning of "description" or the notion of description I elaborated in Chapters 1 and 2 (on Wittgensteinian "description," which I myself would call "interpretation," see Ben-Menahem 1998).

language used in the description (Kukla and Lance 2009, 59).[15] As such, the factic description of an object comes accompanied by an acceptance of responsibility on the part of the person doing the describing: a responsibility to correctly use the descriptive words and procedures in question to generate reliable factic propositions that can be evaluated and, if true, trusted and believed. Factic description also comes with an acknowledgment of the capacity and perhaps even the right of others to call us to account if we do not do so (Moran 2005, 11). But this very responsibility means that the specifically *personal* aspects of a factic description fall away, leaving us with an *impersonal* record of a shared perceptual judgment.

When a speaker describes something to a listener, the speaker's concern is to disclose the object as the object it is, to bring it before all parties in a way that they all affirm and accept. This might not actually happen; for instance, the listener might respond by describing the object in a different way, and a debate might ensue about the correct way to describe the object in question ("That's a mallard." "No, it's a wood duck."). But the very structure of that exchange *presumes* that there is at least one correct way of describing the object, and that the standards and criteria for such a correct description are shared in a way that supports the making of impersonally true claims. In such circumstances there is a way of resolving the question of whether that is a mallard or a wood duck that does not reduce to one party *imposing* an answer on the other, but instead depends on all parties accepting a common descriptive vocabulary: definitions, procedures, and the competent use of language. That common vocabulary, in turn, enables different parties to take up and share an orientation towards an object, a way of intelligibly comporting ourselves such that the object shows itself as the object that it is: "it speaks to one's understanding...'See me as I am,' it (so to speak) says to one; 'namely, as characterized by *these* properties'—and it displays them" (McDowell 1998a, 468). An act of description therefore allows parties to share information and clear up ambiguities, thus facilitating practical outcomes: "Bring me that pen." "Which one?" "The red one."

In that way, a description of whatever sort is concerned, in the first instance, with an *object*—either physical or conceptual—and its characteristics. Descriptions are I–it relationships. By contrast, an explanation is less concerned in the first instance with an object than it is with the interlocutor; it is an I–Thou relationship (Buber 1971). Acts of description are about sharing information and producing a shared orientation towards an object; acts of explanation arise from and respond to entirely different problem-situations. The problem-situation for an explanation

---

15 This can be contrasted to "observatives" (Kukla and Lance 2009, 62), which always "terminate in *someone's* first-personal experiences." "I see a mallard!" isn't a description, but an observative, just because in order for it to be a description, there would have to be something that the statement describes...and what would *that* be, exactly? Instead, the observative gives us a report of first-personal experience, and perhaps suggests how we could each also have that experience: in this case, by looking where the observer is pointing. We get confused about this because we often *subsequently* reason backwards from the seeing of the mallard to a description of the kind of animal that it is, but it is simply bizarre to presume that when we see the mallard, we first see an unqualified animal or even a neutral duck and only subsequently describe that entity as a mallard.

is an incapacity to do something, and an act of explanation is an act intended to *enhance the capacity* of the recipient to do something. A good explanation seeks to develop the kind of understanding that is practically exhibited in the listener actually doing something. A successful explanation, then, is one that gives the recipient an enhanced capacity to *do*, and the success of an explanation ultimately has to be judged on whether or not it contributes to the intended increased capacity, and by whether it intervenes in the problem-situation in a way that allows the recipient to address the problem.

While this is different from our usual *scholarly* or broadly speaking "scientific" way of evaluating an explanation, which places more emphasis on the form and internal consistency of a proffered explanation and on its relation to other at least provisionally accepted explanations, it is a good deal closer to the way we evaluate explanations in a *teaching* context. The best evidence that an instructor has successfully explained something to a student is that they are able to do something that they couldn't do before, whether that is solving an equation or evaluating an argument or producing an analysis or something else. And it is also much more like what Manning argued the point of studying international affairs was: to help others to become aware of the "received assumptions, received, that is, in the relevant, official milieu" by which "the social cosmos is organized already to a certain extent" (Manning 1962, 9). This in turn would allow them to play the international society game correctly, or at least to appreciate the game as an informed spectator. They would know the rules, as exhibited through their being able to use them correctly.

Interpretive explanation thus responds to a different problem-situation than causal explanation does. Over the previous two chapters I have argued that the generic problem-situation calling for a causal explanation is some version of "What is the impact of X on Y?" or, in the imperative form, "Can we affect Y by altering X?" The entire apparatus of statistical-comparative IR scholarship might be thought of as a vast neopositivist machine designed to sift through data seeking answers to that sort of question, albeit more focused on the evaluation of hypothetical nomothetic claims for their conformity with the facts, and less focused on constructing case-specific explanations of particular outcomes. But what makes a causal explanation causal is not whether it tests hypotheses or relies on notions of statistical significance; what makes an explanation causal is that it is intended to equip the recipient with the capacity to *make something happen* in the world, to manipulate entities and objects so as to achieve some particular outcome rather than another (Woodward 2005). As such, it responds to a question not about the rules (e.g., "What are the laws governing the use of force internationally?") but about effectiveness: "Should we launch a pre-emptive strike in this situation or not?"

Those sorts of causal questions are not what the interpretivist strain of English School scholarship prioritizes, and they were not what drove Manning's thinking. Instead, Manning's project is an interpretive explanation, inasmuch as the point of the exercise is to help his readers and students to engage in and appreciate "the game of let's-play-states" by revealing the "theoretical 'structure'" or "'constitution'" of international society. The problem-situation is that the listeners—in

Manning's case, largely his students—do not know how to "go on" in international society, and do not know how to play the game yet. The targets of his explanatory activity, Manning makes clear, are the "sensibly real" individual people who are the players of this game and the bearers of those social relations that sustain and are sustained by the game, because "the big protagonists, the sovereign states, whose given-ness the process presupposes," only have "their influential presence…in the order of the intelligibles, apprehensible to the imagination and not to the eye" (ibid., 166). Unlike, say, Robert Jackson's (2003) or Alex Wendt's (1999) accounts in which *states* are the players of the international-affairs game, for Manning, states remain merely notional rather than sensibly real and thus cannot possibly be the players sitting above the board; states are internal to the game (Aalberts 2010, 257–58). As such Manning's interpretive explanation is, appropriately, not directed at states, but at human beings playing the game of sovereign states; one can explain to a human being how to play chess, but it would make little sense to explain the game to the queen or to a pawn.[16]

In addition to presupposing a capacity for grasping and being affected by teaching and training through language, an interpretive explanation like Manning's is carefully bounded by its steadfast refusal to engage in any comparative assessment of the effectiveness of *ways* of playing the game. There is no analysis of different strategies in Manning's account, and no judgment that one rather than another approach to the game of sovereign states is likely to be more or less effective in any particular circumstance. Instead, as in his student Hedley Bull's account of "the anarchical society" (1977) and much of the English School work that takes after it, there is what we might call a catalog of permissible moves, derived from rich historical study, that serves in the end to answer a question like "How do we do this?" The kind of problem-situation that calls for an interpretive explanation revolves centrally around a question like this one, or, more generally, around a perplexity about "finding our feet" (Ruggie 1998) or "going on" (Shotter 1996). Manning's interpretive explanation is directed at an audience who doesn't yet know the rules of the game, and aims to convey to them a sense of how to play. The concern, so to speak, is less with how to win than with how to play—how to make a valid move, how to correctly use terms and concepts, how to be part of the ongoing flow of the setting or social arrangement being explained *by* the speaker *to* the listener.

"Going Concerns"

All of which is to say that an account like Manning's is concerned not merely with *describing* the rules of international society—the game of let's-play-states—but with equipping the student, the reader, or whomever the recipient of the explanation is, with the capacity to play the game, or at least to appreciate the game as an informed connoisseur. Whether the recipient plays effectively or ineffectively

---

16   Unless, of course, we were to regard states as having something akin to a mind towards which an explanation could be directed — a position Wendt has sometimes (2003; 2004) taken.

is less important than whether the resulting play is correct or incorrect: whether it unfolds according to the rules or not. Manning's connoisseur of cricket is not described as someone who can comparatively assess strategy and tactics, but as someone who appreciates the history of the game as a whole and thus understands the context of any particular match. There is not a shred of concern with causality here, but instead a concern with the hermeneutic horizons of those to whom international affairs are being explained. And there is a presumption that learning to play that game is a worthwhile activity. While most of Manning's analysis relies on adducing empirical examples that illustrate that the notional actor-hood of the sovereign state does actually inform and structure contemporary international affairs sufficiently that elaboration and elucidation of that principle is essential for making sense of the game, he occasionally raises the specter of revolutionary disorder as a reason for sticking to the game as it presently exists, and suggests that if the sovereign state is to be superseded, that will only happen through the formation of a world community outside of the presently existing game (Manning 1962, 176–80).[17] Since Manning's concern is with equipping people to play *this* game, he sets aside the question of alternative games, because they are, in this approach, logically irrelevant. Counterfactual speculation about other games that might be played is helpful to such an explanatory project only if such speculation improves the listener's grasp of the rules of the "going concern."[18]

Keeping the intention of an interpretive explanation front and center in the analysis helps to clarify why this kind of "thick description" is *not* description in the factic sense. In an interpretive explanation, there is always a concern with a set of ongoing meaningful practices, and that set is a "going concern" to the extent that those meaningful practices continue to go on—which in turn requires actors who draw on the available "rules and resources" (Giddens 1984) in similar ways. An interpretive explanation aims to make the listener able to participate, in principle if not in practice, in that "going concern": in a setting or social arrangement. So what has to be conveyed in an interpretive explanation is the capacity to "go on" appropriately, whether the putative object of explanation is an artifact whose meaning is being explicated, or a setting or social arrangement in which the listener wants to participate. The two are closely linked, of course, inasmuch as my explication of the meaning of (e.g.) this piece of colored cloth at least implicitly comes with a reference to the organized community of actors for whom the object has a certain meaning as a national flag. Perhaps the boundaries of that community are clear from the context ("this is *our* flag and deserves *our* respect" vs. "this is *their* flag and this is how *they* show respect to it"), and perhaps they are not ("you should respect the flag!"), but whenever we interpret some object, we are doing

---

17 Which calls to mind Manning's student Hedley Bull's (1977) argument about the priority of order over justice in international affairs. Manning's concerns are in many ways not very far removed from core English School substantive commitments that persist into the present.

18 Although criticizing the rules of the "going concern" was quite far from Manning's own stance, I would argue that critiquing a "going concern" first requires a valid interpretive explanation of that setting or social arrangement. See below.

something quite distinct from factually describing it, inasmuch as our concern is with meaning—understood as rules for appropriate action—and not with anything perceivable or observable.

Now, this can get quite tricky in practice, because when we are explicating the meaning that some artifact has for a community, what we actually have available to us are the ways that the relevant actors act towards it. Sometimes that involves written instructions, like the United States Flag Code,[19] but it almost never suffices to simply cite such documents as definitive without examining how they are actually used in practice, and providing factic descriptions of that use. The document, for instance, states in §8(i) that the U.S. flag "should never be used for advertising purposes in any manner whatsoever," but virtually every Independence Day sale in the U.S. features an image of the flag in some capacity; the document also states in §9 that

> During the ceremony of hoisting or lowering the flag or when the flag is passing in a parade or in review, all persons present in uniform should render the military salute. Members of the Armed Forces and veterans who are present but not in uniform may render the military salute. All other persons present should face the flag and stand at attention with their right hand over the heart, or if applicable, remove their headdress with their right hand and hold it at the left shoulder, the hand being over the heart. Citizens of other countries present should stand at attention. All such conduct toward the flag in a moving column should be rendered at the moment the flag passes.

But in practice not everyone does this, *especially* not "citizens of other countries present" on most occasions.

A good interpretation of the meaning of the U.S. flag would thus have to look closely at what people actually—factually—do and how they act towards the flag, including what role if any this written flag code plays in their deliberations, and conclude from this what *actual* meaning the flag holds for the people in question. Remembering the problem-situation of an interpretive explanation is helpful here: the listener wants to know how to "go on" appropriately in the setting or social arrangement in question, so an explication of the meaning of the flag would have to be a set of instructions to the listener about how to act in the future as the flag is raised or lowered, or when deciding how to advertise a holiday sale. Those instructions cannot merely be a record of how actors have *previously* acted, although that factual record is not unimportant. After all, the problem of how to "go on" only arises when the way forward is not clear—when habit is disrupted by novelty, and creativity is called for (Dewey 1985, 123). Just as the statistical analysis of word frequencies and the use of those frequencies to generate sentences differs from speaking a language, the factic description of a set of written rules or a series of observed activities differs from an interpretive explanation of a "going

---

19 "U.S.C. Title 4—Flag and Seal, Seat of Government, and the States" (n.d.)

concern." While the former might allow you to *simulate* it, the latter makes possible your *participation in* it.

Thinking of the explication of rules as part of an interpretive explanation also helps to resolve some tensions that crop up all too often in the various analyses of the role of "norms" in international affairs, particularly those that attempt to use a norm as a causal factor in the explanation of behavior. Treating a norm as a causal factor means treating an explication of the rules in a given community as though it were a factic claim: as though a claim like "there is a norm against targeting civilians in international society" were a *description* that could be factically true or false. Such a conception immediately runs into well-known problems of definition and measurement, since behavior is not a reliable indicator of whether a norm exists (Kratochwil 1989); there may be a norm against robbery, assault, and battery, for example, but this doesn't mean that these things don't occur. Norms are "counterfactually valid," meaning that violations of a norm don't disprove the norm so much as they call for justifications by the actors involved as to why they violated the norm in the first place. So in practice, scholars looking to construct causal explanations of behavior involving a norm—the actors did as they did because there was a norm, and they would have done something else in the absence of that norm—often use a proxy, like an actor's having signed an international convention, as their operative indicator of whether a norm exists or not (e.g., Morrow 2007). This of course makes the causal argument into something like "signing a treaty affects behavior," taking us further away from the meaningful practices that an interpretive explanation foregrounds.

The other alternative pursued by scholars working with norms as causal factors is to ascertain what kind of action or outcome would be expected *if* a particular norm were in force, and then reasoning from the presence of that outcome or action to the existence of the norm in question—especially if other factors point in different directions. Martha Finnemore's (1996) classic study of norms in international society takes this approach, for instance in explaining the construction of science bureaucracies by countries that have little rational need for them in terms of a global norm about what kinds of agencies and capacities a sovereign state ought to have. Although she highlights the lobbying and advising activities of various U.N. agencies, her argument hinges on "a new understanding of necessary and appropriate state behavior"—a change in norms—"rather than any functional need" that states had or that international agencies were catering to (ibid., 65). Like others making similar arguments that causally explain outcomes in terms of norms (e.g., Price 1995; Tannenwald 1999), Finnemore provides documentary evidence of a norm's existence by citing treaties, conventions, and public declarations, but the causal pathway here involves actors deliberately incorporating the norm into their activities rather than any putative effect of those documents themselves.

But in order to make an argument like this work, we have to treat a norm as a discrete object, rather than treating it as a practical guide for "going on" appropriately in context (Hofferberth and Weber 2015). This is a methodological move rather than a theoretical one; what is at issue here is not the question of what a social norm or rule "really is," but what explanatory purpose we have in apprehending things in one way rather than another. In a causal-explanatory context, where our goal is to explain why/how we get one outcome rather than another and to do so in a way that equips the recipient with the capacity to alter the outcome by changing the causal factor, "norm" *has to* mean some object that can be factically described. In a causal explanation, causal factors are necessarily objects like this, as they could not be manipulated to have a different value or condition unless they were *in fact* in one condition or another: the volume knob on the stereo is pointing to 2 or to 8,[20] the states involved in a dispute have relatively equal or relatively unequal military resources, a country is or is not a democracy. As long as we want our causal explanation to be consonant with the facts, we have no alternative but to treat both outcomes and causal factors as objects that can be factically described.

So a claim about something being a "norm"—or a "rule"—means one thing when used in a causal explanation, and quite another when used in an interpretive explanation. In a causal explanation it is a factic description, and as such makes the most sense when utilized by observers standing outside of the situation rather than participating in it. If I am explaining to you how to make something happen—how to produce a peaceful resolution to a conflict, for instance—then both you and I are treating the conflict that we are hoping to resolve as something that is at arm's length from us. Making something happen by manipulating one factor in order to alter another puts us both into the position of standing outside of the factors in question, relying on their causal powers to produce the outcome we want. When I bake a cake I treat the ingredients as objects I can manipulate according to a recipe, and my correct execution of the instructions in the recipe (which is a causal explanation in imperative form) depends on using the factually correct ingredients and on having factually true measurements of those ingredients. Likewise, when we seek to resolve a conflict by altering the norms in question from "wars of territorial conquest are noble enterprises" to "sovereign borders should be respected," we need to factically describe what the norm is or is not, so we can change it if it needs changing.

A further ambiguity arises when we confuse this causal-explanatory strategy with the kinds of claims that *actors themselves* make in the course of their acting in particular ways, or with the conceptually similar claims that are offered—either by the actors themselves or by third-party analysts, like Manning in his lectures and writings—as guidelines for properly acting as a member of the relevant community. If we are playing chess and I move my rook along the diagonal rather than along a row or column, and you tell me that I have violated the rules, you are not stating a fact but offering an explanation of proper chess play: if I want to play chess correctly, I shouldn't move my rook like that. You are offering me the rules as a guideline for proper play, and the test of that explication of the rules (and the interpretive explanation of which they are a part) is whether acting according to them allows me to "go on" as part of the community of people who play chess

---

20 Or perhaps to 11, although this would also represent a rather profound—and profoundly funny—misunderstanding of how volume knobs work. Kudos to Tony Lang for pushing me to retain this observation.

properly.[21] Exactly the same can be said of an advisor telling a military decision-maker not to target civilians because of a norm or a rule of international law prohibiting such activity: the advisor is offering an instruction for "going on" as a member of the international community (Nuñez-Mietz 2016). This is distinct from the factic question of whether there is a document saying that one should not target civilians or a norm to that effect that is operative in international society, just as the instructions for acting as a member of the chess-playing community are distinct from the factic question of what is codified in official handbooks and the like. In both cases, the interpretive explanation may *use* true factic claims—facts—as part of the grounds for recommending one course of action over another ("the document contains these words" or "people generally act in this way"). But the evaluation of the explanation always means assessing whether it allows the listener to act as a member of the community in question would act. This is not a factic question, but a practical one.

Of course, if the "going concern" referenced in an interpretive explanation is no longer a living community, or not treated as a living community, it is no longer possible to participate in the community in order to practically assess whether any particular explication of its rules permits one to "go on" appropriately in context. In this situation, the discussions of a community's rules and norms take on something more like a factic descriptive character. The record of actors doing things, including codifying rules and using those codes in their discussions with one another, can be straightforwardly described. The thickness of "thick description" falls away, and with it much of the explanatory character of an interpretive explanation. After all, if there is no community to act as a member of, if there is no ongoing game to join in playing, then the validity of an account can only be assessed by comparing it to the known facts and seeing if it lines up. If we remember the way that description is necessarily wrapped up with a community's descriptive vocabulary, then not having a living community to engage with—or not engaging with a community that is actually living and ongoing, in effect treating it as though it were not coeval with one's own (Fabian 1983; Inayatullah and Blaney 1996)—opens the possibility that when we are talking about some community, what we are actually talking about is our own imaginary version of that community. Just as only practical engagement with objects can keep a causal explanation grounded in the problem-situation of making things happen, only practical engagement with a community can keep an interpretive explanation grounded in the problem-situation of "going on" appropriately.

Positionality: Speakers, Listeners, and Communities

Both the need for practical engagement with a community and the possibility of becoming detached from the ongoing activities of that community illustrate that

---

21 "Properly," of course, according to that community. Chess is a fairly formalized game and the rules are well specified and codified, but consider instead the presence of "house rules" in a card game: this is how *we* play the game, even though it might not be how *others* play it.

interpretive explanations have a logical structure that is quite distinct from the structure of causal explanations. Causal explanations only feature one kind of relationship between the knowing subjects and the objects of knowledge, with both speaker and listener located "outside" of those objects so that they can manipulate the inputs and produce outcomes, in principle if not in actuality. Causal explanations thus have factic endpoints—both the causal factors and the caused outcomes can be described factically—even though they themselves are not facts but instructions. Both using and evaluating a causal explanation requires both of these pieces of factic data, together with the logically general claims that support the case-specific explanation. Explaining why civil resistance succeeded in forcing the Shah of Iran from power where a violent campaign did not, for example (Chenoweth and Stephan 2011), means factically establishing that one movement was violent where another was not, and establishing that the Shah was in fact forced from power, together with the general causal claims about nonviolent movements leading to successful outcomes while violent movements prevent such successes from occurring.

But interpretive explanation is not so simple, because either the speaker or the listener, or both, can be located either "inside" *or* "outside" of the community in question, whether the explanation is an explication of the meaning of an artifact (which is indirectly about the community maintaining that meaning) or a more direct admonition about how to act as a member of a community. Although in practice this gets tangled up, it is useful to schematically or analytically distinguish four different ways in which speakers and listeners might be positioned with respect to a community. The overall goal is the same through all of these forms of interpretive explanation, but how that plays out is shaped by whether the speaker and the listener are "outsiders" or "insiders."

Varieties of interpretive explanation.

	Speaker "outside"	Speaker "inside"
Listener "outside"	Translation	Socialization
Listener "inside"	Consulting	Discernment

Starting in the upper left-hand corner, we find the position that Manning occupies vis-à-vis his students and readers. This is, broadly speaking, a position of *translation*, where the audience are relative "outsiders" to the domain being explained, and the explainer, having gained enough knowledge of what it is like "inside" to serve as a reliable source, is similarly located "outside." "There is a sense," Manning noted, "in which education is something suppled, by those who have for longer been finding their way around, to assist the explorations of others who have been at it less long" (1962, ix), which places the teacher in the position of a guide or a translator. Interpretively explaining in this situation is very much like drawing a map and showing someone how to use it, taking the meaningful practices under investigation and translating them into terms that the listener can grasp.

The structure of the situation underpins a potential problem: since both speaker and listener are "outsiders," they might find themselves talking about a community and its meaningful practices in terms that are more or less completely alien to that community itself. The resulting representation might even be "a corporate or institutional self-deception, in which much of what we take the be the subject matter of our science is imaginary in the same way as the 'worlds' created by science fiction" (Shotter 1993a, 76). At worst, especially in an institutionalized academic context, this becomes the kind of "orientalism" decried by critics like Edward Said (1979): scholars citing other scholars, reproducing a conventional wisdom that may amount to little more than structured ignorance (as in Southern 1962). But while such interpretive explanations may not be worth much as a practical guide to "going on" in the community in question, it *is* a set of instructions for "going on" *in the community to which speaker and listener belong*, and revealing of the rules and norms of the community *doing the interpreting*. It would be a mistake to treat Frank Herbert's novel *Dune* as a reliable guide to "going on" in Islamic desert societies, but as a primary source for disclosing the ways that the community of Anglophone readers in the 1960s understood such societies—and thus, implicitly, a set of instructions for "going on" as a member of *that* community—it is a very useful document.

Traditionally, this problem has been addressed—especially in anthropology and sociology—under the heading of the "double hermeneutic" (Giddens 1984): what we do in interpreting another community's meanings is to make sense of how they make sense. In Clifford Geertz's (2000, 58) formulation, what we investigate when we find ourselves in the position of an outsider explaining to another outsider "is what they [those inside the community] perceive 'with' —or 'by means of,' or 'through'—or whatever the word should be." The danger is losing sight of either of these hermeneutic circles, and losing touch either with the audience for the explanation or with the community we are explaining. The classic solution is *fieldwork*, which functions in an interpretive explanation as a way of ensuring that the explanations on offer have been tried out as ways of "going on" in the community and been judged successful. This in turn allows the interpretive explainer to occupy something of a *liminal* position with respect to both communities—the one they and the listener are not a part of, and the one that they and the listener are a part of—and use their experiences in the field as a way of critiquing and refining the conceptual equipment that they use when explaining (exemplary works along these lines include Kondo 1990 and Tsing 2004).

But the condition of possibility for this kind of reflexive criticism is that the interpretive explanation of another community be a valid one, i.e., that it not be simply something invented for the purposes of making a point, but that it be based in fieldwork factually performed and that it function as a reliable guide for "going on" in that community.[22] The practical context for an interpretive explanation always involves this connection to a community; in the case of an outsider

---

22 This is the difference between a novel and piece of critical scholarship delivered in narrative form: the latter has a necessary practical connection to a community in a way that a novel need

explaining to another outsider, this means offering a reliable guide to the community in terms that the listener can work with, even if those terms are not the same ones that the community itself uses, and even if that reliable guide is then used as an object of critique. The possibility of "going on" appropriately anchors any valid interpretive explanation. What matters is not the similarity of language between insiders and outsiders, but the practical results of acting according to the instructions, and whether the resulting actions are understood as appropriate by the community in question.

By contrast, the *socialization* position in the upper-right-hand corner does rely on similar language between the community and the listener, because the point of an interpretive explanation in which an "insider" explains to an "outsider" is to bring the outsider into the community. In effect, the explanation teaches the listener the language. This is what happens when a distinguished practitioner of diplomacy or international development or a similar field of professional practice addresses a group of students and seeks to train them—to help them become practitioners themselves, even if in a limited way. Here the emphasis is less on translation and more on helping the listeners to learn to speak the language themselves. This was not really Manning's own position with respect to international affairs, since he did not have a set of practical experiences to draw on, and his own professional commitments were clearly on the academic side of things. But we can easily conclude that it would have been Manning's position vis-à-vis those of his students who were planning to become professional academics themselves. Specifying the relevant community is an indispensable part of laying bare the structure of an interpretive explanation, and with an account like Manning's, it is certainly reasonable to ask whether he was acting as a translator of the "going concern" of international society, or as an agent of socialization into a community of academic discourse about international affairs. How we assess the validity of his explanations is shaped by this specification, but in either case, the ultimate assessment is whether the interpretive explanation helps the listener "go on" appropriately in context or not.

Things get a little trickier on the bottom row of the table, where the listener is already a participant in the meaningful practices and "going concern" of the community. An explanation of a domain offered to participants from the outside—answering the question "How should *we* go on?" since the listeners are participants, rather than the question "How would *they* go on?" which would be appropriate for listeners located outside of the domain—arises in the kind of relationship that external consultants have to their clients. Consultants are often retained to provide an outsider's perspective, clarifying to the participants aspects of their own practice that they might not have recognized or realized, and often using a conceptual vocabulary that is distinct from the vocabulary of the participants themselves to do so. Such consultants differ from "experts" who typically bring causal knowledge to bear on gaps in participants' efficacy and aim to equip them to be more effective—to

---

not (but sometimes does, depending on the kind of novel that it is). See, in this respect, Naeem Inayatullah's "Foreword" to Dauphinee (2013).

explain causally, relying on their expert authority to underpin the credibility of their advice (Sending 2015; Goetze 2017). Consultants engaged in interpretive explanation, by contrast, are in a sense mirroring the participants' meaningful practices back to themselves, clarifying the mission and values animating those practices. This mirroring offers the participants suggestions about how to "go on," and their validity depends on their acceptance by the participants: whether the participants find these suggestions a compelling account or not. As with other interpretive explanations, the community participants determine whether the suggestions are a valid set of instructions for "going on" or not; the only difference here is that the participants are the recipients of the explanation too.

And if both the speaker and the listener are "insiders," members of the community, an interpretive explanation looks even less like an explanation and more like an argument. Answering the question "How should *we* go on?" when all of the parties to the exchange are community members becomes a form of collective *discernment*, a determination of what we all ought to do going forward. That determination necessarily involves moral and ethical considerations, as any controversy about the most effective way to achieve a certain goal logically depends on some level of agreement about the goal to be pursued and the desirability of that goal. Interpretive explanations in this context thus have as their primary task the clarification of appropriate goals, drawing on the various cultural resources available in the community to craft compelling accounts of who we are and what we ought to therefore be doing (Sewell 1992; Tilly 2002). In so doing, this kind of interpretive explanation takes advantage of the weakly shared cultural and rhetorical commonplaces that characterize a given community, drawing out their meanings as practical suggestions for determining appropriate future actions (Shotter 1993b, 170–71). In this sense, an interpretive explanation offered by community members to other community members takes advantage of the contestable character of community rules and norms (Wiener 2018) and functions as a practical intervention into that ongoing contestation.[23]

Consultation and discernment thus share a logical form with other kinds of persuasive speech acts where the goal is to convince the listener to adopt the speaker's position. Persuasive argument generally is part of what John Shotter (1993b) calls "the cultural politics of everyday life," and interpretive explanation is no exception. But what sets interpretive explanations apart from persuasive argument more generally is that the intent of an interpretive explanation is not merely for the listener to accept the conclusion, but to accept the proposed meaning as well. With other kinds of persuasive argument—such as that involved in attempts to rhetorically coerce one's opponents (Krebs and Jackson 2007), or that involved in framing an issue in one's preferred way (Snow 2022)—the point is to have a causal impact on future action, by ruling some options unacceptable and others acceptable. Interpretive explanation in the discernment mode goes further, since the acceptance of an interpretive explanation by the listener entails the stabilization of a way of "going on"

---

23 It is also important to distinguish between an interpretive explanation intended to shape future actions, and a causal explanation that relates particular deployments of commonplaces to outcomes, inasmuch as the latter is not an intervention into the community's ongoing discernment—at least, not a direct intervention.

in the future. So interpretive explanations of particular environmental issues as connected to climate justice (as in Wilkens and Datchoua-Tirvaudey 2022), or the expansion of the concept of security to encompass notions beyond the territorial integrity of sovereign states (as in Lau 2023), offer direct modifications of the conceptual equipment that "we"—speaker and listener alike—can subsequently use to make sense of things in the future.

It should not come as a surprise that the validity and value of an interpretive explanation depends on the judgment of the listener as to whether the explanation is useful. Because the purpose of an interpretive explanation is to allow the listener to "go on" appropriately in context, the ultimate test of such an explanation is *always* dependent on how useful people find it to be when participating in the relevant community. We should not be misled by the way that interpretive explanations offered to "outsiders" sometimes look like descriptions of settled social practices, where interpretive explanations offered to "insiders" sometimes look like statements about what something means. Both often appear to be phrased as though they were factic claims, but *they are not*—which we can clarify by specifying the relevant community and the relationship of speaker and listener to that community.

And although there are significant methodological differences between all of these types of interpretive explanation on the one hand and causal explanation on the other, we should not conclude that interpretive explanations are just group opinions and as such can never be *true*, where causal explanations can be true (or false). Such a conclusion is the result of conceptual confusion. Causal explanations may have factic endpoints, but they are not themselves facts, inasmuch as their validity ultimately depends on their practical value as instructions for making things happen. Interpretive explanations are the same in this respect, demonstrating their value in practice as instructions for "going on." The tricky thing is that interpretive explanations don't have factic endpoints in the same way that causal explanations do, since "going on" appropriately in context is a condition that can only be experienced from the inside instead of being observed from the outside. Causal explanation presumes arms-length non-participation with the factors being manipulated just as interpretive explanation presumes participation in the relevant community. But a judgment about the validity—the "truth"—of *any* explanation rests on an assessment of its practical value, and as such there are no methodological grounds for maintaining that only causal explanations can be true or false. Manning's analysis of international society is no less *intrinsically* valuable than a quantitative analysis of patterns of state behavior, as both can support explanations that are, in their separate ways, potentially valid.

Manning's Position

Since Manning is offering an interpretive explanation, figuring out whether it is valid or not depends on specifying the relevant community whose rules he is explicating, and the positions that he and his listeners occupy with respect to that community. Doing so in Manning's case can, I will argue, also clarify the mistake that he made in his testimony to the International Court of Justice: he treated the situation as one of translation, when he should have treated it as one of discernment. One simply cannot be an outsider talking to other outsiders when making statements on such a public stage.[24]

In the classroom and in his writings on international affairs for both academic and public audiences, Manning occupies the position of a translator of the language of international society—the game of let's-play-states—for an audience that doesn't yet know how to play the game. In so doing, Manning does not claim that his knowledge derives from long practical experience *in* international affairs, so it would be difficult to think of his goal as trying to socialize his students and readers into a domain of which he was already a part and they aspired to be a part. And his work is not, for the most part, directed at self-identified "insiders" to the world of international affairs; he is not engaged in policy consultation, and he does not treat his audience as a group of fellow interlocutors with whom he is engaged in a collective effort to discern how we collectively should "go on." Instead, Manning occupies the traditional "academic" vocational position of the relatively detached scholar seeking to clarify and understand: here is this domain I have been exploring, let me explain it to you, by telling you what I have learned about its rules and its organizational principles, translating them into terms you can understand—an interpretive explanatory act that it is intended to equip you to similarly move around in that domain, at least in principle.

Interpretive explanations that function as translations inevitably arrest, or idealize, or caricature the domain which they are explaining. There is no way to capture the entire richness of an actually existing social arrangement in a finite explanation, precisely because any instructional setting where the concern is to equip the recipient to "go on" has to provide some set of guidelines or principles to use as a starting-point, but "the rules are no game" (Geertz 2000, 25) and those guidelines and principles are never exhaustive or comprehensive. The point is to help the recipient play the game, not simply to be able to say (factually) what the rules *are*. That in turn means that interpretive explanations are always to some degree stylized, illustrative, oversimplified, but for a *pedagogical* purpose.[25] Within the confines of the idealized academy, where the purpose is generally some variant of the capacity to think clearly about the issues under consideration, the oversimplified detachment of an interpretive explanation conducted as a translation has both a benefit and liability: the benefit is what John Dewey (1920, 150–51) referred

---

24 I am not suggesting that Manning was unaware what he was doing. Indeed, he likely was using his academic cachet as a way to defend his morally reprehensible views about racial differences and natural hierarchies, and wouldn't have regarded his actions as a mistake. But I *am* suggesting that clarifying his actions as a methodological mistake is a valuable exercise. I will take up this point in more detail in Chapter 6.

25 Causal explanations too have their oversimplifications and idealizations, but because such explanations intentionally terminate in in-principle manipulability, there are different methodological strategies for dealing with these issues, including ideal-typification, Bayesian inference, laboratory isolation, and the central limit theorem. These do not and cannot play the same role in interpretive explanations.

to as the liberating power of abstraction, by virtue of which we are able to extract from one situation lessons that might be helpful in another situation; the liability is that we might be so enamored of and entranced by our intellectual constructs that we come to confuse them with actuality (Shotter 1993a, 76–77). Whether the institutionalized habits of the academic life, or the practices that sustain and are sustained by a scholarly vocation, are or can be sufficient to disrupt this tendency towards reification remains a matter of some controversy (Levine 2012; Hamati-Ataya 2018). But at any rate, within the metaphorical and sometimes even physical walls of the academy, there are opportunities for regarding this kind of interpretive explanation as a more or less purely *intellectual* exercise, and thus regarding the commitment to the established rules of the "going concern" under investigation as more of a practical convenience and a logical requisite than as a moral claim.

Not so outside of the academy, and not so with interpretive explanations that can't act as translations because they are not—or not any longer—addressed to outsiders by outsiders, but by insiders to insiders. When someone like C. A. W. Manning addresses an international tribunal, or publishes an article on apartheid in a policy journal like *Foreign Affairs*, all pretext of simply explicating a set of constituent rules for a discrete domain evaporates; the situation switches to one of discernment, and all involved are "insiders" trying to determine how *we, collectively* should "go on." In such a context, to explicate a set of rules is to advocate adopting that set of rules, and to explain how to "go on" in some way is to urge others to "go on" similarly. Outside of the academy there is not even the possibility of regarding statements about appropriate ways of conducting oneself as anything other than attempts at moral suasion, irrespective of what subjective motivations the speaker may have. Weber's admonition that "if you speak about democracy at a public meeting, you do not make a secret of your personal position; on the contrary, you have to take one side or the other explicitly, that is your damned duty and responsibility" (Weber 1994, 14, translation mine)[26] catches up just this difference between the academic and political realms, and Manning's speaking and writing about the apartheid system in political contexts like these can therefore *only* be understood as advocacy.

And this is especially telling in a case where the speaker, on other, more clearly academic occasions, argued that authoritarian leaders were more likely to arise in less "mature" democracies and in countries "of little political experience" precisely because of the absence of settled norms and rules preventing such "unscrupulous" behavior, and wondering why "colonial administration, or as some may still prefer to call it, imperial rule, has not nowadays a sympathetic press," even though (he suggests) it might be in some ways better than the alternatives (Manning 1962,

---

26   The Livingstone translation (Weber 2004, 20), which I generally quite like, has instead: "If you speak about democracy at a public meeting there is no need to make a secret of your personal point of view. On the contrary, you have to take one side or the other explicitly; that is your damned duty."—as though the speaker had a choice about whether their speaking in such a context would "count" as advocacy. Instead, I take Weber's point to be something like: your words are serving as political weapons in that context anyway, so you ought to be explicit about that.

184–85). As *academic* questions, these both might in principle be considered somewhat dispassionately, without thereby functioning as advocacy on behalf of a division of humanity into mature and immature polities.[27] Such a stance requires the institutional protections of the academy to help ensure a division in thought between on one hand an account of how some domain to which we are outsiders is organized and how we ought to act in order to fit into it, and on the other hand practical-moral suasion intended to *organize* ourselves in some distinct way. Blurring that boundary is the mistake here: a category mistake[28] of equating intellectual constructs with valuable social objects, in this case a category mistake made (deliberately?) by Manning himself.

But Manning's sin, for which he is in my view justifiably for the most part expunged from the catalog of founding fathers of the field, should not lead us to disregard the remainder of his analysis, which remains a useful record of how things *were* organized at a particular point in time, and how one ought to act if one wanted to "go on" in that context. An interpretive explanation is necessarily normative within the context it is explaining, but that need not mean that it is ethical in some larger, more globally imperative sense (Adler 2019, 266–67). Explaining how to play chess, or "sovereign states," or colonial-imperial racial hierarchy, can after all just as easily be treated as part of an argument for *not* playing any of those games—an argument that is first and foremost based in a valid account of the game and how to play it. That in Manning's hands it was not should not mean that we are fated, or methodologically compelled, to do likewise. Nor does it mean that the interpretive strain of the English School is methodologically limited to shoring up the present "going concern" of international affairs by treating its rules and practices as sacrosanct. On the contrary, such scholarship can and should go beyond Manning in promoting and provoking ethical reflection on the socially sustained games that it insightfully and competently—interpretively—explains.

---

27 It may not be accidental that both of these are, or come close to being, *causal* questions, of the sort that I have argued that Manning's interpretive approach ought to have nothing to say about. Here we have traces of a second methodological mistake.

28 Or, reification in the strict, narrow sense of Whitehead's "fallacy of misplaced concreteness."

6   Evaluating Claims and Explanations

> In days to come the mountain of the LORD's house shall be established as the highest
> of the mountains and shall be raised above the hills; all the nations shall stream to it.
> Many peoples shall come and say, "Come, let us go up to the mountain of the LORD,
> to the house of the God of Jacob, that he may teach us his ways and that we may walk
> in his paths." For out of Zion shall go forth instruction and the word of the LORD from
> Jerusalem. He shall judge between the nations and shall arbitrate for many peoples;
> they shall beat their swords into plowshares and their spears into pruning hooks;
> nation shall not lift up sword against nation; neither shall they learn war any more. O
> house of Jacob, come, let us walk in the light of the LORD!
>
>   —Isaiah 2:2–5[1]

It may seem odd to open the concluding chapter of a book on facts and explanations
with a prophetic passage from a scriptural text, despite the passage being themat-
ically connected to international affairs and specifically to wars between nations.
Indeed, the connection is more than just thematic; Ralph Bunche Park, located
across the street from the United Nations headquarters building in New York City,
features a wall on which a portion of verse 4 ("they shall beat their swords into
plowshares and their spears into pruning hooks; nation shall not lift up sword
against nation; neither shall they learn war any more") is inscribed, and in 1959 the
Soviet Union gifted a sculpture titled "Let Us Beat Swords into Ploughshares" to
the U.N.[2] So it would appear that what we have here in this passage is some kind
of claim about international affairs, although precisely what kind of claim it is—
descriptive, explanatory, or something else—and whether it should be evaluated as
bearing any connection to facts remains unclear.

    The passage, and indeed the entire book of Isaiah, participates in a prophetic
tradition whereby speakers pronounce judgment on the present by envisioning a
future in which divine justice has been served, typically in the form of "the destruc-
tion of the entire nation as a punishment for its sins" which might or might not be

---

1 This translation is from the New Revised Standard Version Updated Edition, via www.biblegateway.com.
2 "Let Us Beat Swords into Ploughshares | United Nations Gifts" (n.d.)

DOI: 10.4324/9781003455912-6

"avoidable through repentance" (Whybray and Hill 1993). Sometimes, as in this passage, the prophet also presents a vision of a future in which things have been made right, in this case a future in which all of the nations have placed themselves under the authority of "the God of Jacob" and have ceased to quarrel with one another. Understood as a factic description, claims like this are false—competent speakers of the relevant language would not agree that the condition which the prophet is describing is the actual condition facing either the prophet or their audience—but as the claim is set in a future yet to be, we might be tempted to regard it as a fallible factic description of a future state of affairs. While this would be feasible, such a construal would miss the most important aspect of a prophetic claim: that it seeks to alter the course of the present by invoking the future, and thus places itself outside of the boundaries of description, or prediction, factically understood (Rohr and Martos 1987, chap. 4). Isaiah—the narrator of the text, which since the text was revised and redacted over centuries is not by any means a reference to a single historical individual (Becker 2021)—is admonishing the readers of the text to change their present ways and thus to prevent disaster and usher in a better alternative. So while the accounts of the *present* in a prophetic statement might well be treated factically, the epistemic status of the vision of the *future* is somewhat more complicated.[3]

Perhaps, then, we should construe a prophetic claim as a kind of causal explanation, in which listeners are offered a set of instructions for making outcomes happen. Isaiah's indictment of the present is that the Jewish audience being addressed has strayed from the proper worship of the LORD, and that the whole "house of Jacob" should repent and return to the correct path. As such, and regardless of whether we think the audience consists of pre-exilic or post-exilic Jews (Joachimsen 2021), the admonition remains the same:

On that day people will throw away to the moles and to the bats their idols of silver and their idols of gold, which they made for themselves to worship, to enter the caverns of the rocks and the clefts in the crags, from the terror of the LORD and from the glory of his majesty, when he rises to terrify the earth.

In effect, throw away the idols now and perhaps avoid the divine terror that will be inflicted otherwise. And there are benefits too, including the divine arbitration of disputes. So the causal explanation would be something like: the problems of the present, including wars between the nations, are due to a lack of proper subordination to the deity ("the LORD"), and changing our ways now will produce a better future state of affairs.

Like any causal explanation, this set of instructions has factic endpoints together with a logically general causal claim connecting them. The present-day endpoint is the lack of proper subordination to the LORD, which can be treated as a factic

---

3 Antonio Gramsci (1971, 171) suggested that predictions of social outcomes should always be treated this way: not as "elegant conjectures" but as part of "a 'programme' for whose victory" the predictor is working, such that the "prediction is precisely an element contributing to that victory."

description as long as we have shared standards for what proper subordination would look like; the future endpoint is either divine wrath or the absence of war, and here again these might be factic descriptions which could be evaluated at a future time. The general causal claim, which seems to run throughout much of this scriptural text, is that obedience to the LORD produces good outcomes—a fairly straightforward example of a causal claim in imperative or directive form. As long as we accept this general causal claim, we can use it to construct an explanation both for the present state of affairs (war between nations) and for either the future of wrath (if there is not proper subordination) or the future of no war.

The question is whether one *should* accept the general causal claim. In a community of faith centered on the proposition that outcomes are in the hands of a deity whose wrath can be avoided or whose favor can be curried, the question almost never arises. And when it does—say, when believers and nonbelievers alike were slaughtered during the sacking of Rome (Augustine 1984)—the theological response is often to suggest ways that the general causal claim should continue to be accepted alongside the notion that humility is the proper response to a divine will that cannot be reduced to purely human parameters.[4] Sometimes bad things happen to believers; but sometimes good things happen. As long as there is *some* grounding of the causal claim in lived experience—as long as *sometimes* good things happen to believers—then the community can accept the claim even if it comes along with scope conditions that make it less than perfectly reliable in all circumstances. Were the claim *completely* divorced from practical experience, it could not serve as part of a meaningful causal explanation in the first place.

Indeed, no small amount of theological discussion over millennia has been devoted to the question of why any single instance of asking a deity for some boon, or one moment where proper subordination to a deity's rules did not produce a beneficial outcome, should not be grounds to question that events are ultimately in the hands of that deity. These discussions only do not seem to us like ways of talking about the boundaries and character of a general causal claim because we have by and large restricted general causal claims to a very narrow realm of empirical reliability: the 95 percent confidence interval, that commonly accepted measurement of statistical significance that only admits extremely robust correlations and covariations into the cathedral of valid knowledge (Ziliak and McCloskey 2008). Any general claim that falls short of that level of reliability—to say nothing of a general claim that comes with a caveat that it might not hold in any given situation for reasons beyond our mortal understanding—gets rejected, and any explanation using such a claim becomes prima facie invalid.

A good many "new atheist" intellectuals (Hart 2009) suggest that this is *precisely* how we should regard scriptural claims of all kinds: as causal explanations based on hypothetical causal claims that simply do not stand up to an evidence-based evaluation. From here it is a small step to conclude—as vocal critics of

---

4 In the particular faith tradition informing this example, perhaps the clearest statement of the need for humility in the face of an incomprehensibly expansive deity is in the conclusion of the book of Job (chapters 38–41).

religion like Richard Dawkins (2008) often do—that the problem with such causal explanations is that they make reference to unobservable notions (such as a divine being) in the first place, and that no such explanation could *ever* be valid or valuable. Such critics thus subtly shift the terms of the argument away from the question of whether the set of instructions contained in a causal explanation provide a good recipe for making an outcome happen, and towards the question of whether the explanation uses notions that accord with a particular way of apprehending the world: what Max Weber (1994) would call a *disenchanted* world in which valid knowledge is circumscribed by empirical fact on all sides, and everything other than fact is suspect.

As I have argued throughout this book, however, a reduction of all valid knowledge to true factic claims would render the very idea of a valid explanation incoherent. Explanations of whatever type rely not just on facts, but on logically general claims connecting those facts in ways that make possible a set of instructions. We get this confused in an era of "big data" and ever more sophisticated computer algorithms for spotting patterns in that data (Kratochwil 2021). In no small part because ever-increasing computer processing power and the widespread availability of quantitative descriptions make it relatively easy to gather such data and analyze it, we all too easily slip from the description (the *factic* description) of such patterns into the explanation of outcomes. There has also been a profound shift in what level of reliability we expect of a causal explanation and the recipe that it provides; we now expect almost perfect reliability, rejecting chance and happenstance such that Machiavelli's declaration (1994, 74) a mere five centuries ago that fortune controlled about half of the outcome of our actions sounds odd to our ears. Ian Hacking calls this the "taming of chance" (1990), and points out that our tolerance for uncertainty both in our lives and in our public policies is considerably less now than it used to be.

My point is not that we should tolerate more uncertainty and be less insistent that our causal explanations rely on general causal claims that have undergone a severe round of empirical vetting. My point instead is that our preference for causal explanations that aspire to this kind of reliability is not a simple matter of accumulating more facts about the world. It is a more profound change in the way that we relate to the world. Rather than us having "discovered" that no divine authority controls the cosmos, we have instead adopted a way of construing valid knowledge that would *only* have room for such divine authority and control *if* it could be relied on to produce results as efficiently and effectively as, say, the physical principles incorporated into our instructions for baking bread or brewing beer. What Nietzsche (1978) called the "death of god" is less an identifiable event than a replacement of one broad understanding of the world with another (Allan 2018).[5]

---

5 Note that Allan calls all of the broad understandings of the world that he analyzes "cosmologies," despite the ways that our contemporary understanding of the world is in many ways the *opposite* of a "cosmology" in the classical sense of a world that is meaningfully ordered. The disenchanted world we inhabit is, I would say, more like an *anti-cosmology* than a cosmology. But that's an argument for another day and definitely for another book.

To put this another way: as Wittgenstein once pointed out, we should not be too hasty in concluding that a community that celebrates "rites of daybreak" understands such rites as a reliable way to make the sun rise—after all, such rites are celebrated "toward morning, when the sun is about to rise," and not "during the night" when the people "simply burn lamps" (Wittgenstein 1993, 136). *We* read their daybreak actions as causally intended but based on a faulty causal claim about the sun rising, but only because we regard making things happen—the key intention of causal explanation—as requiring relatively decontextualized instructions with a very high degree of reliability. *We* think that a valid causal explanation has to give instructions that when followed produce an outcome as close to all of the time as possible, and that following those instructions has to have an independent effect. So a community celebrating rites of daybreak when the sun is about to rise, like a community praying for the health and healing of someone undergoing a medical procedure, could only *really* be causal if the rites or prayers reliably produced an outcome regardless of what else was going on. Otherwise, the rites and prayers are epiphenomenal to the outcome, and since we have knowledge about sunrises and surgeries that does not involve rites and prayers, these cannot be valid causal explanations of observed outcomes.

When we read claims like this, we have collapsed "sacred" and "temporal" knowledge into one realm, and applied standards of high empirical reliability to issues that might once have been understood as involving faith or tradition rather than guaranteed results. This kind of category confusion results in problematic claims about, for example, relying on prayer *instead of* professional medical practice, or expecting to resist a disease or avoid a natural disaster through *nothing but* willpower. At the same time, the too-hasty declaration that the boundaries of causal knowledge are set by the current state of the art in the scientific community— the kind of declaration that leads to the dismissal of indigenous knowledge of, say, plant cultivation (Kimmerer 2016, 158–60) as something that couldn't possibly be valid because it operates with theories and concepts that are unfamiliar to disenchanted science—compounds the problem, reinforcing the notion that only claims that look like statistically significant empirical generalizations can possibly be valid causal claims.

So if we regard the prophetic claims in the Isaiah passage as advancing a causal explanation rooted in a causal claim about the consequences of proper subordination to the LORD, we can only sensibly do so if we resist the temptation to treat that causal claim as a most-of-the-time-reliable empirical generalization. Or rather, we can only treat the causal claim as if it were such an empirical generalization at the cost of some significant *misunderstanding* of the text. And while there is nothing *logically* preventing us from lifting a claim out of its context and evaluating it in a way different from how it was originally intended, there is perhaps an *ethical* problem in doing so. If we are going to make sense of the passage in context, we have to take seriously the occurrence in the same scriptural compendium of statements like

Forever, O LORD,
Your word stands high in the heavens.

For all generations Your faithfulness.
You made the earth firm and it stood.
By Your laws they stand this day,
for all are Your servants.
(Psalm 119, 89–91[6])

Such a declaration that everything and everyone is *already* under the jurisdiction of the divine law sits oddly alongside the diagnosis in the Isaiah passage that present-day troubles arise from improper subordination to divine law—but the oddity vanishes, or at least strongly recedes, if we understand the causal claim to be something other than an empirical generalization. If instead the causal claim were a statement of confidence in divine power, rooted in experiences of feeling safe and secure in the arms of divinity,[7] then there is little problem in treating the Isaiah passage as a causal explanation. If the notion of divine influence over the outcome of events is part of the common stock of causal claims maintained by a community—maintained because it is validated in experience, even if that experience doesn't fit the strictures of statistical significance—the prophet's admonition makes sense and might be compelling. And as long as we resist the temptation to treat the passage as though it were a causal explanation produced through an exclusive reliance on causal claims understood as empirical generalizations, there is no reason why it can't be *valid* causal explanation.[8]

Now, the obvious objection to this way of reading the passage is surely something like: what *we*—we moderns, we (social) scientists, we educated people[9]— mean by "valid causal explanation" is wrapped up with notions of high reliability that require causal claims to be in some sense empirical generalizations, so a causal explanation that rests on causal claims involving a benevolent divine power that is always in control regardless of what the outcome is in any particular situation can't possibly be anything that we would consider valid. To which I would respond: it can't possibly be valid *according to one sense of validity*, and whether it is valid or not does not make the explanation any more or less a causal explanation. The disagreement here is not over causality, or over the dependence of causal explanations on causal claims. The disagreement is over the character of a valid causal claim, and over whether a particular community's set of definitions and procedures ought

---

6 Translation by Robert Alter (2009).
7 Both Wittgenstein (1965) and James (1902) would likely concur on the importance of this experience to a religious sensibility.
8 Paige Sweet (2020) points out that this is what it means to theorize *from* a social location and a set of experiences.
9 It is in this respect no accident that John Searle (1995, 6) bounds his account of (non-socially constructed) reality by referring to the atomic theory of matter and the evolutionary theory of biology as not "optional for us as citizens of the late twentieth and early twenty-first century" and as conditions of "being an educated person in our era." But like most mind–world dualists, he does not seem to appreciate how such a declaration reveals our standards to be, in the end, *our* standards, and he thus ignores the consequent space for translation across standards that this opens up.

to have priority over others. Certainly it is the case that if we define "causal claim" as a statistically significant empirical generalization, then the causal claims on which the Isaiah passage rests are suspect; if we were to test the general causal claim by ascertaining whether subordination—either to "the God of Jacob" in particular, or more generally to the *same* divinity, defined as adhering to the same religion—was associated with the relevant good outcomes, namely, an absence of war between nations, the empirical evidence (Russett, Oneal, and Cox 2000; Fox 2002) would suggest that it does not.

Treating a causal claim as an empirical generalization answers the question of how to evaluate it by, in effect, converting the causal claim into a factic claim and thus establishing that validity means that the claim cannot be sensibly disagreed with by competent speakers of the relevant language. In that case, a causal claim would be a factically true description of a general empirical pattern, *and nothing else*. But doing this presumes that the generality of a causal claim is empirical generality, when we have seen earlier[10] that the relevant generality for a causal explanation is *logical* generality, which is not necessarily *empirical* generality. The equation of these two kinds of generality is a presumption that we make in some but not all of our knowledge-producing endeavors, and the logical implication of our definitions and procedures is not itself a sufficient argument for preferring our definitions and procedures over others. Just as the candle on my desk can be factually described in different but not contradictory ways depending on the purpose of the description, and just as true factic claims can be made using different vocabularies without those claims somehow collapsing into or being reducible to one another, causal claims need not be exclusively treated as factic descriptions of empirical patterns. Treating a claim as factic is a *choice*, or a hermeneutic *commitment*, and that choice or commitment *itself* has to be justified instead of merely presumed.

So why not regard the Isaiah passage, and by extension any piece of scripture or any explanation rooted in anything but reliable empirical generalizations, as simply not causal, but interpretive: as a guide to what some community *believes* rather than an explanation that might be in any sense valid? While doing so makes our explication of apparent explanations that don't measure up to our standards into something more pedagogical—if you want to "go on" appropriately in that context, you need to profess agreement with this claim—it does so at the cost of foreclosing the position I have been developing throughout this book in favor of either epistemic relativism or the loud assertion that only our way of knowing is actually valid. If meaningful worlds are hermetically sealed such that they can contain "truths" that contradict the "truths" upheld in other meaningful worlds, then we have no alternative to an unending clash in which each side seeks to establish their own set of standards as the definitive ones. And if we instead translate an unfamiliar causal explanation that uses standards of validity for causal claims different from our standards as though it were not actually a causal claim, we are presuming that our present way of living and being in the world is more "in touch

---

10   In Chapters 3 and 4, above.

with reality" than those alternatives. But translating the explanation as causal—albeit as accompanied by a different set of meanings for notions like "general" and "manipulate"—opens up a dialogue.

The ensuing challenge is to have the correct dialogue, and not to fall back into the one-objective-world or the multiple-incommensurable-worlds stances. Suzanne Klein Schaarsberg's (2023, 12) account of "contemplactivists" whose response to world events is to meditate and thus to surface an "'interbeing' in which everything is everything else" illustrates the complexity here. The people she studied and worked with strive for a non-dual awareness within which subject and object simply aren't separate entities, and as such, the distinction between an "internal" change of attitude and an "external" action in the world simply dissolves. As such, nothing that such "contemplactivists" do or believe ought to be regarded as a causal explanation, or ought to be translated into our language as a causal explanation, since what we mean by a causal explanation is all wrapped up with manipulability and a distinct, even if only provisional, externality of knower to known. But Klein Schaarsberg also reports that her interlocutors believe that "this recognition of interconnectedness or interbeing…will create social change," and that a particular group that she studied believed that "their meditation had a broader, calming effect on their surroundings" (ibid., 14). What are we to do with such statements, which look very much like causal explanations that follow the same logic as I have been developing over the past several chapters? We cannot simply relegate them to the realm of "belief" (and thus suspend any question of their validity) without maintaining that only our standards for evaluating causal explanations are correct, and we cannot treat them as explanations to be evaluated according to our standards without committing serious hermeneutic violence and ignoring all of the ways that the community in question is operating with a very different set of assumptions. So instead, we should proceed carefully, interpretively explaining the context within which the explanation makes sense *before* we determine just how to translate it into our terms.

Such care is always a good first step, but it can lead to very different outcomes. When confronted with a causal explanation that seems odd—say, the notion that the sharpness of razor blades is due to their being "kept inside small cardboard pyramids," as "pyramidologists" maintain (Sagan 1997, 221)—it is certainly worthwhile to ask the speaker a bit more about what they mean. Are they suggesting that a general causal claim about the relationship between pyramids and razor-blade sharpness is *valid*, and if so in what sense are they using the word "valid"? If such questioning takes the conversation to a place similar that involving the community of faith implied as the intended readers by the Isaiah text, and if the person advancing that explanation turns out to be operating with very different notions than we are, then simply translating the causal explanation and the causal claim which it utilizes into our terms and evaluating it would be a fraught enterprise.[11] But if such questioning discloses that the speaker *shares* our understanding of causal explanations as involving reliable

11 For Sagan himself, admittedly, this is not fraught at all, since his abundantly clear position is that science deals with reality, and pseudoscience—of which "pyramidology" is an example—is

manipulability (even if "reliable" here means something other than statistically significant—not all of *our* notions of reliability mean this, after all, so we have a variety of possible ways to translate their explanation into our terms), then there is absolutely no problem in evaluating the explanation in those terms to see if it is valid, and in determining that it is not.[12] Just because some community earnestly and vigorously proclaims a causal explanation for something does not suffice to make it a valid explanation, but the latter judgment requires making sure that we have properly translated the explanation. Interpretive explanation, in this sense, necessarily *precedes* causal explanation, unless our way of speaking were somehow the only possible way of speaking—which it clearly is not.

Reading in Context

Leading with interpretive explanation is especially important in our disenchanted world, or in what Charles Taylor (2007) might call a secular age, since we have something of a default interpretive frame through which to read claims and explanations of all sorts. Because a disenchanted world is one of more or less pure immanence, in which anything beyond the tangible and the empirical has been relegated to the realm of the fantastic and can thus for all practical purposes be safely ignored, that default frame is *factic*. A true factic claim relies for its validity only on a practical consensus about definitions and procedures; given a community of competent speakers of the relevant language, there can be no disagreement about a fact, and nothing beyond the community and its descriptive practices needs to be involved.[13] Even when definitions and procedures change—hopefully in a progressive direction (Lakatos 1970)—the resulting set of novel true factic claims is no less immanent than the previous set was, and does not rely on anything beyond the world grasped by the community's descriptive practices.[14] So there is, if not a direct connection, at least a continuity of sensibility between factic claims and a disenchanted world, as both are attempts to do entirely without the transcendent (Bain 2023, 8-10). In such a world, the only sensible way to cash out the "reliability" of a causal explanation is statistically, and there can be no room for faith

nothing but superstition and error. His thinking thus does not even have a space for genuinely different ways of worlding.

12 I challenge any reader to develop a practical explanation in which the sharpness of a razor blade has anything whatsoever to do with whether or not it is stored in a pyramid-shaped container.

13 In many ways this mirrors Bruno Latour's (1987, 23) characterization of facts as "indisputable assertions," but for Latour this is an effect of social arrangements and relations of power rather than a logical consequence of competent language use. As a sociologist of knowledge, Latour is more interested in explaining why no one disagrees; my more philosophy of knowledge approach concentrates instead on establishing the parameters of sensible disagreement, including a clarification of where that cannot happen.

14 Even a scientific realist construal of true factic claims as related to the mind-independent character of the object described must admit that such claims have to be made using the transitive language of our present grasp of reality (Bhaskar 1998). So true factic claims are still reliant on our descriptive practices, even if those practices are themselves related to some mind-independent character of objects.

in a divine power that remains in control or persistently present even if it cannot be manipulated as effectively as mundane worldly factors can be.

The trouble is that not all claims are helpfully understood as factic, if by a helpful understanding we mean something like an earnest effort to grasp the intention of the claim in context. I am not merely referring to claims made in and by communities that are not as enthusiastic about disenchantment and the immanent frame as we are, but also to claims that *we ourselves* make. Aesthetic and ethical claims, certainly, lose something when moved into a factic idiom, as though it were possible to evaluate a claim about the wrongness of murder or the profundity of a musical composition by adducing empirical evidence. In practice, what we do when we make such translations is to subtly shift the claim by redefining words: "wrongness" becomes "people think something is wrong" and "profundity" becomes "people think something is profound," both of which can be measured through survey research techniques. While there is nothing in principle wrong with doing this, we should be clear about what we are doing when we do it: we are converting ethical and aesthetic claims into (factic) descriptions of people's responses to questions. As such we are no longer evaluating the original claims, but their converted analogues: "everyone thinks that murder is wrong" is not the same claim as "murder is wrong," and "virtually no one thinks that Marillion's composition 'This Strange Engine' is profound" is entirely compatible with the only apparently contradictory claim that "Marillion's composition 'This Strange Engine' is profound."

Aesthetic and ethical claims are the comparatively easy cases, even though the persistence of such claims in a disenchanted world poses some tricky questions.[15] The harder case, which I have been developing throughout this book, is that *explanatory claims*—both causal and interpretive—are not factic claims either. Explanations rely on and incorporate facts about specific situations, but they also rely on general principles (causal claims and delineations of rules) that don't really function as factic descriptions. Instead, these general principles provide guides for future action in virtue of their having been lifted and distilled from practical experience; they go *beyond the facts*, and serve as the foundation for future recipes or instructions—explanations—in virtue of their logical generality, or what John Dewey (1920, 150–51) once called the liberating power of abstraction. Explanations, therefore, are inescapably hybrid combinations of factic claims and general principles that, *even if* they are derived from statistically significant generalizations, necessarily contain something non-factic.

In some ways this should not be news to scholars and students in international studies. Almost half a century ago, Kenneth Waltz pointed out in the first chapter of *Theory of International Politics* (1979) that "theories" explain "laws," and by laws Waltz meant empirical generalizations. Theories, in this conception, are the repositories of general causal claims from which we draw to explain specific outcomes,

---

15 Perhaps chief among such questions is: do ethical and aesthetic claims represent some kind of *resistance to disenchantment*, or perhaps some sign that disenchantment is not the whole truth of who we are?

whether those outcomes are general empirical patterns (such as the recurrence of war in the international system) or more localized actions (such as the formation of a countervailing coalition in response to a rising power). Of course, those theories can be equally if not more helpful in constructing explanations of outcomes that *don't* correspond to the general causal claims in question, setting up questions about why a particular actor did *not* respond to systemic pressures in the expected way—questions that can then be answered by examining the situation to ascertain what else combined with those pressures to generate the specific outcome in question (Goddard and Nexon 2005; Wæver 2009). This is theory as ideal-type, causal claims as abstract baselines rather than falsifiable predictions, and explanation as configurational (Weber 1999a; see also Jackson 2017).

So as long as there has been an understanding of causal claims as empirical generalizations in the field, there has been an alternative too—an alternative that doesn't eschew causal explanation, but which understands causal claims differently. This understanding is not in any way unique to international studies, or to the social sciences more broadly. Philosophers of natural science have long agreed with Nancy Cartwright's (1983) argument that if we understand the laws of physics as empirical generalizations, then we have to conclude that those laws *lie*: the core elements of physics are not empirical generalizations as much as they are specifications of causal powers, proclivities, and tendencies that can be variously realized in different contexts (Aronson, Harré, and Way 1995). That in turn makes the task of causal explanation into something quite distinct from the simple and straightforward subsumption of a case to a law, even to a law hemmed in with scope conditions that limit its range of applicability.[16] The point is less that one or the other of these understandings of what a causal claim is and how it should be used in a causal explanation are correct, and more that both remain what William James (1907) might call "live possibilities" and that neither can claim an exclusive monopoly on causal explanation. What is common to both—the logical structure of a causal explanation—is that valid general causal claims have to be combined with true factic descriptions (facts) about specific situations in order to generate a compelling causal explanation. But this structure is indifferent to the question of precisely *how* we validate general causal claims and combine them with facts; that is more a matter for particular communities to work out in practice.

As for interpretive explanations, it is even clearer that they are not factic claims, and that the general claims on which they rely are something quite different from empirical generalizations. Clifford Geertz (2000, 69–70) summarizes a good

---

16   Despite the efforts of some contemporary scholars to distinguish an approach to causal explanation focusing on "inference" from the Hempelian strategy of subsumption under a general law (e.g., Lawler and Waldner 2023), I would argue that there is little philosophical or conceptual difference between an empirical generalization of broad empirical scope and an empirical generalization over a more modest domain—especially as both are used the same way in constructing a causal explanation and making possible the consideration of counterfactual outcomes. Exorcising the ghost of logical positivism requires more than the adoption of more modest empirical claims that still aspire to be something more robustly certain in the progressive future.

deal of the common sense among ethnographers when he argues that the goal of participant-observation is make sense of the "modes of expression" employed by a group of people, and that this is "more like grasping a proverb, catching an allusion, seeing a joke—or, as I have suggested, reading a poem—than it is like achieving communion." Interpretive explanation is thus more about instructing someone in how to act appropriately in context than it is about factically describing anything, just as learning to speak a language is distinct from factically delineating patterns of word use. From interpretive policy analysis (Yanow 1996) to accounts of different conceptions of international order (Spruyt 2020) to interrogations of the character of international law (Kratochwil 2014)—as well as the classic English School approach to the institutions of international society (Bull 1977)—interpretive explanations abound in the field writ large. Although all such explanations feature combinations of general claims (the rules of the game, or other general specifications of what makes sense) and factic descriptions of specific situations, as instructions for "going on" appropriately in context they cannot be reduced to factic claims and cannot be evaluated as though they were descriptions.

Hence, when confronted with a claim, rather than simply assuming that it is intended to be a factic description and evaluating it as such, we have a series of determinations to make:

1) Is the claim a *description*, or an *explanation*, or something else? A description aims to bring an object before us, while an explanation aims to give instructions to someone. And these two categories don't exhaust the kinds of possible claims, so we need to remain open to the possibility that the claim in question isn't either of these, but might be an ethical or an aesthetic claim or perhaps something else that I haven't discussed here.

2) If the claim is a description, is it *factic* description, i.e., a description that intends to be one with which competent speakers of the relevant language cannot sensibly disagree? A description might, after all, be poetic or humorous any number of other things. But if it is a factic description, then evaluating the claim means using words in the appropriate way, and perhaps translating the claim into our own language in order to do so. If a descriptive claim can be translated, then its truth or falsity is a relatively straightforward determination in our language; if a descriptive claim can't be translated into our language, then it can only be evaluated in its own language. Factic descriptions that are true in one language cannot be false in another unless something has gone wrong in the translation, and apparent contradictions between descriptive claims are either the result of mistakes or are a sign of complementarity.

3) If the claim is an explanation, is it a causal explanation or an interpretive explanation, or is it something else? Causal and interpretive explanations, at least, have a similar logical structure, combining factic descriptions of specific situations with general claims that in important ways go beyond the facts and hence support the consideration of counterfactual outcomes and courses of action. But they differ considerably based on their intention: causal explanations aim to give someone the capacity to make something happen, while interpretive

explanations aim to give someone the capacity to "go on" appropriately in context. And while it is always appropriate to subject the factic parts of a causal or an interpretive explanation to the same kind of scrutiny as we would apply to any other factic description, it remains an open question whether to treat the general claims involved in the explanation as though they too were factic descriptions. Indeed, this may only be appropriate for certain kinds of causal explanation, and rarely if ever appropriate for any kind of interpretive explanation.

Remembering that we already have these various categories and classifications available to us in our intellectual tradition means that we are not actually fated to shove every claim we encounter into just one box. To the contrary, we have *options*, and an intellectual task: to figure out what someone else is saying, and to do so in a way that begins with an acknowledgment of the diversity of intentions that might animate a claim. Once a determination is made, there are a series of logical implications about how to proceed with evaluating the claim that proceed from that determination: if we understand a claim to be a factic description, we need to subject it to the ordinary rules of competent language use, and if we understand a claim to be an explanation, we need to ascertain whether it succeeds in giving the recipient the practical capacity at which it aims. All of these types of evaluation depend on community deliberation, insofar as the ordinary rules of competent language use—no less than the precise operational definition of a word like "succeeds"—depend on the concrete practices in which we are involved. But the major moment of discretion comes at the outset, when we first determine what kind of claim is being made and what its intention is.

As such, it is entirely correct to say that interpretive explanation has a certain philosophical *priority* over causal explanation and even over factic description. We have to make sense of a claim before we can do anything with it, after all, and that process of making sense is precisely what interpretive explanation is all about. My interpretation of a claim, just like my interpretation of an object or a phenomenon—my *reading* of that claim, so to speak—is, practically speaking, an explanation offered for how you ought to read and understand the claim. If I am outside of the relevant community whose rules I am drawing on to produce my reading, and you are also outside of it, the resulting reading is about how *they* understand the claim, and that brackets the question of validity or indeed of the evaluation of the claim per se, in favor of an assessment of whether my reading has in some sense "gotten it right" and allowed you to go on appropriately in that community in the future. My insider reading offered to you, an outsider, socializes you and teaches you how to be a part of the community; my outsider reading offered to you, an insider, might clarify your practices in helpful ways. And my insider reading offered to you, a fellow insider and a member of the same community, is part of an ongoing deliberative process whereby we collectively determine how we ought to go on and how we ought to understand the claim.

What I have aimed to do throughout this book is to elucidate a conceptual language that can preserve the diversity of intentions animating the kinds of claims that people make about objects and phenomena in the world, but also avoid the spurious relativism or the brash assertion of superiority that is all too often hastily invoked as a response to that diversity. The diversity of intentions that can animate claims does not mean that the validity of any particular claim is a matter of arbitrary subjective opinion, any more than the meaning of a word is a matter of purely personal preference. Just as there are no such things as private languages (Wittgenstein 1958, secs. 244–315), there are no such things as factic descriptive claims and fact-incorporating explanatory claims whose validity depends purely on personal opinion. While that in no way means that true factic claims are somehow transhistorically valid, it does mean that such claims depend for their validity on a community of practice that is larger than the individual speaker. It also means that valid fact-incorporating explanations depend on a community that can both ascertain the truth of the factic claims involved and determine whether the resulting instructions produce the correct capacity for future action. Facts, and fact-incorporating explanations, are thus shown to be community-dependent without being reduced to the arbitrary declarations of that community, or of anyone within it.

In this light, the problem with which the book began—the problem of so-called "alternative facts"—is dissolved by the conceptual vocabulary I have developed here. To understand some claim as factic is to usher in a set of procedures for evaluating that claim that involve careful definitions of terms and the careful and methodical collection of appropriate information. None of those definitions or procedures involve *wanting* the claim to be factually true, let alone *pretending* that the claim is factually true because if it were true it would confer advantages to one's preferred position—and pretending through a kind of "scientization" (Dixit 2022, 65) that makes a claim superficially *appear* to be well-supported by evidence. Counterfeit facts arise from our collective forgetting that factic claims bring certain obligations along with them, first among those being an obligation to be clear in how words are used, and not to use words in ways that the audience understands in different ways without pausing to work out the discrepancy. So if we are, as we should be, worried about large numbers of people bandying about counterfeit facts as though they were genuine facts, what we should do is to *enforce those obligations*. The first step in doing so is to be clear as to what those obligations are, and the vocabulary I have developed throughout this book is, I hope, a contribution to doing just this.

This may not be enough. Clarity about obligations and the logical entailments of particular kinds of claims can only help if we share a commitment to remaining in community and collectively working out standards of competent linguistic practice. It is all too easy to respond to the difficulties of doing so by defecting, and forming a separate community in which a different set of standards reigns: by cutting cables to assemble our own teams, so to speak. Although this doesn't actually succeed in producing a separate and inconsistent set of facts and fact-incorporating explanations, when combined with a relaxation of the standards implicitly invoked when a factic or fact-incorporating explanatory claim is advanced, and when reinforced by the kind of media echo chambers characteristic of our present predicament, it can certainly postpone the reckoning and allow a counterfeit fact to remain in circulation instead of being simply discarded. So what we need is both clarity and commitment. Logical and conceptual elaboration can really only generate the former—but at least it can, perhaps, do that. And if nothing else it can highlight the need for the latter, even if it cannot itself produce that commitment. But maybe, just maybe, being aware of the need can inspire a revitalizing of the commitment in practice to being in community, which is ultimately where such a commitment has to be actualized in any event.

Postscript

The effort to lock down the interpretation of a piece of text by appending yet more text to the beginning and the end of that text is, perhaps, foredoomed to failure. Nevertheless I am called to make the attempt. "Do, or do not; there is no try"—certainly, but also: "there's a divinity that shapes our ends, rough-hew them though we will."

Part of why this book has taken so long for me to complete is that I did *not* want to write a book called *Postfoundational Pragmatism and International Studies: Towards a New Notion of Knowledge*. That book—traces of which undoubtedly remain, especially in the middle chapters of this one—would have been concerned to sketch out a definite position within existing academic debates, and would have proceeded through a series of detailed engagements with other programmatic statements in the field, together with a defense of that position vis-à-vis those alternatives. Rather than participating in the "rock 'n' roller cola wars" (Joel 1989) of intra-academic debate and the fractal dynamics they co-constitute (Abbott 2001), I decided early on—inspired by Wittgenstein, Dewey, Weber, and, behind them, Nietzsche—to proceed instead by developing a series of examples and drawing out the logic of inquiry tacitly informing them already. My aim throughout was and is to achieve a measure of clarity, and not merely to add one more "contribution" to a field already overstuffed with them.

I have also worked to develop a set of concepts that will be useful for thinking across, or outside of, the various intellectual camps that structure our everyday academic discussions. The definition of a fact as a descriptive claim with which competent speakers of the relevant language cannot sensibly disagree is, I would say, equally compatible with a mind-world dualist *and* a mind-world monist (as in Jackson 2016) philosophical ontology; it's just that a dualist and a monist would disagree on whether that absence of sensible disagreement is ultimately rooted in factors external or internal to social and linguistic practice. "Alternative facts" as a concept does not, in my view, go far enough in making sense of why all sides of such a disagreement regard their own "facts" as *actual* facts while denigrating their opponent's "facts" as deluded misconstruals; hence, "counterfeit facts," which I would say does go far enough. The notion of a "factic" claim reinforces the account of both how counterfeit facts work (by borrowing the value invested

DOI: 10.4324/9781003455912-7

in facts in our disenchanted world) and why each side of a dispute works to establish apparent "facts" that reinforce their own position. The practical character of explanation, and the difference between the generation of specific explanations and the evaluation of the general claims that support such explanations, is nothing that either neopositivists or "interpretivists" ought to object to—after all, both Hempel and Geertz (to reference a "classic" author in each tradition) maintained this distinction, and the very idea of a "general explanation" in either a causal or an interpretive sense is, I have endeavored here to demonstrate, ambiguous at best, and logically incoherent at worst.

So a significant part of what I hope that readers take away from this book is this conceptual vocabulary. As an exercise in methodology and not in theory, this vocabulary is intended to prevent us from confusing theoretical claims—*any* theoretical claims, in *any* idiom or *any* tradition—with factic descriptions. The (logical) consequence is that theoretical claims are to be understood instead for their *explanatory* value: as scientific ontology (as in Jackson and Nexon 2013). Doing so has implications for how we might go about building or constructing theory, and what it means to "theorize" something. For instance: the common piece of advice handed to students starting to develop a proposal—to take a case in which they are interested and ask, "Of what is this an instance?"—tacitly presupposes that theory is in some fundamental sense descriptive rather than explanatory, and it might therefore be better to start by asking, "What might explain this?" I am leaving those implications mainly as matters for the reader to ponder, although it should be apparent from the way I have presented the argument throughout this book that I would urge that explanation be central to those activities.

The other thing I hope that readers will take away from this book is the importance of beginning with the possibility that a speaker making a claim that seems odd or bizarre might be operating with a different set of commitments and presuppositions than we are—but not using that as an excuse to refuse to question or to engage. We should assume that our interlocutors are speaking a language instead of merely making sounds, and we should assume that their language might not be ours. Then as we look for points of contact and overlap, as well of points of difference, we will put ourselves in the best position to figure out whether what they are saying is correct or incorrect, or whether it is instead complementary to what we would say. This will, I hope, also sensitize us to counterfeit facts and the kind of explanations built out of them, since it is always in order to analyze the logic of a claim and to interrogate its validity. Doing so is more challenging than simply imposing our own terms and standards, and requires more courage than simply "agreeing to disagree" which is precisely what we *cannot* do with factic claims and fact-incorporating explanations. *Engagement*, rather than dismissal or dogmatism, requires much more effort. But this kind of ongoing contentious conversational connection, however tenuous, is perhaps the only thing that has a chance of healing this fractured world.

References

Aalberts, Tanja E. 2010. "Playing the Game of Sovereign States: Charles Manning's Constructivism Avant-La-Lettre." *European Journal of International Relations* 16 (2): 247–68. https://doi.org/10.1177/1354066109343986.

Abbott, Andrew. 1988. "Transcending General Linear Reality." *Sociological Theory* 6 (2): 169–86.

———. 1992. "What Do Cases Do? Some Notes on Activity in Sociological Analysis." In *What Is a Case?*, edited by Charles C. Ragin and Howard S. Becker, 53–82. Cambridge: Cambridge University Press.

———. 2001. *Chaos of Disciplines*. Chicago: University of Chicago Press.

———. 2001. *Time Matters: On Theory and Method*. Chicago: University of Chicago Press.

Achinstein, Peter. 1985. *The Nature of Explanation*. New York: Oxford University Press.

———. 2010a. "Can There Be a Model of Explanation?" In *Evidence, Explanation, and Realism: Essays in Philosophy of Science*, 143–67. Oxford; New York: Oxford University Press.

———. 2010b. *Evidence, Explanation, and Realism: Essays in Philosophy of Science*. Oxford; New York: Oxford University Press.

Ackerman, Gary A., and Michael Burnham. 2019. "Towards a Definition of Terrorist Ideology." *Terrorism and Political Violence* 33 (6): 1160–90. https://doi.org/10.1080/09546553.2019.1599862.

Adler, Emanuel. 2019. *World Ordering: A Social Theory of Cognitive Evolution*. Cambridge Studies in International Relations. Cambridge: Cambridge University Press.

Adler, Emanuel, and Michael Barnett. 1998. "A Framework for the Study of Security Communities." In *Security Communities*, edited by Emanuel Adler and Michael Barnett, 29–65. Cambridge: Cambridge University Press.

Adler, Emanuel, and Vincent Pouliot, eds. 2011. *International Practices*. Cambridge: Cambridge University Press.

Agius, Christine, Annika Bergman Rosamond, and Catarina Kinnvall. 2020. "Populism, Ontological Insecurity and Gendered Nationalism: Masculinity, Climate Denial and Covid-19." *Politics, Religion & Ideology* 21 (4): 432–50. https://doi.org/10.1080/21567689.2020.1851871.

Allan, Bentley B. 2018. *Scientific Cosmology and International Orders*. Cambridge Studies in International Relations. Cambridge: Cambridge University Press. https://doi.org/10.1017/9781108241540.

Alter, Robert, trans. 2009. *The Book of Psalms: A Translation with Commentary*. New York: W. W. Norton & Company.

Anderson, Abigail, Sophia Chilczuk, Kaylie Nelson, Roxanne Ruther, and Cara Wall-Scheffler. 2023. "The Myth of Man the Hunter: Women's Contribution to the Hunt across Ethnographic Contexts." *PLOS ONE* 18 (6): e0287101. https://doi.org/10.1371/journal.pone.0287101.

Anscombe, G. E. M. 1963. *Intention*. 2nd ed. Cambridge, MA: Harvard University Press.

———. 1993. "Causality and Determination." In *Causation*, edited by Ernest Sosa and Michael Tooley, 88–104. Oxford; New York: Oxford University Press.

Aronson, Jerry L., Rom Harré, and Eileen C. Way. 1995. *Realism Rescued: How Scientific Progress Is Possible*. Chicago: Open Court.

Augustine. 1984. *Concerning the City of God Against the Pagans*. New York: Penguin Classics.

Autesserre, Séverine. 2014. *Peaceland: Conflict Resolution and the Everyday Politics of International Intervention*. Cambridge: Cambridge University Press.

Bain, William. 2023. "Political Theology and International Relations: From History to Emancipation." *International Studies Quarterly* 67 (4): 1–10. https://doi.org/10.1093/isq/sqad097.

Balcetis, Emily, and David Dunning. 2006. "See What You Want to See: Motivational Influences on Visual Perception." *Journal of Personality and Social Psychology* 91 (4): 612–25.

Barad, Karen. 2007. *Meeting the Universe Halfway: Quantum Physics and the Entanglement of Matter and Meaning*. Durham, NC: Duke University Press.

Barnett, Michael, and Martha Finnemore. 2004. *Rules for the World: International Organizations in Global Politics*. Ithaca, N.Y.: Cornell University Press.

Beach, Derek, and Rasmus Brun Pedersen. 2013. *Process-Tracing Methods: Foundations and Guidelines*. Ann Arbor, MI: University of Michigan Press.

Beauvoir, Simone de. 2011. *The Second Sex*. Translated by Constance Borde and Sheila Malovany-Chevallier. 1st edition. New York: Vintage.

Becker, Uwe. 2021. "The Book of Isaiah: Its Composition History." In *The Oxford Handbook of Isaiah*, edited by Lena-Sofia Tiemeyer, 37–56. Oxford University Press. https://doi.org/10.1093/oxfordhb/9780190669249.013.2.

Ben-Menahem, Yemima. 1998. "Explanation and Description: Wittgenstein on Convention." *Synthese* 115 (1): 99–130. https://doi.org/10.1023/A:1005016201213.

Bennett, Andrew, and Jeffrey T. Checkel, eds. 2014. *Process Tracing: From Metaphor to Analytic Tool*. Strategies for Social Inquiry. Cambridge: Cambridge University Press. https://doi.org/10.1017/CBO9781139858472.

Bernstein, Richard J. 1978. *The Restructuring of Social and Political Theory*. Philadelphia: University of Pennsylvania Press.

———. 1983. *Beyond Objectivism and Relativism: Science, Hermeneutics, and Praxis*. Philadelphia: University of Pennsylvania Press.

Bevir, Mark, and Asaf Kedar. 2008. "Concept Formation in Political Science: An Anti-Naturalist Critique of Qualitative Methodology." *Perspectives on Politics* 6 (03): 503–17. https://doi.org/10.1017/S1537592708081255.

Bhaskar, Roy. 1975. *A Realist Theory of Science*. London: Verso.

Bhaskar, Roy. 1998. *The Possibility of Naturalism*. London: Routledge.

Blake, Aaron. 2017. "Kellyanne Conway Says Donald Trump's Team Has 'Alternative Facts.' Which Pretty Much Says It All." *Washington Post*. January 22. https://www.washingtonpost.com/news/the-fix/wp/2017/01/22/kellyanne-conway-says-donald-trumps-team-has-alternate-facts-which-pretty-much-says-it-all/.

Boghossian, Paul. 2007. *Fear of Knowledge: Against Relativism and Constructivism.* Oxford: Oxford University Press.

Bogost, Ian. 2012. *Alien Phenomenology, or What It's Like to Be a Thing.* Minneapolis, MN: University of Minnesota Press.

Brennan, Jason, and Philip Magness. 2019. *Cracks in the Ivory Tower: The Moral Mess of Higher Education.* New York: Oxford University Press.

Broz, J. Lawrence, and Seth H. Werfel. 2014. "Exchange Rates and Industry Demands for Trade Protection." *International Organization* 68 (02): 393–416. https://doi.org/10.1017/S002081831300043X.

Buber, Martin. 1971. *I and Thou.* Translated by Walter Kaufmann. New York: Touchstone.

Bull, Hedley. 1977. *The Anarchical Society.* New York: Columbia University Press.

Bump, Philip. 2016. "Donald Trump Will Be President Thanks to 80,000 People in Three States." Washington Post. December 1. https://www.washingtonpost.com/news/the-fix/wp/2016/12/01/donald-trump-will-be-president-thanks-to-80000-people-in-three-states/.

Bush, George W. 2005. "President Bush's Second Inaugural Address." NPR.Org. 2005. http://www.npr.org/templates/story/story.php?storyId=4460172.

Butler, Judith. 1999. *Gender Trouble: Feminism and the Subversion of Identity.* New York: Routledge.

Buzan, Barry R., Charles O. Jones, and Richard Little. 1993. *The Logic of Anarchy.* New York: Columbia University Press.

Carnap, Rudolf. 2012. *The Unity of Science.* Reissue. London: Routledge.

Cartwright, Nancy. 1983. *How the Laws of Physics Lie.* Oxford; New York: Oxford University Press.

———. 2007. *Hunting Causes and Using Them: Approaches in Philosophy and Economics.* Cambridge; New York: Cambridge University Press.

Carus, A. W. 2010. *Carnap and Twentieth-Century Thought: Explication as Enlightenment.* Cambridge: Cambridge University Press.

Chenoweth, Erica, and Maria Stephan. 2011. *Why Civil Resistance Works: The Strategic Logic of Nonviolent Conflict.* New York: Columbia University Press.

Chernoff, Fred. 2014. *Explanation and Progress in Security Studies: Bridging Theoretical Divides in International Relations.* Stanford, CA: Stanford University Press.

Cillizza, Chris. 2017. "Sean Spicer Held a Press Conference. He Didn't Take Questions. Or Tell the Whole Truth." *Washington Post.* January 21. https://www.washingtonpost.com/news/the-fix/wp/2017/01/21/sean-spicer-held-a-press-conference-he-didnt-take-questions-or-tell-the-whole-truth/.

Comas, Jordi, Paul Shrivastava, and Eric C. Martin. 2015. "Terrorism as Formal Organization, Network, and Social Movement." *Journal of Management Inquiry* 24 (1): 47–60. https://doi.org/10.1177/1056492614538486.

Dauphinee, Elizabeth. 2013. *The Politics of Exile.* Reprint edition. New York: Routledge.

Davies, Sara E., and Sophie Harmon. 2024. "WHO and COVID-19: Stress-Testing the Boundary of Science and Politics." *International Relations* online first. https://doi.org/10.1177/00471178241248548

Dawkins, Richard. 2008. *The God Delusion.* New York: Mariner Books.

Demetriou, Chares. 2009. "The Realist Approach to Explanatory Mechanisms in Social Science: More than a Heuristic?" *Philosophy of the Social Sciences* 39 (3): 440–62.

Descartes, René. 1993. *Discourse on Method and Meditations on First Philosophy.* Translated by Donald Cress. 3rd ed. Indianapolis, IN: Hackett Press.

Deudney, Daniel, and G John Ikenberry. 2018. "Liberal World." *Foreign Affairs* 97(4): 16-24.

Deutsch, Karl W. 1957. *Political Community and the North Atlantic Area: International Organization in the Light of Historical Experience.* Princeton, N.J.: Princeton University Press.

Dewey, John. 1910. *How We Think*. Mineola, N.Y.: Dover Publications.

———. 1920. *Reconstruction in Philosophy*. New York: Kessinger Publishing.

———. 1985. *How We Think, Revised Edition*. Electronic Edition. The Later Works of John Dewey, 1925–1953, Volume 8, 1933. Carbondale and Edwardsville, IL: Southern Illinois University Press.

———. 1999. *Individualism Old and New*. Amherst, N.Y.: Prometheus Books.

———. 2007. *Essays in Experimental Logic*. Edited by D. Micah Hester and Robert B Talisse. Carbondale, IL: Southern Illinois University Press.

Dixit, Priya. 2016. "Securitization and Terroristization: Analyzing States' Usage of the Rhetoric of Terrorism." In *State Terror, State Violence. Staat – Souveränität – Nation*, edited by Bettina Koch, 31–50. Wiesbaden: Springer. https://link.springer.com/chapter/10.1007/978-3-658-11181-6_3.

———. 2022. *Popular Culture, and Far-right Extremism in the United States*. Basingstoke: Palgrave Macmillan.

Dray, William H. 2000. "Explanation in History." In *Science, Explanation, and Rationality: The Philosophy of Carl G. Hempel*, edited by James H. Fetzer, 217–42. Oxford; New York: Oxford University Press.

Druckman, James N. 2001. "Evaluating Framing Effects." *Journal of Economic Psychology* 22 (1): 91–101. https://doi.org/10.1016/S0167-4870(00)00032-5.

Dunne, Tim. 1998. *Inventing International Society: A History of the English School*. London: Palgrave Macmillan.

Elman, Colin, and Miriam Fendus Elman, eds. 2003. *Progress in International Relations Theory: Appraising the Field*. Cambridge, MA: MIT Press.

Fabian, J. 1983. *Time and the Other: How Anthropology Makes Its Object*. New York: Columbia University Press.

FairVote.org. 2016. "Faithless Electors Fizzle, But Leave Uncertainty." FairVote. December 21. https://www.fairvote.org/faithless_electors_fizzle.

FairVote.org. 2019. "Faithless Electors." 2019. https://www.fairvote.org/faithless_electors.

Fetzer, James H. 2000. "The Paradoxes of Hempelian Explanation." In *Science, Explanation, and Rationality: The Philosophy of Carl G. Hempel*, edited by James H. Fetzer, 111–37. Oxford; New York: Oxford University Press.

Feyerabend, Paul. 1993. *Against Method*. 3rd ed. London: Verso.

Finnemore, Martha. 1996. *National Interests in International Society*. Ithaca, N.Y.: Cornell University Press.

Foucault, Michel. 1980. *Herculine Barbin*. New York: Random House.

Fox, Jonathan. 2002. "Ethnic Minorities and the Clash of Civilizations: A Quantitative Analysis of Huntington's Thesis." *British Journal of Political Science* 32 (3): 415–34.

Frostenson, Sarah. 2017. "A Crowd Scientist Says Trump's Inauguration Attendance Was Pretty Average." Vox. January 24. https://www.vox.com/policy-and-politics/2017/1/24/14354036/crowds-presidential-inaugurations-trump-average.

Galison, Peter. 1990. "Aufbau/Bauhaus: Logical Positivism and Architectural Modernism." *Critical Inquiry* 16 (4): 709–52.

Geertz, Clifford. 1973. *The Interpretation of Cultures*. New York: Basic Books.

———. 2000. *Local Knowledge: Further Essays in Interpretive Anthropology*. New York: Basic Books.

George, Alexander L., and Andrew Bennett, eds. 2005. *Case Studies and Theory Development in the Social Sciences*. Cambridge, MA: MIT Press.

Gerlach, Phillip. 2017. "The Games Economists Play: Why Economics Students Behave More Selfishly than Other Students." *PLOS ONE*. https://doi.org/10.1371/journal.pone.0183814.

Gerring, John. 2005. "Causation: A Unified Framework for the Social Sciences." *Journal of Theoretical Politics* 17 (2): 163–98. https://doi.org/10.1177/0951629805050859.

———. 2012. *Social Science Methodology: A Unified Framework*. Cambridge; New York: Cambridge University Press.

Ghebreyesus, Tedros Adhanom. 2020. "WHO Director-General's Opening Remarks at the Media Briefing on COVID-19 – 11 March 2020." 2020. https://www.who.int/direc tor-general/speeches/detail/who-director-general-s-opening-remarks-at-the-media-brief ing-on-covid-19---11-march-2020.

Giddens, Anthony. 1984. *The Constitution of Society*. Berkeley, CA: University of California Press.

Gifford, Don. 1991. *The Farther Shore: A Natural History of Perception, 1798–1984*. New York: Vintage.

Goddard, Stacie E., and Daniel H. Nexon. 2005. "Paradigm Lost? Reassessing Theory of International Politics." *European Journal of International Relations* 11 (1): 9–61.

Goetze, Catherine. 2017. *The Distinction of Peace: A Social Analysis of Peacebuilding*. Ann Arbor, MI: University of Michigan Press. https://doi.org/10.3998/mpub.7484138.

Goffman, Erving. 1990. *Asylums: Essays on the Social Situation of Mental Patients and Other Inmates*. New York: Anchor Books.

Goldenberg, Julieta, and Rogers Brubaker. 2024. "Emerging Pronoun Practices After the Procedural Turn: Disclosure, Discovery, and Repair." *Sociological Science* 11 (March): 91–113. https://doi.org/10.15195/v11.a4.

Goldstein, Joel K. 2016. "One of the Smallest Electoral College Victories." *Huffington Post* (blog). December 13. https://www.huffingtonpost.com/entry/one-of-the-smallest-electo ral-college-victories_us_5850168fe4b0151082221eea.

Goldstein, Judith, and Robert Gulotty. 2014. "America and Trade Liberalization: The Limits of Institutional Reform." *International Organization* 68 (02): 263–95. https://doi.org/ 10.1017/S0020818313000490.

Gramsci, Antonio. 1971. *Selections from the Prison Notebooks*. New York: International Publishers.

Greenblatt, Stephen Jay. 2007. *Learning to Curse: Essays in Early Modern Culture*. New York: Routledge.

Grynaviski, Eric. 2013. "Contrasts, Counterfactuals, and Causes." *European Journal of International Relations* 19 (4): 823–46. https://doi.org/10.1177/1354066111428971.

Guido, Maria. 2017. "'Alternative Facts' Get the Meme Treatment They Deserve." Scary Mommy (blog). January 23, 2017. https://www.scarymommy.com/alternative-facts-get- the-meme-treatment-they-deserve/.

Guzzini, Stefano. 2011. "Securitization as a Causal Mechanism." *Security Dialogue* 42 (4–5): 329–41. https://doi.org/10.1177/0967010611419000.

Hacking, Ian. 1990. *The Taming of Chance*. Ideas in Context. Cambridge: Cambridge University Press. https://doi.org/10.1017/CBO9780511819766.

Hacking, Ian. 2014. *Why Is There Philosophy of Mathematics at All?* Cambridge: Cambridge University Press. https://doi.org/10.1017/CBO9781107279346.

Hall, Ian. 2015. "Interpreting Diplomacy: The Approach of the Early English School." In *System, Society, and the World*, edited by Robert W. Murray, Second, 34–39. Bristol: E-International Relations. http://www.e-ir.info/2015/12/05/edited-collection-system-soci ety-and-the-world-exploring-the-english-school/.

Hamati-Ataya, Inanna. 2018. "The 'Vocation' Redux: A Post-Weberian Perspective from the Sociology of Knowledge." *Current Sociology*, February, 0011392118756472. https://doi. org/10.1177/0011392118756472.

Hansen-Magnusson, Hannes, and Antje Vetterlein, eds. 2023. *The Routledge Handbook on Responsibility in International Relations*. 1st ed. Abingdon: Routledge.

Hanzlick, Randy, ed. 1997. "Cause-of-Death Statements and Certification of Natural and Unnatural Deaths." College of American Pathologists.

Hanzlick, Randy, John C. Hunsacker III, and Gregory Davis. 2002. "A Guide for Manner of Death Classification." National Association of Medical Examiners.

Haraway, Donna. 1990. *Simians, Cyborgs, and Women: The Reinvention of Nature.* New York: Routledge.

Harré, Rom, and Edward H. Madden. 1975. *Causal Powers: A Theory of Natural Necessity.* London: Blackwell Publishers.

Hart, David Bentley. 2009. *Athiest Delusions: The Christian Revolution and Its Fashionable Enemies.* New Haven, CT: Yale University Press.

Hausman, Daniel, and James Woodward. 1999. "Independence, Invariance and the Causal Markov Condition." *The British Journal for the Philosophy of Science* 50 (4): 521–83. https://doi.org/10.1093/bjps/50.4.521.

Heidegger, Martin. 1927. *Being and Time.* San Francisco, CA: HarperCollins.

Hempel, Carl G. 1942. "The Function of General Laws in History." *The Journal of Philosophy* 39 (2): 35–48.

———. 1965. "The Function of General Laws in History." In *Aspects of Scientific Explanation and Other Essays*, 231–44. New York: Free Press.

———. 2001. *The Philosophy of Carl G. Hempel: Studies in Science, Explanation, and Rationality.* Edited by James H. Fetzer. Oxford; New York: Oxford University Press.

Hickman, Larry A., Stefan Neubert, and Kersten Reich, eds. 2009. *John Dewey between Pragmatism and Constructivism (American Philosophy.* 3rd ed. New York: Fordham University Press.

Hobbes, Thomas. 1651. *Leviathan.* New York: W. W. Norton.

Hofferberth, Matthias, and Christian Weber. 2015. "Lost in Translation: A Critique of Constructivist Norm Research." *Journal of International Relations and Development* 18 (1): 75–103. https://doi.org/10.1057/jird.2014.1.

Hoffman, Bruce. 2006. *Inside Terrorism.* Revised and expanded. New York: Columbia University Press.

Holland, Paul W. 1986. "Statistics and Causal Inference." *Journal of the American Statistical Association* 81 (396): 945–60. https://doi.org/10.2307/2289064.

Horowitz, Alexandra. 2010. *Inside of a Dog: What Dogs See, Smell, and Know.* New York: Scribner.

Huelss, Hendrik. 2017. "After Decision-Making: The Operationalization of Norms in International Relations." *International Theory* 9 (3): 381–409.

Hyde, Susan D., and Nikolay Marinov. 2014. "Information and Self-Enforcing Democracy: The Role of International Election Observation." *International Organization* 68 (02): 329–59. https://doi.org/10.1017/S0020818313000465.

Illari, Phyllis. 2011. "Mechanistic Evidence: Disambiguating the Russo–Williamson Thesis." *International Studies in the Philosophy of Science* 25 (2): 139–57. https://doi.org/10.1080/02698595.2011.574856.

Inayatullah, Naeem, and David L. Blaney. 1996. "Knowing Encounters: Beyond Parochialism in International Relations Theory." In *The Return of Culture and Identity in IR Theory*, edited by Yosef Lapid and Friedrich Kratochwil, 65–84. Boulder, CO: Lynne Rienner.

International Olympic Committee. 2021. "Omega Debuts New Technologies at London 2012 – Olympic News." International Olympic Committee. July 13, 2021. https://olympics.com/ioc/news/omega-debuts-new-technologies-at-london-2012.

Ish-Shalom, Piki. 2008. "Theorization, Harm, and the Democratic Imperative: Lessons from the Politicization of the Democratic-Peace Thesis." *International Studies Review* 10 (4): 680–92. https://doi.org/10.1111/j.1468-2486.2008.00825.x.

Jackson, Patrick Thaddeus. 2006. *Civilizing the Enemy: German Reconstruction and the Invention of the West*. Ann Arbor, MI: University of Michigan Press.

———. 2016. *The Conduct of Inquiry in International Relations*. 2nd ed. London: Routledge.

———. 2017a. "Causal Claims and Causal Explanation in International Studies." *Journal of International Relations and Development* 20: 689–716. https://doi.org/10.1057/jird.2016.13.

———. 2017b. "The Production of Facts: Ideal-Typification and the Preservation of Politics." In *Max Weber and International Relations*, edited by Richard Ned Lebow, 79–96. Cambridge: Cambridge University Press. https://doi.org/10.1017/9781108236461.004.

Jackson, Patrick Thaddeus, and Daniel H. Nexon. 2009. "Paradigmatic Faults in International-Relations Theory." *International Studies Quarterly* 53 (4): 907–30.

———. 2013. "International Theory in a Post-Paradigmatic Era: From Substantive Wagers to Scientific Ontologies." *European Journal of International Relations* 19 (3): 543–65. https://doi.org/10.1177/1354066113495482.

Jackson, Robert. 2003. *The Global Covenant: Human Conduct in a World of States*. New York: Oxford University Press.

James, William. 1902. *The Varieties of Religious Experience: A Study in Human Nature*. Centenary Edition. London: Routledge.

———. 1907. *Pragmatism: A New Name for Some Old Ways of Thinking*. Heritage Illustrated Publishing.

Joachimsen, Kristin. 2021. "The Book of Isaiah: Persian/Hellenistic Background." In *The Oxford Handbook of Isaiah*, edited by Lena-Sofia Tiemeyer, 176–97. Oxford: Oxford University Press. https://doi.org/10.1093/oxfordhb/9780190669249.013.11.

Joel, Billy. 1989. *We Didn't Start The Fire*. New York: Columbia Records.

Kaczmarska, Katarzyna. 2019. "Reification in IR: The Process and Consequences of Reifying the Idea of International Society." *International Studies Review* 21 (3): 347–72. https://doi.org/10.1093/isr/viy016.

Kaczmarska, Katarzyna. 2020. *Making Global Knowledge in Local Contexts: The Politics of International Relations and Policy Advice in Russia*. Worlding Beyond the West. Abingdon: Routledge.

Kaiser Family Foundation. 2023. "The U.S. Government and the World Health Organization." KFF. May 22, 2023. https://www.kff.org/coronavirus-covid-19/fact-sheet/the-u-s-gov ernment-and-the-world-health-organization/.

Katzenstein, Peter, and Rudra Sil. 2008. "Rethinking Asian Security: A Case for Analytical Eclecticism." In *Rethinking Japanese Security*, 249–85. London: Routledge.

Kelanic, Rosemary A. 2016. "The Petroleum Paradox: Oil, Coercive Vulnerability, and Great Power Behavior." *Security Studies* 25 (2): 181–213. https://doi.org/10.1080/09636 412.2016.1171966.

Kim, Hun Joon, and J.. Sharman. 2014. "Accounts and Accountability: Corruption, Human Rights, and Individual Accountability Norms." *International Organization* 68 (02): 417–48. https://doi.org/10.1017/S0020818313000428.

Kimmerer, Robin Wall. 2016. *Braiding Sweetgrass*. Minneapolis, MN: Milkweed Editions. https://milkweed.org/book/braiding-sweetgrass.

King, Chuck. 2019. "Max Scherzer: Pitch Clock Messes with 'fabric' of Baseball." WJLA. February 23, 2019. https://wjla.com/sports/washington-nationals/max-scherzer-pitch-clock-messes-fabric-baseball.

King, Gary, Robert O. Keohane, and Sidney Verba. 1994. *Designing Social Inquiry: Scientific Inference in Qualitative Research*. Princeton, N.J.: Princeton University Press.

Klein Schaarsberg, Suzanne. 2023. "Enacting the Pluriverse in the West: Contemplative Activism as a Challenge to the Disenchanted One-World World." *European Journal of International Relations*, October, 13540661231200864. https://doi.org/10.1177/135406 61231200864.

Kohn, Eduardo. 2013. *How Forests Think: Toward an Anthropology Beyond the Human*. Berkeley, CA: University of California Press.

Kondo, D. K. 1990. *Crafting Selves: Power, Gender, and Discourses of Identity in a Japanese Workplace*. Chicago: University of Chicago Press.

Kratochwil, Friedrich. 1989. *Rules, Norms, and Decisions*. Cambridge: Cambridge University Press.

———. 2014. *The Status of Law in World Society: Meditations on the Role and Rule of Law*. Cambridge: Cambridge University Press. https://doi.org/10.1017/CBO9781139583930.

———. 2021. *After Theory, Before Big Data: Thinking About Praxis, Politics and International Affairs*. London: Routledge.

Krebs, Ronald R., and Patrick Thaddeus Jackson. 2007. "Twisting Tongues and Twisting Arms: The Power of Political Rhetoric." *European Journal of International Relations* 13 (1): 35–66.

Krinsky, John, and Ann Mische. 2013. "Formations and Formalisms: Charles Tilly and the Paradox of the Actor." *Annual Review of Sociology* 39 (1): 1–26. https://doi.org/10.1146/annurev-soc-071312-145547.

Kuhn, Thomas S. 2000. *The Road Since Structure: Philosophical Essays, 1970–1993*. Edited by James Conant and John Haugeland. Chicago: University of Chicago Press.

Kukla, Rebecca, and Mark Lance. 2009. *'Yo!' and 'Lo!': The Pragmatic Topography of the Space of Reasons*. Cambridge, MA: Harvard University Press.

Kurki, Milja. 2008. *Causation in International Relations: Reclaiming Causal Analysis*. 1st ed. Cambridge: Cambridge University Press.

Lakatos, Imre. 1970. "The Methodology of Scientific Research Programmes." In *Criticism and the Growth of Knowledge*, edited by Imre Lakatos and Alan Musgrave, 91–196. Cambridge: Cambridge University Press.

Lapidos, Juliet. 2009. "There Are Four Lights! Revisiting Star Trek: The Next Generation's Eerily Prescient Torture Episode." *Slate* magazine. May 7. https://slate.com/culture/2009/05/star-trek-the-next-generation-s-eerily-prescient-torture-episode.html.

Latour, Bruno. 1987. *Science in Action: How to Follow Scientists and Engineers through Society*. Cambridge, MA: Harvard University Press.

Lau, Raymond Kwun-Sun. 2023. "Operationalizing Human Security: What Role for the Responsibility to Protect?" *International Studies* 60 (1): 29–44. https://doi.org/10.1177/00208817231154054.

Lawler, Janet, and David Waldner. 2023. "Interpretivism versus Positivism in an Age of Causal Inference." In *The Oxford Handbook of Philosophy of Political Science*, edited by Harold Kincaid and Jeroen Van Bouwel, 221–42. Oxford Handbooks. Oxford; New York: Oxford University Press.

Lebow, Richard Ned. 2003. *The Tragic Vision of Politics: Ethics, Interests and Orders*. Cambridge: Cambridge University Press.

———. 2010. *Forbidden Fruit: Counterfactuals and International Relations*. Princeton, N.J.: Princeton University Press.

———. 2014. "What Can International Relations Theory Learn from the Origins of World War I?" *International Relations* 28 (4): 387–410. https://doi.org/10.1177/0047117814556157.

"Let Us Beat Swords into Ploughshares | United Nations Gifts." n.d. Accessed August 11, 2023. https://www.un.org/ungifts/let-us-beat-swords-ploughshares#.

Levine, Daniel J. 2012. *Recovering International Relations: The Promise of Sustainable Critique*. New York: Oxford University Press.

Levy, Jack S. 1989. "Domestic Politics and War." In *The Origin and Prevention of Major Wars*, edited by Robert I. Rotberg and Theodore K. Rabb, 79–99. New York: Cambridge University Press.

Libet, Benjamin, Curtis A. Gleason, Elwood W. Wright, and Dennis K. Pearl. 1983. "Time of Conscious Intention to Act in Relation to Onset of Cerebral Activity (Readiness-Potential): the Unconscious Initiation of a Freely Voluntary Act." *Brain* 106 (3): 623–42. https://doi.org/10.1093/brain/106.3.623.

Long, David. 2005. "C. A. W. Manning and the Discipline of International Relations." *The Round Table* 94 (378): 77–96. https://doi.org/10.1080/00358530500033190.

Machamer, Peter. 2004. "Activities and Causation: The Metaphysics and Epistemology of Mechanisms." *International Studies in the Philosophy of Science* 18 (1): 27–39. https://doi.org/10.1080/02698590412331289242.

Machiavelli, Niccolò. 1994. *Selected Political Writings*. Translated by David Wootton. Indianapolis, IN: Hackett Press.

Manning, C. A. W. 1954. *The University Teaching of Social Sciences: International Relations*. Geneva: UNESCO.

———. 1962. *The Nature of International Society*. London: John Wiley & Sons.

———. 1964. "In Defense of Apartheid." *Foreign Affairs* 43 (1): 135–49. https://doi.org/10.2307/20039084.

———. 1966. *Collective Selfhoods: An Element in the South West Africa Case, Being the Testimony of an Academic South African*. London: The South Africa Society.

Martin, Aryn, and Michael Lynch. 2009. "Counting Things and People: The Practices and Politics of Counting." *Social Problems* 56 (2): 243–66. https://doi.org/10.1525/sp.2009.56.2.243.

McAdam, Douglas, Sidney Tarrow, and Charles Tilly. 2001. *Dynamics of Contention*. Cambridge: Cambridge University Press.

McDowell, John. 1998a. "Lecture II: The Logical Form of an Intuition." *The Journal of Philosophy* 95 (9): 451–70. https://doi.org/10.2307/2564577.

———. 1998b. "Lecture III: Intentionality as a Relation." *The Journal of Philosophy* 95 (9): 471–91. https://doi.org/10.2307/2564578.

McPhail, Clark, and John McCarthy. 2004. "Who Counts and How: Estimating the Size of Protests." *Contexts* 3 (3): 12–18. https://doi.org/10.1525/ctx.2004.3.3.12.

Medina, José. 2004. "In Defense of Pragmatic Contextualism: Wittgenstein and Dewey on Meaning and Agreement." *The Philosophical Forum* 35 (3): 341–69. https://doi.org/10.1111/j.1467-9191.2004.00177.x.

Moran, Richard. 2005. "Getting Told and Being Believed." *Philosophers' Imprint* 5 (5): 1–29. http://hdl.handle.net/2027/spo.3521354.0005.005.

Morris, David Z. 2017. "D.C. Transit Stats Show Weak Demand During Trump Inauguration." Fortune. January 22, 2017. http://fortune.com/2017/01/22/dc-transit-statistics-inauguration/.

Morrow, James D. 2007. "When Do States Follow the Laws of War?" *The American Political Science Review* 101 (3): 559–72.

Musgrave, Paul, and Daniel H. Nexon. 2018. "Defending Hierarchy from the Moon to the Indian Ocean: Symbolic Capital and Political Dominance in Early Modern China and the

Cold War." *International Organization* 72 (3): 591–626. https://doi.org/10.1017/S00208 18318000139.

Navari, Cornelia. 2013. "English School Methodology." In *Guide to the English School in International Studies*, edited by Cornelia Navari and Daniel Green, 205–22. Hoboken, NJ: John Wiley & Sons.

Nebehay, Stephanie. 2020. "WHO Says It No Longer Uses 'pandemic' Category, but Virus Still Emergency." *Reuters*, February 24, 2020, sec. World News. https://www.reuters.com/article/uk-china-health-who-idUKKCN20I0PD.

Nelson, Stephen C. 2014. "Playing Favorites: How Shared Beliefs Shape the IMF's Lending Decisions." *International Organization* 68 (02): 297–328. https://doi.org/10.1017/S00208 18313000477.

Nelson, Stephen C., and Peter J. Katzenstein. 2014. "Uncertainty, Risk, and the Financial Crisis of 2008." *International Organization* 68 (02): 361–92. https://doi.org/10.1017/S0020818313000416.

Nietzsche, Friedrich Wilhelm. 1978. *Thus Spoke Zarathustra: A Book for None and All.* New York: Penguin.

Norman, Ludvig. 2021. "Rethinking Causal Explanation in Interpretive International Studies." *European Journal of International Relations* 27 (3): 936–59. https://doi.org/10.1177/13540661211006454.

Nuñez-Mietz, Fernando G. 2016. "Lawyering Compliance with International Law: Legal Advisers in the 'War on Terror.'" *European Journal of International Security* 1 (2): 215–38. https://doi.org/10.1017/eis.2016.9.

Nuzzi, Olivia. 2017. "Kellyanne Conway Is the Real First Lady of Trump's America." *New York* magazine. March 18. http://nymag.com/intelligencer/2017/03/kellyanne-conway-trumps-first-lady.html.

Official Playing Rules Committee. 2021. "Official Baseball Rules." Office of the Commissioner of Baseball.

Oneal, John R., and Bruce Russett. 2000. *Triangulating Peace: Democracy, Interdependence, and International Organizations*. New York: W. W. Norton & Company.

Onuf, Nicholas G. 1989. *World of Our Making: Rules and Rule in Social Theory and International Relations*. Columbia, S.C.: University of South Carolina Press.

———. 1998. "Constructivism: A User's Manual." In *International Relations in a Constructed World*, edited by V. Kubálková, Nicholas G. Onuf, and Paul Kowert, 58–78. Armonk, N.Y.: M. E. Sharpe.

Pitkin, Hanna F. 1973. *Wittgenstein and Justice: On the Significance of Ludwig Wittgenstein for Social and Political Thought*. Berkeley, CA: University of California Press.

Popper, Karl. 1979. *Objective Knowledge: An Evolutionary Approach*. Vol. Revised. Oxford: Oxford University Press.

———. 1996. *Myth of the Framework: In Defence of Science and Rationality*. London: Routledge.

Pratt, Simon Frankel. 2020. "Reification, Practice, and the Ontological Status of Social Facts." *International Theory* 12 (2): 231–37. https://doi.org/10.1017/S175297192 0000081.

Price, Richard. 1995. "A Genealogy of the Chemical Weapons Taboo." *International Organization* 49 (1): 73–103.

Quinton, Sean. 2017. "Don't Blink: The Science of a 100mph Fastball." *The Seattle Times*, March 31. https://projects.seattletimes.com/2017/mariners-preview/science/.

Reisch, George A. 2005. *How the Cold War Transformed Philosophy of Science: To the Icy Slopes of Logic*. Cambridge: Cambridge University Press.

Rescher, Nicholas. 1997. *Objectivity: The Obligations of Impersonal Reason*. Notre Dame, IN: University of Notre Dame Press.

Richardson, Alan W. 2006. "The Many Unities of Science: Politics, Semantics, and Ontology." In *Scientific Pluralism*, edited by Stephen H. Kellert, Helen E. Longino, and C. Kenneth Waters, 1–25. Minneapolis, MN: University of Minnesota Press.

Ringer, Fritz K. 1997. *Max Weber's Methodology: The Unification of the Cultural and Social Sciences*. Cambridge, MA: Harvard University Press.

Rohr, Richard, and Joseph Martos. 1987. *The Great Themes of Scripture: Old Testament*. Cincinnati, OH: Franciscan Media.

Rousseau, David L., Christopher Gelpi, Dan Reiter, and Paul K. Huth. 1996. "Assessing the Dyadic Nature of the Democratic Peace, 1918–88." *The American Political Science Review* 90 (3): 512–33.

Ruggie, John Gerard. 1998. "Introduction: What Makes the World Hang Together?" In *Constructing the World Polity*, 1–39. London: Routledge.

Russett, Bruce. 1993. *Grasping the Democratic Peace*. Princeton, N.J.: Princeton University Press.

———. 2005. "Bushwhacking the Democratic Peace." *International Studies Perspectives* 6 (4): 395–408. https://doi.org/10.1111/j.1528-3577.2005.00217.x.

Russett, Bruce, John Oneal, and Michael Cox. 2000. "Clash of Civilizations, or Realism and Liberalism Déjà Vu? Some Evidence." *Journal of Peace Research* 37 (5): 583–608.

Sabato, Larry, Kyle Kondik, and Geoffrey Skelley. 2017. *Trumped: The 2016 Election That Broke All the Rules*. Lanham, MD: Rowman & Littlefield.

Sagan, Carl. 1997. *The Demon-Haunted World: Science as a Candle in the Dark*. New York: Ballantine Books.

Saguy, Abigail C., and Juliet A. Williams. 2022. "A Little Word That Means a Lot: A Reassessment of Singular They in a New Era of Gender Politics." *Gender & Society* 36 (1): 5–31. https://doi.org/10.1177/08912432211057921.

Said, E. 1979. *Orientalism*. New York: Vintage Books.

Sandal, Nukhet Ahu. 2011. "Religious Actors as Epistemic Communities in Conflict Transformation: The Cases of South Africa and Northern Ireland." *Review of International Studies* 37 (3): 929–49.

Saylor, Ryan. 2020. "Why Causal Mechanisms and Process Tracing Should Alter Case Selection Guidance." *Sociological Methods & Research* 49 (4): 982–1017. https://doi.org/10.1177/0049124118769109.

Schaffer, Frederic Charles. 2015. *Elucidating Social Science Concepts: An Interpretivist Guide*. New York: Routledge.

Schwartz-Shea, Peregrine, and Dvora Yanow. 2012. *Interpretive Research Design: Concepts and Processes*. New York: Routledge.

Searle, John. 1995. *The Construction of Social Reality*. New York: Free Press.

Sending, Ole Jacob. 2015. *The Politics of Expertise*. Ann Arbor, MI: University of Michigan Press. https://www.press.umich.edu/4016693/politics_of_expertise.

Sewell, William H. 1992. "A Theory of Structure: Duality, Agency, and Transformation." *American Journal of Sociology* 98 (1): 1–29.

Shotter, John. 1993a. *Conversational Realities: Constructing Life through Language*. Thousand Oaks, CA: Sage.

———. 1993b. *Cultural Politics of Everyday Life*. Toronto: University of Toronto Press.

———. 1996. "'Now I Can Go On': Wittgenstein and Our Embodied Embeddedness in the 'Hurly-Burly' of Life." *Human Studies* 19 (4): 385–407.

Singer, Benjamin J., Robin N. Thompson, and Michael B. Bonsall. 2021. "The Effect of the Definition of 'Pandemic' on Quantitative Assessments of Infectious Disease Outbreak Risk." *Scientific Reports* 11 (1): 2547. https://doi.org/10.1038/s41598-021-81814-3.

Snow, David A. 2022. "Framing and Social Movements." In *The Wiley-Blackwell Encyclopedia of Social and Political Movements*, 1–7. New York: Wiley-Blackwell. https://doi.org/10.1002/9780470674871.wbespm434.pub2.

Soniak, Matt. 2017. "What's the Difference between 'Mostly Sunny' and 'Partly Cloudy'?" Mental Floss, June 27. http://mentalfloss.com/article/56820/whats-difference-between-mostly-sunny-and-partly-cloudy.

Southern, R. W. 1962. *Western Views of Islam in the Middle Ages*. Cambridge, MA: Harvard University Press.

Spruyt, Hendrik. 2020. *The World Imagined: Collective Beliefs and Political Order in the Sinocentric, Islamic and Southeast Asian International Societies*. LSE International Studies. Cambridge: Cambridge University Press. https://doi.org/10.1017/978110 8867948.

Stump, Jacob L., and Priya Dixit. 2013. *Critical Terrorism Studies: An Introduction to Research Methods*. London: Routledge.

Suganami, Hidemi. 1996. *On the Causes of War*. Oxford: Clarendon Press.

———. 2001. "C. A. W. Manning and the Study of International Relations." *Review of International Studies* 27 (1): 91–107.

———. 2008. "Narrative Explanation and International Relations: Back to Basics." *Millennium – Journal of International Studies* 37 (2): 327–56. https://doi.org/10.1177/0305829808097643.

Sweet, Paige L. 2020. "Who Knows? Reflexivity in Feminist Standpoint Theory and Bourdieu." *Gender & Society* 34 (6): 922–50. https://doi.org/10.1177/089124322 0966600.

Tannenwald, N. 1999. "The Nuclear Taboo: The United States and the Normative Basis of Nuclear Non-Use." *International Organization* 53 (3): 433–68.

Tanney, Julia. 2000. "Playing the Rule-Following Game." *Philosophy* 75 (292): 203–24.

Taylor, Charles. 2007. *A Secular Age*. Cambridge, MA: Harvard University Press.

Teles Fazendeiro, Bernardo. 2023. "The Question of Truth: How Facts, Space and Time Shape Conversations in IR." *European Journal of International Relations*, May, 13540661231173858. https://doi.org/10.1177/13540661231173858.

Terris, Ben. 2017. "The Ballad of Sean Spicer: He Snagged the Washington Dream Job, but at a Price." *Washington Post*, July 21, sec. Style. https://www.washingtonpost.com/lifest yle/style/the-ballad-of-sean-spicer-he-snagged-the-washington-dream-job-but-at-a-price/ 2017/07/21/2ae13da8-6e3e-11e7-9c15-177740635e83_story.html.

Tilly, Charles. 1998. *Durable Inequality*. Berkeley: University of California Press.

———. 2002. *Stories, Identities, and Political Change*. Lanham, MD: Rowman & Littlefield.

Torigian, Joseph. 2021. "A New Case for the Study of Individual Events in Political Science." *Global Studies Quarterly* 1 (4): 1–11. https://doi.org/10.1093/isagsq/ksab035.

Tsing, Anna Lowenhaupt. 2004. *Friction*. Princeton, N.J.: Princeton University Press. https://press.princeton.edu/books/paperback/9780691120652/friction.

Tworek, Heidi. 2021. "The Impact of Communications in Global History." In *What in the World? Understanding Global Social Change*, edited by Mathias Albert and Tobias Werron, 195–210. Bristol: Bristol University Press.

"U.S.C. Title 4 - Flag and Seal, Seat of Government, and the States." n.d. Accessed July 28, 2023. https://www.govinfo.gov/content/pkg/USCODE-2021-title4/html/USCODE-2021-title4.htm.

Van Fraassen, Bas C. 1977. "The Pragmatics of Explanation." *American Philosophical Quarterly* 14 (2): 143–50.

———. 2004. *The Empirical Stance*. New Haven, CT: Yale University Press.

Wæver, Ole. 2009. "Waltz's Theory of Theory." *International Relations* 23 (2): 201–22.

Waismann, Friedrich. 1979. *Wittgenstein and the Vienna Circle: Conversations*. New York: Rowman & Littlefield.

Waldner, David. 2007. "Transforming Inferences into Explanations: Lessons from the Study of Mass Extinctions." In *Theory and Evidence in Comparative Politics and International Relations*, edited by Richard Ned Lebow and Mark Lichbach, 145–75. New York: Palgrave Macmillan.

Wallace, Tim, and Alicia Parlapiano. 2017. "Crowd Scientists Say Women's March in Washington Had 3 Times as Many People as Trump's Inauguration." *The New York Times*, January 22, sec. U.S. https://www.nytimes.com/interactive/2017/01/22/us/politics/wom ens-march-trump-crowd-estimates.html.

Waltz, Kenneth N. 1979. *Theory of International Politics*. New York: McGraw-Hill.

Weber, Max. 1976. *Wirtschaft Und Gesellschaft*. Edited by Johannes Winckelmann. Vol. 5th. Tübingen: J. C. B. Mohr.

———. 1994. *Wissenschaft Als Beruf • Politik Als Beruf*. Edited by W.J. Mommsen and W. Schluchter. Tübingen: J. C. B. Mohr.

———. 1999a. "Kritische Studien Auf Dem Gebiet Der Kulturwissenschaftlichen Logik." In *Gesammelte Aufsätze Zur Wissenschaftslehre*, edited by Elizabeth Flitner, 215–90. Potsdam: Internet-Ausgabe, http://verlag.ub.uni-potsdam.de/html/494/html/.

———. 1999b. "Die 'Objektivität' Sozialwissenschaftlicher Und Sozialpolitischer Erkenntnis." In *Gesammelte Aufsätze Zur Wissenschaftslehre*, edited by Elizabeth Flitner, 146–214. Potsdam: Internet-Ausgabe, https://www.uni-potsdam.de/verlagsarchivweb/html/494/html/index.html.

———. 2003. "The 'objectivity' of Knowledge in Social Science and Social Policy." In *The Essential Weber: A Reader*, edited by Sam Whimster, 359–404. London: Routledge.

———. 2004. *The Vocation Lectures*. Indianapolis, IN: Hackett Press.

Wendt, Alexander. 1999. *Social Theory of International Politics*. Cambridge: Cambridge University Press.

———. 2003. "Why a World State Is Inevitable." *European Journal of International Relations* 9 (4): 491–542. https://doi.org/10.1177/135406610394001.

———. 2004. "The State as Person in International Theory." *Review of International Studies* 30 (2): 289–316.

White, Jeremy. 2021. "How AI Will Help Keep Time at the Tokyo Olympics." *Wired*. https://www.wired.com/story/omega-olympics-beach-volleyball-time/.

Whybray, R. N., and David Hill. 1993. "Prophets." In *The Oxford Companion to the Bible*. Oxford: Oxford University Press. https://www.oxfordreference.com/display/10.1093/acref/9780195046458.001.0001/acref-9780195046458-e-0591.

Wiener, Antje. 2018. *Contestation and Constitution of Norms in Global International Relations*. Cambridge: Cambridge University Press. https://doi.org/10.1017/978131 6718599.

Wight, Colin. 2006. *Agents, Structures and International Relations: Politics as Ontology*. Cambridge: Cambridge University Press.

Wilkens, Jan, and Alvine R C Datchoua-Tirvaudey. 2022. "Researching Climate Justice: A Decolonial Approach to Global Climate Governance." *International Affairs* 98 (1): 125–43. https://doi.org/10.1093/ia/iiab209.

Wilson, Peter. 2004. "Manning's Quasi-masterpiece: The Nature of International Society Revisited." *The Round Table* 93 (377): 755–69. https://doi.org/10.1080/003585304200 0300223.

Winch, Peter. 1990. *The Idea of a Social Science and Its Relation to Philosophy.* London: Routledge.

Wittgenstein, Ludwig. 1958. *Philosophical Investigations.* 2nd ed. Oxford: Blackwell.

———. 1965. "A Lecture on Ethics." *The Philosophical Review* 74 (1): 3–12. https://doi.org/10.2307/2183526.

———. 1990. *Last Writings on the Philosophy of Psychology.* Vol. One. Oxford: Blackwell.

———. 1993. *Philosophical Occasions: 1912–1951.* Edited by James Carl Klagge and Alfred Nordmann. Indianapolis, IN: Hackett Pub Co.

Woodward, James. 2005. *Making Things Happen: A Theory of Causal Explanation.* New York; Oxford: Oxford University Press.

World Health Organization. 2009. "Pandemic Influenza Preparedness and Response: A WHO Guidance Document."

Yanow, Dvora. 1996. *How Does a Policy Mean?* Washington, D.C.: Georgetown University Press.

Zarakol, Ayse. 2010. *After Defeat: How the East Learned to Live with the West.* Cambridge Studies in International Relations. Cambridge: Cambridge University Press. https://doi.org/10.1017/CBO9780511921421.

Ziliak, Stephen T., and Deirdre N. McCloskey. 2008. *The Cult of Statistical Significance: How the Standard Error Costs Us Jobs, Justice, and Lives.* Ann Arbor, MI: University of Michigan Press.

Index